CW00553288

A TROJAN
FEAST

THE FOOD AND DRINK OFFERINGS OF
ALIENS, FAERIES, AND SASQUATCH

Joshua Cutchin

ANOMALIST BOOKS
*San Antonio * Charlottesville*

An Original Publication of ANOMALIST BOOKS

A TROJAN FEAST
Copyright © 2015 Joshua Cutchin

ISBN: 978-1938398353

Book design by Seale Studios

Cover image by Gail Rau

For information, go to AnomalistBooks.com, or write to:
Anomalist Books, 5150 Broadway #108, San Antonio, TX 78209

CONTENTS

Science is a maw, or a headless and limbless stomach, an amoeba-like gut that maintains itself by incorporating the assimilable and rejecting the indigestible… By a process of sorting over data, rejecting the objectionable, and taking in the desirable, Science saves itself great pains, because a bellyache is something that is only a gut in torment.

– Charles Fort, American writer and researcher on anomalous phenomena (aka "Fortean phenomena")

FOREWORD

Anomalies have a right to be strange, even an obligation. The popularity of UFOs and unknown animals owes much to their strangeness, but it helps when that strangeness is of an accessible sort. An understanding of UFOs as spaceships from another planet mirrors our own spacefaring ambitions and accommodates widespread expectations based on conventional science. If Sasquatch belongs to a relict population of hominids inhabiting remote corners of the globe, that prospect too is both plausible and exciting. Visitors from space and prehistoric survivors add spice to an otherwise bland world without straining our grasp on how it works. Such notions allow ufologists to act as physical scientists in search of extraterrestrial technology and cryptozoologists to assume the role of field naturalists hunting a furtive animal, keeping the inquiries respectable and no-nonsense. Many people interested in such anomalies, many investigators engaged in their study, relish strangeness as long as it remains limited to a congenial sort, but act as ramrods of nuts-and-bolts or tracks-and-turds rectitude whenever their chosen anomalies deviate from a strictly materialistic paradigm.

The image of a machine worked well for flying saucers during the 1950s. Any testimonies to the contrary were dismissed as errors and hoaxes or ignored altogether. Yet witnesses repeatedly described bizarre events that sounded more appropriate for ghosts and magic than machinery, until the lid finally blew off during the 1960s and 1970s. Jacques Vallee compared encounters with UFO occupants and abductions to the folklore of fairies and demonology; John Keel wove UFOs with Men in Black and Mothman into a weird and widening tapestry of things strange that seemed too uncanny in their similarities to doubt that they were related. It was the era of High Strangeness, so well described by Jerome Clark in his encyclopedia, when UFOs, mystery animals, and everything else strange transformed into facets of a paranormal Mystery greater than any of its particular manifestations.

Anomalies thrive on the personal encounter. It is their lifeblood; some would say, their only substance. Some anomalies appear to be physical phenomena, behave like physical events, even leave physical evidence in their wake. The UFO that registers on radar or burns a hole in the clouds reassures the orthodox ufologist that a technological device underlies the reports, and justifies a ufology that pays attention only to physical phenomena. Yet witnesses continue to report paranormal manifestations hand in hand with apparently material events, separable only by brute force. Jerome Clark refers to these cases as experience anomalies. The experience is their fact; the events described are too bizarre and irrational to belong to any accepted scheme of understanding. Experience anomalies do not belong to this world yet multiple witnesses can see them, people in multiple cultures share them. They are impossible, yet they happen.

The usual efforts to understand the high-strangeness aspects of anomalies typically begin with enthusiasm, only to end in exhaustion and confusion, the inquirer led astray and mired down much like the traditional victim of mischievous fairies. A newcomer to the fray, Joshua Cutchin takes a new path to explore this tangled wilderness. Like others before him, he notes the striking similarities of fairy lore and UFOs, especially in accounts of entity encounters and abductions. Sasquatch reports join as subjects of comparison because they also share some of the same plots and motifs. The relationships among these three bodies of narrative provide the problem he sets out to solve. What is novel in his approach is the particular relationship he pursues—it is the role of food and drink in human encounters with aliens, fairies, and mystery hominids. If the approach seems narrow and unpromising at first, in Cutchin's hands the argument opens repeated insights into the ways food and drink connect the actions of anomalous beings.

Anomalists quickly noted a similarity between the "supernatural lapse of time" motif and the missing time experience in UFO abductions. Cutchin highlights the overlooked agency of food in both cases, one in which the visitor to fairyland becomes trapped there by partaking in the fairies' food or drink, the other in which ingestion of some liquid or pill from aliens causes amnesia or unconsciousness in the abductee. The thread leads onward to healing or aphrodisiac liquids, the fruit of knowledge that expands awareness, and ointments that reveal an invisible world. Some food exchanges between humans and entities seem benign; others, like rumors that aliens eat cattle or even humans, cast doubt on entity motives and call attention to long-running themes of deception and harmful allurement. For Cutchin the trail leads to psychedelics and the shamanic initiation as an extreme example of human consciousness reordered by ingested materials. While drugs may figure into the symbolism and strangeness underlying entity encounters, he does not reduce the experiences to drug-induced hallucinations. He raises the possibility that genuine entities communicate with humans by symbolic means, through the agency of ingested substances that appear as food to the consumers but are really "food mirages." Whether the intent is helpful or harmful remains unknown, but the method is an old one, a way of outsiders gaining entry into human consciousness by means of a Trojan Horse in the form of a "Trojan Feast."

Readers may or may not agree with Cutchin's conclusions. He offers them only as suggestions and states that his primary task is to identify connections. With this goal he scores an outstanding success, discovering one unsuspected link after another and demonstrating that the uncomfortable bizarreness of entity encounters is more than nonsense after all. The humble subject of food in anomalistic accounts serves, in his measured, learned, and lucid argument, as proof that high strangeness events may be uncertain and discordant, but not incomprehensible.

— Thomas E. Bullard

INTRODUCTION

There is communion of more than our bodies when bread is broken and wine drunk. – M.F.K. Fisher

Astri Olsdatter disappeared for five days in June 1720.[1]

The young girl of 15 was herding cows in Norway's Aadalen Valley when she noticed what appeared to be her employer, farmer Niels Scharud. Scharud's appearance was accompanied by a peculiar music drifting from the mountains; after asking if she could hear the melody as well, the man requested the girl leave the herd behind and follow him.

As his employee, Astri naturally obliged. They soon came upon a large straight road where four men awaited them, each clad in a red shirt, black trousers, and blue stockings, their blonde hair covered by "black round caps." Before Astri's eyes, Scharud's countenance changed to resemble his fellow captors, and she suddenly found herself *inside* the mountain, a large metallic door swinging shut behind her.

The girl began to sob. It wasn't long before someone she identified as a priest arrived to console her, encouraging her to be "joyful on account of all the glory she could see and take part of."

He then put a cup to her lips, and entreated her to drink. Astri refused.

After being led to a comfortable "armchair," a woman appeared who claimed to be the priest's wife. Plate-in-hand, she offered Astri some food, but the girl again refused. The woman looked deep into Astri's eyes and, after a time, again presented a cup and entreated her to drink.

During her stay in this metallic subterranean realm, the mountain people asked Astri to eat or drink on no less than eight separate occasions, to no avail. The entities tried a variety of tricks: they presented a sumptuous feast, took on the guise of Astri's

aunt and mother, even offered her betrothal and riches, if only she
would partake of their food and forget her old life.

The girl's refusals eventually led the mountain people to return
Astri to the Scharud farm, where she was nursed back to health.
Upon returning to her parents, she was astonished to learn that
five days had passed, as the entire ordeal had felt no longer than 12
hours. She did not recall eating any strange hallucinogenic berries
or falling asleep before her encounter, and claimed no history of
sleepwalking.

The account of Astri Olsdatter is not presented here because
it is an airtight case above scrutiny, but rather because of how well
it illustrates a disturbing trend that has persisted for millennia
in folklore and modern accounts alike: cases where humans are
insistently offered food by humanoid entities.[2]

The Food Taboo

Cultures across the world historically hold a prohibition, or
taboo, on eating food in the "land of the dead," lest the consumer be
detained indefinitely. Such superstitions are particularly widespread
throughout Europe, the most famous of which is the Celtic belief
that, upon entering the faerie realm—closely associated with the
underworld—anyone who partakes of fae food or drink will be
trapped in their land forever. Lady Wilde tells in *Ancient Legends,
Mystic Charms, and Superstitions of Ireland* about a young girl who
is led down to faerie land after meeting their prince:

> At the end of the stairs they came upon a large hall,
> all bright and beautiful with gold and silver and
> lights; and the table was covered with everything
> good to eat, and wine was poured out in golden
> cups for them to drink. When she sat down they all
> pressed her to eat the food and to drink the wine;
> and as she was weary after the dancing, she took
> the golden cup the prince handed to her, and raised

it to her lips to drink. Just then, a man passed close to her, and whispered—

"Eat no food, and drink no wine, or you will never reach your home again."

So she laid down the cup, and refused to drink. On this they were angry, and a great noise arose, and a fierce, dark man stood up, and said—

"Whoever comes to us must drink with us."[3]

Warnings to abstain in the land of the dead can be found in Jewish, Teutonic, and Nordic traditions. In the Finnish *Kalevala*, for example, the hero Väinämöinen shrewdly rejects a tankard of beer offered to him during his journey to the Underworld.[4]

In Asia, Mesopotamian mythology speaks of the hero Adapa, who refused food from the god Anu; though it promised immortality, he would have never returned to the mortal world.[5] The Japanese goddess Izanami died in childbirth and ate food in the afterlife, never to return to the living.[6]

Indigenous peoples in the South Pacific hold similar beliefs. On the island of New Caledonia, tradition says that the newly deceased will remain in the spirit world if they eat there. The Maori of New Zealand tell of a young man granted permission by the gods to visit his dead lover under the condition that he not consume anything offered to him.[7]

These beliefs are also reflected in the views of North American tribes such as the Haida, Tsimshian, Pawnee, and Cherokee people.[8] The Kwakiutl of Alaska speak of *buk'wus*, the "woodman," who entices passersby to share in his feast.[9] Anyone foolish enough to do so is trapped in the spirit world, eventually becoming a *buk'wus* themselves.[10]

The widespread nature of this belief begs the question of its origin. Scholars often point to the myth of Persephone, daughter of Demeter, the Greek goddess of grain. When Hades, god of the underworld, abducted the young virgin, her distraught mother blighted the harvest, cursing the fertility of man and beast alike. Hermes, sent by Zeus, asked Hades to release Persephone; he obliged, though not before secretly giving her a cursed pomegranate seed. Hades encouraged Persephone to consume the seed, an act that imprisoned her in the underworld for eternity. She briefly emerges each spring to rejoin her mother.[11]

While the Persephone story may explain the universality of belief across the Eurasian landmass, it cannot account for the propagation of the food taboo (as it shall be known henceforth) to such far-flung locales as North America and the South Pacific.[12] Anthropologists have proposed a wide variety of possible reasons for this shared global superstition, including the notion that to eat with a people is to gain a certain kinship with them: to contort a phrase, "we are with whom we eat."[13]

"Commensality, a willingness to eat together, is a powerful social glue in pre-industrial societies," says Diane Purkiss, professor of Keble College, Oxford. "To accept food is to make oneself part of a community."[14] Other possible theories are notions of contagion and contamination, or that the food itself contains transmigrated souls.[15] Food in the mortal realm keeps those who eat it mortal, or at least alive; ergo food in the spirit world keeps its consumers dead.

But what if the food taboo is universal for another reason— what if there is some truth to it beyond mere myth and superstition? What do we make of the fact that these legendary prohibitions of old applied not only to food from the dead, but also food from liminal entities such as faeries and Bigfoot? Even more compelling, what do we make of the fact that individuals claiming alien abduction and contactee experiences in the modern era occasionally report an exchange of food and drink?

Consider the case of Ivan Martynovich, who told his local newspaper that a tall stranger with gray skin and clear blue eyes took him aboard an extraterrestrial craft in September 1990. Like

Astri Olsdatter and the mountain, Martynovich's entry into the ship was sudden and imperceptible. He was shown a quick review of his life on a sort of screen, after which the beings invited him to their homeworld. Martynovich enthusiastically agreed, and once there he marveled at the alien's diet of milk and vegetables. He asked to try some, but was forbidden by the extraterrestrials, who told him that eating their food would "influence" him, and he would be forced to stay on their world. Following a series of warnings about mankind's destructive behavior, Martynovich was returned home that same night.[16]

The similarities of this story to the tales of Astri Olsdatter and Lady Wilde's lost girl are striking. Are we to assume that Ivan Martynovich was a liar and a fan of world folklore—or is something more going on?

About the Book

There are thousands of contemporary accounts involving interactions with non-human entities which, taken in aggregate, show a remarkable amount of cross-cultural uniformity. Individuals with no knowledge of the typical alien, faerie, or Sasquatch encounter detail consistent characteristics between accounts and, while some must certainly be flights of fancy by unstable individuals, many are reported by average citizens or trained observers such as policemen and military personnel. The accounts are occasionally so absurd as to strain credibility—except that anyone wishing their fabrication to be believed would undoubtedly refrain from creating such unbelievable details.

Sadly, we are saddled with a scientific establishment that is perfectly comfortable with Schrödinger's cat being both alive and dead, yet scoffs at thousands of years' worth of eyewitness reports. The responsibility to investigate these cases instead falls upon those open-minded few who are paying attention.

A substantial portion of these humanoid encounters echo aspects of the food taboo, with witnesses receiving both food and drink from strange entities. As one would expect, very few result in anyone being physically trapped in the "land of the dead"—we obviously wouldn't hear such accounts at all—but a striking number of people are impacted by these encounters, and perhaps what they consumed, for the rest of their lives.

Though many have noted this trend, no one has made an in-depth study of the food and drink exchanged between eyewitnesses and non-human entities (hereafter referred to simply as "entity food") until now. By examining the trends shown by these cases and viewing their significance through the lenses of folklore, religion, and psychology, this book will hopefully serve as an important first step toward bringing attention to this oft-overlooked aspect of the unexplained.[17]

CHAPTER 1
LORE: FAERIES

And what you've not to do is this: bite no bit, and drink no drop,
however hungry or thirsty you are; drink a drop, or bite a bit, while in
Elfland you be, and never will you see Middle Earth again.
— Warlock Merlin in "Childe Rowland,"
Fairy Tales by Joseph Jacobs

With its stark beauty and imposing limestone cliffs, the Aran Islands are the perfect place for a vacation, annually attracting thousands of visitors to one of the last bastions of true Celtic culture. The islands possess a rich history, boasting some of Ireland's oldest archaeological remains—the ancient stone forts of Dún Aonghasa and Dún Chonchúir—as well as the first true Irish monastery, founded by Saint Enda circa 484. It is a nexus of Christianity and the ways of old.

Young Brian Collins was on holiday in the islands when he noticed two small men, dressed in green with brown boots, fishing on the shore. Each man was approximately 3.5 feet tall, and they were laughing and speaking Gaelic. Brian took an interest and, after seeing them jump behind the bank they were sitting on, investigated but found no sign of them, save a small pipe. He returned to the house where he was staying and placed the pipe in a locked drawer, from which it disappeared shortly thereafter.[18]

Though it may sound like a tale from centuries ago, Brian's experience happened in the early 1990s. Such sightings occur to this day, and modern attitudes do a great disservice to faeries or, to use the older term, the fae folk.[19] The tiny, winged ladies of Victorian art bear little resemblance to their inspiration, an ethereal race of entities whose wrath was so feared that cultures worldwide refused to use their names, instead creating a host of euphemisms: *wee folk, fair folk, good folk, the gentry.*

To ancient man, faeries were simply a part of life, nature spirits tied to wild places. Treated with respect and given offerings, they could set one's life aright, cleaning homes and aiding in the harvest; disrespected, they could ruin one's luck, blind, kidnap, or kill.

Legends of faeries, like the food taboo, can be found worldwide. Elves, gnomes,[20] pixies, imps, and sprites are the best known, though European cultures describe hundreds with their own designated duties, preferred offerings, and distinct mythology. The Russian *domovoi* trades a well-kept household for milk and biscuits, much like the English *brownie*. Mothers in Dutch Guiana warn their children not to drink from the bottle of the *bakru*, a malicious dark-skinned dwarf, lest they face death.[21] Native Hawaiians tell of the diminutive *menehune*, West Africans of the *azizas*, Chinese of *mogwai*, and the Portuguese of *duendes*. This elaborate worldwide taxonomy is even reflected in the Cherokee lore of the southeastern United States, which describes four types of "Little People" living in rock cliffs, rhododendron thickets, "broom sage," and out in the open.[22]

The umbrella term "faerie" can refer to a nature spirit of any size or shape, including giants and mermaids. They can be tall and elegant, like the *Ellefolk* of Scandinavia, or short and hideous, like trolls and goblins. The *woodwose*, depicted as a hairy wild man brandishing a club, is one entity that contradicts the modern conception of a faerie.[23]

In addition to keeping these spirits appeased with offerings, one can also safeguard against their anger by keeping a piece of stale bread in a pocket,[24] or by exhibiting Christian piety.[25] Iron and salt are also extremely potent deterrents.[26] According to folklorist Alasdair MacGregor, consuming cheese or milk from a cow that had eaten *mothan*, a plant whose true identity is now lost to time, could also ward off fae folk.[27]

A common theme in fae lore is the abnormal passage of time in fairyland. Depending upon the story, time either passes too slowly or too quickly. One Scottish tale speaks of two fiddlers who spent a few hours at a faerie gathering within a hill and emerged one hundred years later, crumbling into dust.[28] In many stories of this type, this rapid aging is brought upon by consuming mortal food after returning from fairyland.

Numerous theories have tried to explain the myths, mostly focusing on the Celtic tradition. One popular explanation is that faeries are the shared racial memory of a secretive people who coexisted with early Celts on the British Isles. Others contend that faeries represent departed souls, given their longstanding association with the dead. The introduction of Christianity confused the matter further, as the early church was quick to lump pagan deities with faeries, labeling the lot of them as either demons or fallen/demoted/neutral angels.

At any rate, such explanations do little to explain why these beliefs are shared by other cultures, and are absolutely useless in the face of modern accounts. In 1936, an Icelandic hiker mired in a snowstorm stumbled upon a farmhouse in the woods. The owner identified himself as one of the *huldufólk*, or hidden people, and gave the hiker food and a room for the night. The hiker departed the next day after breakfast, and when he glanced back, the house had vanished.[29]

Iceland is known for its enduring belief in the fae folk. An oft-cited 1998 study by the newspaper *Dagblaðið Vísir* claimed that 54.4% of Icelanders surveyed believed in elves,[30] and it is not at all uncommon today for road construction to deviate around a rock believed to house the *huldufólk*.

Faeries and the Food Taboo

On September 16, 1759, Jacob Jacobsson returned from an

errand for his father when, much to his surprise, he discovered a large, broad road before him, winding its way through the Swedish countryside. The road had not been there earlier, and so the young man set out to investigate, eventually finding himself in a settlement of large houses. He entered one of the buildings and "saw crowds of little people, running back and forth," supervised by a tall attractive woman who entreated him to their feast. Jacobsson declined, and when asked if he should like to remain with the little people, said aloud, "God, help me back home to my father and mother!"

One of the faeries demanded his removal on account of rudeness, and Jacobsson found himself back where the road began, though it was now gone. Four days had passed, and Jacobsson later made a formal statement of his encounter to the local reverend.[31]

Besides exercising common sense, Jacobsson was likely familiar with the prohibition of eating food in fairyland. As mentioned earlier, this version of the food taboo is frequently cited in paranormal research, and is common in faerie lore. Perhaps the most famous story is that of "Jemmy Doyle in the Fairy Palace," recorded in *Legendary Fictions of the Irish Celts*, where the protagonist stumbles into a feast at a fae castle on his way home. As in Lady Wilde's account, he is warned against partaking (this time by a dead relative), and instead spills his tumbler of punch between his coat and waistcoat, enabling his return.[32]

Doyle's deception was a wise choice, as there are serious repercussions for refusing fae hospitality. One apocryphal story tells of a man who was found dead on a country road after refusing milk offered by the *banshee*,[33] while a Scottish tale details a young lady who was imprisoned for declining buttermilk from a faerie. She was told her release would come after she spun all the wool and ate all the meal in her prison; however, both commodities replenished themselves nightly, and she was only able to escape after wetting her left eye with saliva prior to each day's work (fairytale logic at its finest).[34]

Perhaps the most surprising thing about the food taboo in

faerie folklore is that, outside of legends, there are few actual reports of people being trapped in fairyland. As mentioned, any permanent abduction would be impossible to verify, so perhaps the belief reflects the time dilation experienced in the company of faeries, though it is not necessary to eat their food to experience such. An alternate suggestion is that the penalty of "staying" is more metaphorical than literal. For example, an Apache legend tells of two boys who took food from where the mountain spirits lived—while they were able to return home, they could no longer eat the food of mortals.[35]

The *elle-maids* of Scandinavia and Germany dance alongside roads at night, their beauty enticing travelers to drink their wine. Any who do are driven insane.[36] One man traveling from Seden to Odense in Denmark drank the wine but lived the rest of his short life restless and mad, eager to return to the *elle-maids*.[37]

Insanity and death are certainly forms of imprisonment. It seems equally likely that the true punishment is a lasting internal change: after partaking of faerie food, one cannot "return home" to the way things were. The lives of Adam and Eve were irrevocably changed after consuming the Forbidden Fruit, and it seems the consumption of entity food—be it godly, fae, alien, or Sasquatch— has a similar affect.

Not all faerie food leads to dire consequences, however. Disregarding the *elle-maids*, food and drink offered by faeries outside the realm is generally considered safe for consumption. Folklorist Ruth Tongue cites the story of a kindly farmer who mended a child-sized ped, or spade, that he found broken. Unknown to him, it belonged to a faerie, and he later returned to find a small cake in the ped's place. He ate the food in spite of his comrade's warnings, deeming it "proper good" and suffering no ill effects (it should be noted that the farmer only expressed appreciation and not thanks, as overt gratitude allegedly leads to bad luck).[38]

The children of Sandy MacDonald saw faeries in 1912 near Ardnamurchan, a remote peninsula in the Scottish Highlands. The two boys were playing by the water when two tiny figures in green miraculously appeared. The entities invited the boys to their nearby boat, where a tiny woman and her rat-sized dog could be seen in the cabin. The lads declined, and were instead treated to "a few loaves of faery bread, each about the size of a walnut" (it is interesting that the boys were by the sea, since fossilized sea urchins are sometimes referred to as "fairy loaves," and roughly correspond to the size of the bread described).[39]

After they ate, one of faeries said, "We are departing now... We will not be coming back here any more, but others of our race will be coming." The boys were snapped out of their trance by their sister, who arrived shortly thereafter, and neither seemed further affected from eating the loaves.[40]

Such accounts indicate that the food's power is tied to the entity's intent. Folklorist Katharine Briggs, citing E.M. Leather's *The Folk-Lore of Herefordshire*, provides an example in the story of Herla, ancient king of the Britons. Though Herla emerged from a faerie wedding feast centuries after he entered,[41] "there seems no suggestion that the passage of time was caused by this communion... the intention does not seem to have been unfriendly."[42]

The Nature of Faerie Food

What is the food given by faeries, that it should cause so much strife? Though it often has the appearance of baked goods, wine, or milk, legend alludes to the use of *glamour*, or illusion, utilized by faeries to appear different than they truly are, and similar spells are cast upon what they offer as food. Alasdair MacGregor wrote in *The Peat-Fire Flame: Folk-tales and Traditions of the Highlands and Islands* of a woman who abstained from food in fairyland, and afterwards "came to examine the food offered her by the Men of Peace, [and] she found it to consist 'only of the refuse of the earth.'"[43]

Such concepts can be traced back to early legend. The aforementioned Scandinavian hero Väinämöinen, upon rejecting beer in the Underworld, "gaz'd awhile upon the tankard; Lo! within it frogs were spawning, worms about its sides were laying."[44] In the story of St. Collen, the seventh-century Welsh saint visited the King of Faeries, and declared, "I do not eat the leaves of a tree!" when he saw the "food" for what it truly was.[45] Witches, conflated with faeries by the Christian church, ascribed similar attributes to the Devil's food—one of the famous Pendle witches reported in 1612 that "although they did eat [at their masses], they were never the fuller nor better for the same."[46]

This theme reappears in modern accounts. Abdul Mutalib disappeared in January 1982 from his guard post at a recruit training center near Kuala Lumpur. A search was mounted to no avail, and locals whispered of the *buni*, elemental beings who, in their minds, were responsible for several such disappearances. Abductees who returned spoke of "a distant place" and "delicious food"—though when they vomited, only worms and grasses came up.[47]

If the food offered by fairies is illusory, what do they themselves actually consume? Varying reports point to "barley meal, poisonous mushrooms, goat milk, red deer meat, silver weed roots, heather stalks, toadstools, and weeds,"[48] or a diet similar to a mouse.[49] UFOlogist Jacques Vallée often identified meat and pure water as the primary food source of the faeries, citing the writings of anthropologist W.Y. Evans-Wentz.

Most literature, however, posits that they feed on the essence, also called the *toradh* or *foyson*, of food.[50] Parallels to the *foyson* concept can be found with the Arabic *djinn*, which "eat human food, stealing its energy."[51] Food without its *foyson* is unfit for human consumption. Evans-Wentz, in his seminal *The Fairy-Faith in Celtic Countries*, was told that food left for faerie offerings was "not allowed to be eaten afterwards by man or beast, not even pigs... The underlying idea seems to be that the fairies extract the spiritual essence from food offered to them, leaving behind the grosser elements."[52] The book also details housecats who drank milk left out for *piskies* and became sick.[53]

The folklore bears similarities to a 1970 case in Chile, where a small creature was seen gliding through a family's livestock pasture. The next day, ten of their llamas were found exsanguinated. The family attempted to cook one of the animals, but the meat tasted foul; even the vultures who ate the remaining carcasses were seen to vomit, and the family had no choice but to burn all that remained.[54]

Subsiding on *foyson* allows faeries to consume living animals without apparent harm. One Welsh farmer watched the *Verry Volk* slaughter his ox, then resurrect it, minus a piece of leg bone they had misplaced. The next day the animal appeared healthy, save a slight limp.[55]

It is easy, and perhaps sensible, to write off the concept of *foyson* as a way to explain why most offerings left for faeries remain physically untouched. We will return to this subject, as well as those of offerings and food theft, in further depth later.

CHAPTER 2
LORE: ET & BIGFOOT

My royal lord,
You do not give the cheer: the feast is sold
That is not often vouch'd, while 'tis a-making,
'Tis given with welcome: to feed were best at home;
From thence the sauce to meat is ceremony;
Meeting were bare without it.
– Lady MacBeth, MacBeth, Act 3 Scene IV

The average reader is likely more familiar with Bigfoot and alleged extraterrestrial visitation than the historical depiction of faeries; therefore, the following chapter will serve as a brief "crash course" in basic concepts to establish a baseline for the rest of our discussion. Other researchers and authors have built strong cases for the existence of these phenomena—it is recommended that readers familiarize themselves with such literature to grasp the full complexity and validity of modern day sightings.

Extraterrestrials

Though similar sightings have taken place since time immemorial, UFOs made their official debut in the 20th century as "flying saucers" sighted by Kenneth Arnold on June 24, 1947. The phenomenon immediately embedded itself in popular culture, and today it is difficult to find anyone in the Western world who isn't familiar with the unidentified flying objects (UFOs) and their occupants, purported extraterrestrials from another planet. For the sake of clarity, the term "alien" will be used to describe these beings for the remainder of this book, though it is not an endorsement of the extraterrestrial hypothesis (ETH).

Shortly after Arnold's sighting the contactee movement took hold, and hundreds of individuals stepped forward claiming interactions with non-earthly intelligences. Like UFO sightings, these encounters had been occurring for centuries, but their golden era truly was the 1940s and 1950s. Contactees spoke of their positive meetings with tall, blonde, humanlike "Space Brothers" who often brought messages of hope or wisdom. The contact was frequently claimed to be ongoing.

These encounters took on a sinister tone with the first widely publicized alien abduction. In September 1961, Betty and Barney Hill claimed they were forcibly taken aboard an extraterrestrial craft while driving through rural New Hampshire. A series of hypnosis sessions revealed that the Hills were subjected to medical examinations by the entities on board the craft, though their recollection of the beings themselves was hazy.

Today, the typical abduction scenario is a popular culture meme with which we are all familiar. A blinding light shines through your bedroom window; short, large-eyed aliens (referred to as "the Greys") appear at your bedside; you miraculously pass through the window or roof and wind up on an operating table. The Greys perform a medical exam, often sexual, supervised by a taller humanoid, and you wake up in your bed, often with no conscious recall but with trace physical evidence in the form of scoop marks or misplaced clothing.

In truth, nearly every contactee and abductee report has at least one atypical element that stands out as particularly bizarre. These frequently incorporate mystical aspects that seem more akin to near-death or out-of-body experiences (recall Ivan Martynovich's life review, for example). Generally speaking, the contactee experience is positive, voluntary, and extremely personal, while abductions tend to be negative, forceful, and coldly impersonal.

Some have argued that, while food is common in contactee scenarios, it does not feature very often in abductions. In a 2004 post on the *UFO UpDates* site, researcher Nick Pope wrote that while food shows up in contactee encounters, it "does not feature much in the abduction literature."[56] With all due respect to Pope, injections, force-feeding, and ointment all still feature quite prominently in abduction accounts. Each of these can easily be argued as variations of food exchange, especially considering how the UFO phenomenon constantly re-contextualizes itself in different cultures and eras.

One such case is that of Geraldo Bichara, a guard at Escola de Sargentos das Armas in Tres Coracoes, Brazil, whose testimony was examined by investigator Ubirajara Franco Rodrigues. Bichara was making his post-midnight rounds at the school early on August 26, 1962, when he noticed a blue light approaching him. The approach coincided with a power outage and a deafening hum, and Bichara made a futile yell for help. He was immediately paralyzed and finally perceived the source of the light: a dark disc hovering above. He was grabbed by two small figures in hooded orange coveralls and led up a stairwell and into the craft. Once inside, Bichara was subjected to numerous medical exams. In one instance, an object shaped like a beehive with a spout was placed near his face, and he was given a distasteful liquid to drink. He gagged and asked for water, a request which was ignored, and was eventually returned to his post.[57]

In truth, liquids are given so often in abductions that the act could be considered a second-tier hallmark of the phenomenon. The research of the late Karla Turner, her book *Taken* in particular, is filled with accounts of drinks given to abductees. John G. Miller's essay "Medical Procedural Differences: Alien Versus Human" also details the frequency with which liquids are administered.[58]

Abductions and contactee reports have only been attributed to alien beings in the relatively recent past, and although there are plenty of *exchanges* of food, there are very few examples where the food *taboo* is explicitly mentioned. As to the nature of what sort of food is given and what these extraterrestrials themselves eat, those subjects will be covered in greater depth later in this book.

Bigfoot

For centuries indigenous people around the world have spoken of large, hairy hominids that inhabit the wild places of the world. In Russia they are called *Almas*, in the Himalayas *Yeti*, Australia *Yowie*, Sumatra *Orang Pendek*, and in China *Yeren*. In North America, particularly the Pacific Northwest, tribes have a rich folklore regarding the beasts, calling them everything from *Skookum* (a term also synonymous with hearty food) to *Sasquatch*, known colloquially as Bigfoot.

"Sasquatch" is actually an Anglicanized word drawing upon several Native American terms, in particular the Halkomelem *ses'quac*. In general, these creatures are described as 6-to-10-foot-tall, hairy beings that bear an uncanny resemblance both to apes and humans. They are especially famous for their tracks, which appear similar to a human foot, albeit up to 24 inches long. As of May 2014, the Bigfoot Field Researchers Organization (BFRO) had collected well over 4,500 contemporary accounts, which is to say nothing of unreported or historical sightings.[59] While most scientists feel there is little validity to the existence of Sasquatch, there is actually a wealth of physical evidence in favor of Sasquatch's reality, including footprints, audio and visual recordings, and alleged hair samples.

Sasquatch came to the forefront of American popular culture in 1958 when bulldozer operator Gerald Crew found large footprints on a work site in Del Norte County, California. The family of local logger Ray Wallace, following his death, attributed the creation of the prints to him; this admission struck a great blow to the credibility of the phenomenon, if only to those who were unaware of its existence prior to the Crew tracks. In reality, there are plenty of Sasquatch sightings pre-1958, including a story related by future President Theodore Roosevelt, who met an eyewitness with a tale so convincing that the president published it in his book *The Wilderness Hunter.*

Explanations for the sightings range from a relict population of Neanderthals or *Gigantopithecus blacki* to simple misidentification. It is recommended anyone interested in further exploring the evidence for Sasquatch's existence should consult the work of researchers such as John Bindernagel, a wildlife biologist; the late Grover Krantz, who was a professor of physical anthropology at Washington State University; Loren Coleman, author and director of the International Museum of Cryptozoology; and Jeffrey Meldrum, a professor of anatomy and anthropology at Idaho State University.

While some Native American folklore explicitly states that Sasquatch is a biological, flesh-and-blood entity, there are also some tribes that claim the creature is actually a spirit. It is in these myths that the food taboo appears. As noted earlier, the *buk'wus* of Kwakiutl folklore offers "ghost food" to trap the unwary; in some tales, this appears as dried salmon but is, just like faerie food, only tree bark.[60]

A variety of diets have been attributed to the beasts. In folklore, Sasquatch are generally anthropophages, consumers of humans, while modern accounts detail a broad array of food-related activities, including chasing deer, wading for trout, foraging nuts and berries, and dumpster diving for their meals.

One human-devouring representation of Sasquatch is *Tsonoqua*, the "wild woman of the woods" in Kwakiutl mythology, described as a "giant, hairy, bearded, black-bodied, big-breasted, wide-eyed female monster."[61] She guards the Water of Life,[62] and some researchers associate her with Sasquatch. In yet another example of the food taboo, any human children who happen upon her and are foolish enough to eat the food she offers are seized and tossed into the basket on her back.[63]

Though discussed frequently in folklore, detailed accounts of recent Sasquatch abduction are hard to come by, accounts involving food even harder, and credible accounts involving food nigh impossible, especially when compared to faerie or alien stories. Most modern sightings of the beast tend to be brief, and the opportunity to exchange food does not present itself very often.

The most famous testimony involving food is that of Albert Ostman, who swore in a 1957 affidavit that he was abducted by a Sasquatch 33 years earlier. Ostman, working as a prospector in British Columbia, was allegedly picked up and carried while asleep, sleeping bag and all. After three hours he was unceremoniously dropped in a small valley, surrounded by four Sasquatch that he presumed were father, mother, son, and daughter. Over the course of a few days, he was fed "sweet roots" with a "satisfying taste." Interestingly enough Ostman also used consumables to escape, tricking the father into eating his entire can of snuff: the tobacco made the beast ill and, after downing Ostman's coffee ("That did no good," he later said), it fled to a nearby spring for water. The commotion created an opportunity for Ostman's getaway.[64]

The proverbial jury is out on the credibility of the Ostman account. John Green, the researcher who took Ostman's report initially, felt is was valid, while René Dahinden alleged that Ostman's story varied over the years. Both men were legends in the field of Bigfoot study, so there is no telling which was correct.

Just as households of the past used to leave out offerings for faeries, some so-called "habituators" today leave food and trinkets for Sasquatch, their disappearance attributed to the beings. Sometimes gifts are left in exchange—one compelling BFRO report from Washington detailed how ten mice, delicately wrapped in grass packages, were left in exchange for a bag of apples.[65] Such intricate weaving of grass requires more dexterity and intelligence than any known North American fauna possess.

One Bigfoot witness from Michigan recalled a summer in his childhood when chickens were stolen from the coop of his family's farm. The morning after the disappearances, the witness found five to six bullhead catfish at the family doorstep, presumably in recompense for the poultry. It was noted that—though the fish were fresh to the point of "still breathing"—none of the farm cats would touch them.[66]

Perhaps the catfish were missing their *foyson*?

Further Complexities

Six "little men" entered an elderly woman's home in Puerto Rico in January 1991, according to a *Fate* magazine article by Scott Corrales.[67] One of the entities, presumably their leader, instructed the witness to drink something from a vial while he gave her a medical checkup. Corrales included this account in an article on unidentified flying objects (UFOs), although the fact that the beings thoroughly cleaned her house, combined with an absence of spacecraft, seem to echo faerie tradition more than something extraterrestrial.

It is understandable how someone would wonder why three such disparate humanoids—faeries, aliens, and Sasquatch—are included together in one book. The truth is that the lines between these phenomena blur far too often to be mere coincidence. In 1010, an Italian Cardinal-Bishop recorded the account of a boy who was taken by strangers to a great feast, made to eat, and returned safely through the roof—was this the work of faeries or aliens?[68] In one of his hypnotic regressions, Barney Hill said that one of the entities left him with the impression of "a redheaded Irishman"—not exactly someone you would expect to find onboard a spaceship.

Many of UFOlogy's greatest minds have made note of the similarities between the fae folk and aliens. Jacques Vallée addressed many of these parallels in his groundbreaking book *Passport to Magonia*, as have researchers Thomas Bullard and Janet Bord in their respective work. The correspondence between the broad strokes of both phenomena—short beings seen in conjunction with supernatural lights—are clear. Take for example the Irish *trow*, goblins so fond of kidnapping they are also referred to as "the night stealers" or "grey neighbors"[69]... chilling names in light of bedtime abductions by Grey aliens.

Both aliens and faeries have a penchant for leading the unwary astray, only to be instantaneously whisked off to another realm. The time displacement in the faerie realm corresponds to the missing time witnesses claim to experience in conjunction with abductions, and both entities are fond of stealing children (faeries allegedly stole babies from their cradles in the middle ages and replaced them with sickly changelings, while pregnant abductees today report in utero fetus theft). Modern crop circles are yesterday's "fairy rings." Even the minutiae, such as the tall, lithe entity presiding over a host of shorter beings in Jacob Jacobsson's story, are common features in modern abduction reports.

There is also a persistent line of thought among researchers that those with Celtic or Native American ancestry may be more prone to alien abduction. Both of these cultures have a rich folklore describing not only "little people" but hairy hominids as well.

Few individuals with a passing interest in the unexplained are aware that Sasquatch lore crosses the faerie-alien boundaries. While there is certainly a strong case to be made for a terrestrial, flesh-and-bone relict hominid, one cannot toss out folktales of the Celtic *woodwose*, nor the reports of Sasquatch-like entities witnessed in conjunction with UFO activity (see the flap[70] that began in Pennsylvania in 1973, for example). Unexplained livestock mutilations, tied to UFOs in modern thought, have also been attributed to both faeries and Sasquatch in times past. Some Celts and Native American tribes felt that faeries and Sasquatch, respectively, were the souls of the dead, and it is a rarely-addressed fact that deceased relatives are known to appear sporadically in alien abduction reports. Faeries live in faerie mounds, aliens have underground bases, and Sasquatch sleep in caves. Both faeries and aliens can paralyze their victims before absconding with them, while researchers have explored the concept of ultra low-frequency infrasound, seen in predators such as tigers, as a possible method Sasquatch may utilize to stun its prey.

Even the elaborate taxonomy of faeries—a feature that

pushes the boundaries of believability with its *Pokémon*-esque catalogue—is reflected in the Sasquatch and alien fields. Modern alien abductee lore speaks not only of Greys but also human-like entities, reptilians, mantids, and even trolls and gnomes, mirroring the work of Sasquatch researchers like William Jevning, who has classified hairy hominids into manlike, apelike, and doglike (!) categories.

Lastly, in addition to all of these comparisons, let us not overlook the food taboo.

None of this is to claim necessarily that faeries are aliens, or vice versa, nor that Sasquatch isn't a living, breathing animal. Regardless of one's personal beliefs, any researcher should feel vindicated if, upon awakening tomorrow, they read headlines that a flesh-and-blood Sasquatch was captured or a nuts-and-bolts alien spaceship has landed on the White House lawn. However, if we are honest with ourselves, we *must* take notice of these similarities. Such comparisons highlight how the High Strangeness[71] of anomalous experiences cannot be pigeonholed, despite how much we want to force each phenomenon into its own discrete box. The ETH in particular is a tidy explanation for a grossly untidy phenomenon, one often evoking theatre, humor, absurdity, and spirituality on a constant basis.

What we may be dealing with is something far more bizarre—and intimate—than little green men from outer space, undiscovered apes, or mere folklore.

CHAPTER 3
TRENDS

*You will see a sumptuous banquet, but don't eat or drink anything.
Your life depends on it. – Pan's Labyrinth*

In *Passport to Magonia*, researcher Jacques Vallée collected a century's worth of UFO landings (1868 – 1968) in an appendix prefaced as follows: "To compile a catalogue is to invite criticism. Catalogues are obtained by integrating information over a variety of sources, but not every piece of information has an identifiable source; information drawn from a single source is always questionable; information gathered from several sources is generally contradictory."[72]

The following is not a catalogue, as there is little doubt that the compiled data set is incomplete; that said, the research collected for this book represents roughly 350 folkloric accounts and eyewitness testimonies where individuals have received food or drink from non-humans. The cases described in detail are just a handful of the total researched.

Hard numbers are eschewed in this book in favor of a more qualitative approach to the entity food phenomenon. The inclusion of a data table or appendix would, among other complexities, imply that each case is of equal provenance, and that is simply not the truth.

There are several limitations to this study that must be addressed in the interest of transparency. Not every case collected is reliable, and no such claims are made to the contrary. The internet, though a marvelous tool, has certainly made it more difficult to separate the proverbial signal from the noise. As you will see, some cases are of an excellent pedigree (unimpeachable witnesses vetted by respected researchers, for example), while others are of more dubious origin (tabloids and stories collected from the internet). Treating these cases as equals in a data table feels somewhat disingenuous, and it is for that reason that each account mentioned is handled on a case-by-case basis.

Some of these accounts may be fabricated from whole cloth while others may be honest misidentification; in researching the unexplained, often all we have to rely upon are eyewitness reports and our own good judgment. *Caveat emptor.* The sources herein range from the research of independent organizations to out-of-print non-English magazines, and as such the chain of custody on this information is occasionally less than pristine. Still, every best effort has been made to verify these accounts and to provide citations as accurately as possible.

Second, it is unclear how much emphasis can be placed on the importance of entity food reports in the first place. After all, everything on Earth eats, and any lengthy encounter would naturally have to include food for the witness, lest they perish. Consider the countless reports where entities are described breathing; certainly we can all agree that is not a subject worthy of an entire book. This being said, the internal consistency of entity food cases, as we soon shall see, is a strong indicator that this exchange has some significance beyond simple sustenance.

An additional concern is that some of the observed trends may simply be a product of their time, place, and culture, and may not have any special significance to the entity food phenomenon as a whole. For example, faeries in medieval accounts tended to offer wine or bread; both were dietary staples of the era, so their presence is to be expected more than, say, a mango. Similarly, cultural norms may play into how tastes or textures are described, as flavors found palatable in one cuisine are reviled in another. Witnesses may also recall nothing more specific than the act of eating or drinking, or they might remember receiving food yet have no recollection of consuming it.

The final and perhaps greatest concern is that some cases are difficult to categorize, spanning multiple classifications. For example, do we label "fruit juice" a fruit, a beverage, or both? Is a tablet dropped into water considered a drink or a tablet? What about a paste smeared on the mouth, or ointment absorbed through the skin? Should we include force-feeding and injections in a discussion of food, which is usually voluntary and oral? Because of the nebulous nature of categorizing this data, exact statistics will be avoided in this book for the most part, lest we be forced to present several conflicting data sets.

The following reports were collected from a variety of sources. Special acknowledgement should be given to Albert Rosales, who has amassed an incredible database of over 17,000 humanoid encounters from books, magazines, television, and radio, as well as findings from independent investigators, research organizations, and personal correspondence. Without his assistance, this project would have never begun.

Like all anomalous phenomena, this body of research is rife with nuance, and our human penchant for language only seems to compound the complexity. In spite of such limitations, there are nonetheless clear trends that can be ascertained—trends that not only help us to better understand these cases, but also shed light on the unexplained as a whole.

Overall Trends

We will first establish the overall trends before more closely examining each type of entity food.

A few notes:
- Terms such as *correlation* and *significance* have very specific meanings in the field of statistics. No claim is made that such terms in this book are used in a strict social science

sense.

- Some trends (geographic incidence, demographics) may be indicative of UFO, alien, and Sasquatch encounters as a whole and not just the entity food phenomenon. If, to illustrate, there are more Sasquatch encounters in Washington than anywhere else in America, then it stands to reason that more entity food reports featuring Sasquatch would come from Washington.
- The data is only as good as the most descriptive cases—some have important details missing, in particular taste and color, either due to a lack of witness recall or poor investigatory standards. Thus, each of the following trends only includes cases where that information was provided and may skew the findings.
- Although they will be extensively discussed in each of the following chapters, accounts that are explicitly folklore, myths, and legends have been omitted from the tallies below in an effort to concentrate upon eyewitness testimony.

Entities: Most cases involving the exchange of food and drink come from encounters with beings reported as faeries or aliens, with only a few reports associated with large, hairy hominids. As noted by Nick Pope, former steward of the British Government's Ministry of Defence "UFO Desk," alien contactees are more likely to be given something to eat than alien abductees.[73] Abductees are usually given a substance via force-feeding or injection. If not, they consume food under duress while faerie and Sasquatch witnesses, as well as contactees, eat voluntarily.

Food groups: More than 60% of eyewitness accounts collected involve liquids, especially fruit juice. The next most common entity foods are fruits/vegetables, followed closely by grain products, pills, and, least often, meat and cheese. Meat is exceedingly rare and often rare when it appears. Abductees most often describe liquids; contactees most often describe liquids, fruits, and grain products; faeries witnesses describe liquids and grain products; and Sasquatch witnesses note fruits/vegetables and meat.

Color: While there is a very slight lean in favor of food/drinks described as white and clear, there is no strong trend regarding the color of entity food. In addition to white and transparent, reported hues are green, blue, yellow, orange, red, black, brown, and "multicolored," in that order. It should be noted that the aforementioned concern over categorization rears its head again here—some languages use the same word to describe different colors. Take, for example, something as simple as the color green. *Glas* in Old Irish is green or grey, while *glas* in Welsh is blue, both coming from Proto-Celtic *glasto*. Modern Persian lacks a distinction between black, blue, or green. Old Chinese, Thai, old Japanese, and Vietnamese can all describe blue and green with the same word.

Taste: When mentioned, a majority of entity food is described as sweet, tasty, or delicious. "Unpleasant" and "tasteless" are reported next most often, each in equal measure, while the rest of the accounts are more or less evenly divided between "tasteless, sour/tangy, bitter, or strange." Very few cases describe the food as "salty," which is notable when one recalls faeries' aversion to salt.

Demographics: Men outnumber women witnesses in the cases by more than 2:1, a statistic that anyone adopting a psychological approach will be quick to seize upon as Freudian. Witnesses also tend to report recurring contact. Farmers comprise a substantial portion of entity food receivers. While it is expected that anyone working outside would be more likely to run into a nonhuman than someone working in an office environment, it is nonetheless compelling that the people who once relied upon faeries for a healthy harvest are the same individuals who so often receive entity food. Food-related tasks are often interrupted or take place immediately prior to the experience, from the overt (dining, cooking, foraging) to the oblique (hunting, herding, fishing).

Geography: The highest number of eyewitness entity food reports comes from the United States, Russia, and Brazil, with the US slightly leading the trend. This is followed by (in descending order): England/Ukraine, Sweden/Spain, and France. There is a very high incidence of entity food reports from Puerto Rico, which was not included in the United States tally—taken on its own, the territory is tied with Sweden and Spain, astounding for an island of only 3.5 million people. If we took a reductive approach and lumped together the entirety of Latin American reports, the region would skyrocket to first place, outpacing the number of US accounts by a full third. Note that entity food is almost exclusively a Christian-country phenomenon, though that may be more indicative of language barriers and underreporting in non-Christian nations rather than actual incidence. *Also note that this data does not include folkloric accounts.* If it did, it is entirely likely that England and the Scandinavian countries would rank number one, with their rich traditions of faerie mythology.

Timeline and Effects: Though there are cases where it is offered in the middle of an encounter, the exchange of entity food tends to bookend the witness's experience, coming soon after entering or just before leaving the entity's presence. Of these, there is a strong tendency for entity food to be given immediately prior to the end of an event, particularly in the case of liquids. When eyewitnesses note the effect of eating entity food, they usually black out, only to reawaken in more mundane surroundings. Witnesses will often ascribe their subsequent amnesia to the food as well. Less common effects of entity food include stimulation, fullness, sedation, and vomiting/nausea. Even if it is not a direct result of the food or drink given them, witnesses will also report improved health, artistic ability, or psychic ability. That said, if folklore were included, the number one effect would no doubt be some variation on imprisonment in fairyland.

Although widely respected food taboos made it the common course of action in ancient accounts, exceedingly few modern cases were found where witnesses refused entity food, a profoundly disturbing trend. Most of us wouldn't accept food from a human on the subway, to say nothing of a Grey alien on a spaceship. Such behavior suggests that these experiencers must be somehow disinhibited during these encounters, or swept away in the dream-like quality often ascribed to them.

CHAPTER 4
FOOD: LIQUID

A little learning is a dang'rous thing; Drink deep, or taste not the Pierian spring. – Alexander Pope, *An Essay on Criticism*

March 24, 1978: Luis had left the tiny village of Penalva, Maranhão, Brazil to gather guava fruit in the surrounding jungle when, without warning, the young man heard a deafening noise accompanied by a blinding light in the trees. The combination knocked him on his back, and Luis found himself paralyzed, unable to move save his eyes. He slowly ascended into the canopy, passing through the veil of palm fronds and into the noonday sky, until he saw something strange hovering in the clouds: a round object with several domelike protuberances, one of which was glowing. He floated through an open porthole and was gingerly lowered onto the floor of the craft's interior, where he encountered several short beings, no more than three feet tall, each wearing a metallic suit and a visor. Luis felt the UFO shudder and move, only to stop once more some time later.

The witness was then "floated out of the object and came to rest on a flat stone or table." All around him was tall grass, yet above were neither clouds nor stars—only darkness. The last thing Luis recalled before passing out was how the short beings had forced a tube into his nose, placed a ball gag in his mouth, and poured some type of liquid down his throat. When a fisherman found Luis catatonic 81 hours later, he took him to the local hospital, where it was revealed his hair had been singed completely off and that two molars were broken, another two missing entirely.[74]

Luis is one of many purported UFO and faerie experiencers who claim to have received some type of liquid from a non-human intelligence. As noted, the most common food exchanged in humanoid encounters is not food at all but is actually drink, often likened to fruit juice or milk. In Sasquatch reports, liquid is practically nonexistent.

Description, Taste, and Effect

Though a majority of *all* entity food is perceived as sweet, drinks are described as tasting sweet or unpleasant (in particular "bitter") in roughly equal measure. Generally speaking, sweet drinks are thin and associated with contactee/faerie reports, while unpleasant drinks are thick and common in abductions; the trend, however, is by no means absolute. The famous abductee Betty Andreasson recalled a sweet and syrupy liquid dripping into her mouth during one encounter, while there are plenty of experiencers who remember a drink's unpleasant flavor but not its consistency.[75]

As we shall see, sweet drinks in these cases are usually likened to fruit juice, while cases involving thicker liquids often have no earthly analogue. One Brazilian UFO witness was given a viscous, tasteless drink in August 1979,[76] while a 1990 Russian account detailed a liquid that was thick and sour—neither made a comparison to anything they had ever ingested.[77] Equally persistent are cases where victims are suspended in a sort of viscous medium (ostensibly to dampen the effects of space travel on the human body) that also happens to be edible.

Consumption is universally voluntary in contactee and faerie cases while abductees tend to be force-fed, such as Kerry Reid of South Australia, who recalled a "dark, viscous liquid" pumped into his throat during a childhood abduction.[78] Injections can be seen as a variation on this forced-ingestion trope, and are so common in modern abductions that they practically deserve a book unto themselves.

There is no clear frontrunner for the color of entity-administered liquids. While entity food on the whole is slightly more likely to be white, liquids are also green, yellow, or transparent in more-or-less equal measure. "Dark" and blue are the next most common hues, followed by the rare colors purple, orange, and red. Categorization of color, a process one would expect to be straightforward, can prove surprisingly difficult: in one fanciful 1953 account from Ukraine, otherworldly visitors gave the witness a glass of water that, when combined drops from a phial, "turned pink, then blue in color, then transparent again," according to researcher Anton Anfalov of the Yaroslavl UFO Group.[79] To further compound these complexities, many witnesses do not note any specific color at all.

In the 1969 case of José Antonio Da Silva, the witness was taken aboard a craft by several tiny, bearded gnomes with large noses. Once airborne, Da Silva was able to establish rudimentary communication with the beings, who seemed interested in earth's weapons (Da Silva, it should be noted, was a solider). The exchange was interrupted when one of the dwarfs presented a bitter green liquid in a square stone cup, which Da Silva drank only after seeing his captors imbibe. He was returned five days later 200 miles from where he had disappeared.[80]

Da Silva reported that the drink stimulated him, though the beverage Manuel Olaer claimed to have consumed during his September 2, 1958, encounter in the Philippines had the opposite effect. Olaer was allegedly taken from his bedroom as a child by several four-foot-tall extraterrestrials with large grey heads and black, banana-shaped eyes. His last conscious memory prior to waking up in bed was feeling a tube snaked through his nose and throat, from which a "clear gold-filled" liquid was administered.[81]

This gap in memory represents a major theme in these cases, as roughly half of *all* entity food results in amnesia, unconsciousness, or sleepiness. This effect is strongly pronounced among liquids. To many, such substances will undoubtedly evoke uncomfortable comparisons to "date rape" drugs, pharmaceuticals that, when abused, can cause similar symptoms. For example, γ-Hydroxybutyric acid (GHB), legally used to treat narcolepsy, can in sufficient quantities induce retrograde amnesia—the erasure of recent past memories.

A few selected examples illustrate the consistency of induced amnesia throughout contemporary entity reports:

- Puerto Rico, 1980: Iván Morales was suffering from an incurable strain of rheumatic fever when two beings—classic Grey aliens—appeared by his bedside. Without warning, Morales (who had been bedridden for some time) found himself standing inside what he perceived as a transparent alien spacecraft. He claims that they descended beneath the sea and emerged in an underwater cave, where the aliens began to examine him and offered a bitter-tasting yellow liquid to drink. Morales noted that the beverage made him very drowsy, so much so that his conscious memory of the event ends there. Miraculously, he was healed of all his existing ailments.[82]

- One "Jack T." recalled under hypnosis an event ten miles south of Lake Ontario in the summer of 1964 or 1965 where he and a friend were taken by strange entities. The two boys were playing in a deserted park when they were approached by a Grey alien dressed in a shiny, dark blue uniform. It seemed to put them in a sort of trance, communicating that they should come with him to see something interesting. The pair followed the entity to a nearby garage where they were helped into a four-door black Cadillac with tinted windows. Two humanoids in the front then drove them down a swampy dirt road to a disc-shaped craft where the boys were placed in a room together. Each was forced to drink a liquid that made them drowsy, followed by an examination by two shorter entities. They were told never to speak of the event, "because no one would believe them.' They summarily returned to the garage unharmed.[83]

- A family of three adults and two small children were traveling in Oxfordshire on a quiet stretch of highway late one night in 1978 when their car was supposedly intercepted by a flying saucer. The craft's humanlike occupants examined the family; according to the eldest daughter Natasha, "before they left the spaceship, the grown-ups were given a clear, fizzy drink in a glass, 'to help them forget.'" The adults later confirmed this under hypnotic regression, describing the taste as "milky." Natasha had refused the drink outright and as such had the clearest memory of any of the abductees.[84]

- Barbara Warmoth of Franklin, Ohio said she was taken aboard a craft on August 19, 1981, as she was driving along the interstate in broad daylight. The beings, which she had encountered before, were seven feet tall with catlike yellow eyes, long thin noses, pointed chins, and thin lips. Warmouth was placed in a large chair and examined before receiving a glass of greenish liquid. The next thing she remembered was awakening in her car.[85]

- Angie, a recurring abductee who worked with the late Karla Turner, recalled an experience one night in October 1993 where she was awakened at 1:30 a.m. by a loud noise. Her next memory was standing in a forest clearing, accompanied by four other women. A "strange-looking airplane flew toward them and landed like a helicopter," from which men in black uniforms emerged, threw her in the craft, and took her to some sort of compound. Once they had landed, one of these "men" held a brief telepathic conversation with Angie before a strangely hypnotic woman gave her a bitter, dark red liquid. The substance "made her dizzy and sleepy to the point of passing out."[86]

In 1987, a hunter named Kevin stopped to use the bathroom during a trip on the North Canol Road near Macpass, Canada, when he spotted something out of the ordinary: a green cigar-shaped craft hovering just in front of the mountains to the south. He watched until the object disappeared from view, whereupon he was jarred from his reverie by a metallic sound behind him. Thinking there might be another witness to corroborate his sighting, Kevin rounded the bend and saw two five-foot tall beings in blue jumpsuits with "grasshopper" heads. One of the entities raised a device in its left hand and shot a beam of white light that paralyzed him—the next thing he knew they were gone and he was able to move once more. Kevin promptly hopped on his bike and quickly set off for his destination.

After a restless evening of listening to ominous, unsettling sounds outside the trailer, Kevin awoke in a strange environment, this time accompanied by a Grey alien. He asked the being if it planned to experiment on him, to which the Grey telepathically replied that such activities had already taken place. The Grey then directed him toward a window saying, "That bright white star is your home."

After declining an invitation to "go on a trip," Kevin was offered "a clear glass, ¾ full with a yellow liquid," which his host urged him to drink. The beverage, it seemed, would make him forget the experience, though Kevin protested, wanting to remember this once-in-a-lifetime experience.

"I was told it was for my own good that I forget," said Kevin upon later recollection, "So I took three little sips and put the glass down." The next thing he remembered was gaining consciousness by his bike on the side of the road. [87]

Martin Jasek of UFO British Columbia met with Kevin numerous times during his investigation of the case. As physical proof of his experience, Kevin was left with two peculiar, deep scoop marks in his hands. Though he initially remembered very little, it is worth noting that Kevin recalled his experience bit-by-bit over time and not via hypnotic regression, as is often used in abduction cases.

The forced amnesia experienced by alien abductees is echoed in faerie lore. An Irish priest raised in Connemara told Evans-Wentz that "the mind of a person coming out of Fairyland is usually a blank as to what has been seen and done there."[88]

The tendency for amnesia-causing liquids to be offered to witnesses at the end of an encounter is evocative of *nepenthe*, the "drug of forgetfulness" in ancient Greek mythology. One of the *Moirai*, the mythic Fates, was known for offering hapless knights an "elixir of blissful oblivion" that, after drinking, would obliterate their memory and identity.[89] Recall the story of Astri Olsdatter, who was told in one instance that if she were to drink from the cup of the mountain men she would forget about her father and mother.[90]

One of the first individuals to draw this connection between nepenthe and the food offered during humanoid encounters is self-identified abductee Whitley Strieber, perhaps most famous as the author of the best-selling book, *Communion*. In the past few decades Strieber has come under a great deal of fire for his outlandish claims, some of which include entity food. To his credit, however, Strieber has stuck by his story in spite of its more outlandish aspects, and several of his observations are extremely thoughtful and quite germane to our coming discussions.

In *Transformation*, Strieber recalls being "forced to swallow a milky substance that left a horrid taste in [his] mouth" just prior to returning from his December 26, 1985, abduction.[91] This is emblematic of another trend involving liquids: even when they fail to explicitly cause amnesia of the incident, they still tend to precede a return to the "real" world.

Though contradictory to the established mythology, the notion that entity food might have the opposite effect of the food taboo (i.e. release instead of trap the consumer) has precedent in folklore as well. One legend tells of a shepherd boy who joined a ring of faeries dancing on a hillside. He was instantly transported to a faerie palace where all his wishes came true, and was told he could stay so long as he did not drink from the fountain in the garden. He eventually took a sip, of course— as fairytale protagonists are wont to do—and found himself instantly returned to the real world.[92]

On rare occasions liquid will be given at the beginning of an encounter, often in the form of an ointment or paste. In these cases, the entities will often explicitly note that the substance administered will facilitate travel. This is by no means a trivial subject, and will be discussed in greater detail later.

Milk

Milk, a staple of life since time immemorial, is common in faerie lore. Practically all of the fae folk accept milk as an offering, are quick to steal it from farmers, and occasionally offer it directly to humans (recall the man who died for rejecting the *banshee*'s buttermilk).

It isn't always animal milk that faeries offer, however. In one Scandinavian folktale, a young cowherd was fending off sleep when a faerie happened upon him. "You look hungry," she said seductively. "Come, I'll give you something to drink. Take a suck, *if* you dare." She presented her breast and somehow enticed the young man to suckle, whereupon he fell into a trance and "stayed there for an eternity." Somehow he eventually extricated himself from this awkward position, possessing only a foggy memory of the encounter.[93]

Even more enticing was the milk of the Milk-White Milch Cow, a fae bovine with the miraculous ability to never run dry. Any Celtic family lucky enough to happen upon her could drink her milk and be made healthy, wise, or happy, depending upon one's needs.[94]

In the early 1970s in Veracruz, Mexico, several child disappearances were attributed to the *chaneques*, small elemental faeries similar to the aforementioned *duendes*. One child was Arturo Gutierrez, who disappeared at age six after going on a hike with his uncle. The uncle was awaiting trial for murder when the boy reappeared 33 days later in perfect health, saying that he had "been living with the little men. They gave me food and milk with honey in it. We played a lot of games. I was very happy."[95]

As mentioned earlier, there are very few stories where Sasquatch offer liquids, presumably because—if one adopts the biological ape theory—they lack the sophistication to create drinking vessels. Nonetheless, there are still a few interesting connections to make with folklore and anecdotes. Just as Milk-White Milch Cow guarded her magical liquid of life, so *Tsonoqua* holds a special elixir of her own. According to folklorist Cheryl Shearar, if *Tsonoqua* was slain, her skull could be turned into a wash basin, one whose "water gives children anointed with it remarkable strength. She occasionally endows select, fortunate and clever individuals with great wealth."[96]

Several reports exist of hairy hominids suckling humans. Circa 1200, a baby was stolen from its nanny in Sienra, Spain. A hastily organized rescue party quickly located the boy, who was "happily sucking one of the tits" of the *serrana*, or wild woman. There is some dispute as to whether or not this account is describing a bear, although such behavior would seem unlikely from a wild animal.[97] One Indian news source ran a story, no less suspect, of an alleged Yeti abduction that ended in an unfortunate man being "forcibly breastfed." He described the milk as "sour with a mixture of bitterness."[98]

There is also no shortage of extraterrestrial cases where witnesses allegedly consume milk or a "milky" substance.

• A 52-year-old repeat experiencer in Dagestan, Russia, awoke one night in 1990 to find two humanoids dressed head-to-toe in tight-fitting suits. One held a bottle of "some unknown whitish liquid" which she was forced to swallow. The entities disappeared immediately afterward. She later remarked that the beverage tasted like sour milk.[99]

• In 2007, one witness recalled an incident some 33 years earlier when Grey aliens entered the bedroom and administered "some white liquid that had the appearance of milk but had a horrible chemical taste." The witness remembers a Grey alien, larger than its compatriots, hovering close by and communicating good intentions.[100]

• Researcher Albert Rosales had direct correspondence from "Margaret," a mother in Queensland, Australia, involved in multiple encounters. Margaret reported that in 1993 her daughter claimed to have met a "tall woman" who had come through the window and given her "cake and pink milk to drink in a large goblet." Though it is possible these were simple childish flights of fancy, the mother had seen several shadowy figures moving through the home around the time of the incident, and once even caught a glimpse of a tall woman on their property.[101]

• "Godre Ray King" wrote in 1934's *Unveiled Mysteries* that he had encountered "Saint Germain" four years prior while working at California's Mount Shasta. King, whose real name was Guy Warren Ballard, said that Saint Germain was an immortal being who gave him a peculiar creamy fluid to drink called "Life—Omnipresent Life." He also consumed a golden beverage with the consistency of honey. Ballard would later found the "I AM" Activity, a New Age organization.[102]

In addition to consuming the "milky drops" during one of his abductions, Strieber also recalled a peculiar encounter with an entity he refers to as "Master of the Key." Early on the morning of June 6, 1998, an enigmatic man allegedly visited Strieber in his Toronto hotel room and sermonized to him about all matter of topics, including spirituality and the environment. Before leaving, the Master instructed Strieber to "drink a white liquid that he'd had in one of the glasses from the bathroom." Upon awakening, however, Strieber could find no evidence of the liquid in his glass, suggesting that the encounter had taken place in some other, ethereal reality, if it indeed occurred at all.

Not to be crude, but one must wonder if there is any symbolic meaning in a thick, white liquid exchanged between two men. Any homoerotic overtones were lost on Strieber, who equated the beverage with his earlier memories of "the Milk of Nepenthe." He suggested that perhaps the amnesia experienced in these cases is an attempt to dampen "the anguish of remembering the pleasures" of another realm.[103]

Cryptic messages from other worlds are a staple of such experiences. In *Alien Dawn*, Colin Wilson tells of a repeat abductee who was allowed to remember one evening:

> Liquid was injected into her hand below the thumb. When she cried out, she was told, 'There is no pain', and the pain went. Then she was undressed, and a needle driven into her navel. When she asked why this was being done, she was told, 'It is part of the change.' Later she was shown horses on a tiny screen, and told that they had also been changed. So had cows. Then the 'doc' [Grey alien] told her, 'You must eat only cow things.'[104]

While perhaps unrelated to the appearance of milky liquids in abductions, this is nonetheless a compelling anecdote. Aliens have long been proposed as the agents behind unexplained livestock mutilation, and while that topic falls out of the scope of our discussion, it will nonetheless be briefly touched on later, as will the theft of milk by nonhuman entities.

Is there perhaps a symbolic aspect to these reports of milk? Milk has been referred to as the "elixir of life," bestowed by the archetypal mother, central to civilization. "Precious, sustaining, and elusive, milk [in medieval history] was an accompaniment to conversation with divine powers," writes folklorist Deborah Valenze in *Milk: A Local and Global History*. "Wherever milk was found, we can expect to see a mix of bodily and spiritual concerns in the Middle Ages."[105]

Saint Bernard of Clairvaux legendarily received three drops of milk from a statue of the Virgin Mary, creating the notion of Marian lactation as spiritual sustenance in Catholic iconography.[106] How do we reconcile this image with the screen memory[107] from Strieber's *Transformation* where a woman administers "three drops of a clear liquid out of an eyedropper" onto his tongue?[108]

In Vedic tradition, the primordial ocean was comprised of milk and churned by gods and demons. By adding strong herbs to the churning process, the deities were able to coax a magic elixir out of the milk: the moon god Chandra, who was later called *Soma*.[109] Hindu myth describes *Soma* as a god and a plant as well as a drink, a fact not inconsequential to our future discussion.

Armando Zurbarán, the Mexico City contactee from 1954, reported his humanlike hosts preferred a type of milk as their primary source of nourishment, albeit made from plants. Zurbarán's report is typical of the contactee era, a mix of the mundane and bizarre filled with charming details such as an automated "air shower" and an extraterrestrial breakfast. Other fare during his experience included a very terrestrial meal of grilled meat, butter, and cheese, as well as fruit juice that faintly tasted like "mangoes and other tropical fruits."[110]

Juice

Reports of liquids describe fruit juice roughly as often as they describe "milk." For all intents and purposes, descriptions of "fruit juice" are exclusive to alien contactee cases—though if one considers wine a fruit derivative, this assessment should be adjusted to incorporate faerie accounts as well.

Unfortunately, these reports are often quite vague and fail

to describe how the juice tasted beyond "sweet." J. Escobar Faria and Richard Hall reported that one Mr. Rossi of São Paulo was given something resembling fruit juice in 1956 by tall, bald, sexless beings prior to visiting their home planet.[111] Half a world away in 1978, a Ukraine shepherd named Pyetr Matvienko claimed to have stayed well-fed during his visit to another world simply by consuming a drink flavored like "a mixture of fruits;" in a parallel to the elle-maid stories, he became so bored upon his return that he eventually committed suicide.[112] Even Zurbarán, mentioned above, was noncommittal on exactly what flavor he perceived.

A small number of accounts offer greater insight and report a wide array of specific flavors:

• One of the few faerie accounts to feature juice was the 2002 testimony of Audur Gudmundsdóttir, a nine-year-old Icelandic girl who claimed to have interacted with a short woman while playing among some boulders. Gudmundsdóttir had fallen to the ground when one of the rocks opened and revealed a small figure as tall as her waist. The being invited the girl inside, where she gave the girl "a spiral-shaped cake and some funny banana juice." Gudmundsdóttir claimed many interactions with the elves from then on, even bringing her mother a small nail-like object that she claimed was the key to a faerie house.[113]

• In August 1994 Swedish contactee Ante Jonsson received a colorless drink resembling lemonade from a tall "pale man" and several ugly dwarves. This allegedly took place in a modest "restaurant" on an alien planet, accompanied by a meal resembling steak and "some vegetables." Jonsson, whose encounters often featured beverages, was expressly told in a prior event that he would not be able to travel with the entities unless he drank what was given. [114]

• A humanlike entity wearing a silver coverall and black vi-

sor visited the Skogveien, Norway, home of recurring contactee
Arve Jacobsen in November 1984. The being invited Jacobsen
aboard his mothership where he beheld many fantastic things,
including an indoor garden with gigantic pyramid like structures. When he became tired, Jacobsen was given a beverage
that reminded him of raspberries and was rejuvenated.[115]

• In his 1967 book *Stranger at the Pentagon*, Dr. Frank E.
Stranges claimed to have met "Valiant Thor," a being from
Venus visiting Earth with the intention of helping mankind
overcome its destructive impulses. While aboard Thor's spacecraft, Stranges claimed to have eaten high-protein food and
consumed a green drink that tasted of papaya.[116]

• One sensational story tells of a farm engineer from Boro-
voye, Russia, who was on a fishing trip when he and his companion noticed an egg-shaped craft land approximately two
kilometers away. The two decided to investigate, but the witness' friend turned back, and soon he was intercepted by a tall
figure in a grey suit and respirator mask. A conversation en-
sued, and the witness was asked to follow him inside the craft,
where several shorter entities were seen. Upon inquiring what
the aliens ate, the tall being produced a made-to-order apple-
flavored "cactus-seaweed" drink. The witness had an old leg injury healed, and upon returning to his friend had no memory
of the encounter and discovered (to his surprise) that he had
been missing for hours. He recalled the event in full one year
later.[117]

Note the generally positive sentiment in each of these
encounters, a hallmark of the contactee experience. One wonders
how many more witnesses were given some sort of "fruit juice," as
this sweet flavor profile is consistent with tastes in a great number
of cases. Fruit juice also commonly appears in conjunction with
other foods, as we shall see throughout this book.

Though it is impossible to say for certain, there may be a link between the frequency of fruit juice and some classic post-abduction symptoms. A high bone-lead content, often representing a lifetime accumulation of the element, has been noted in the skeletons of some Romano-British cemeteries. This is thought to be in large part due to the consumption of fruit juice from lead or pewter vessels—the acid in the fruit leeched lead into the cup, and would likely have caused chronic lead poisoning.[118]

Lead poisoning symptoms can include memory loss, insomnia, reproductive problems, and tingling in the extremities—all ailments not uncommon to those who claim to have encountered extraterrestrials. A persistent metallic taste in the mouth is another symptom common to both lead poisoning and experiencers. For example, the famous Travis Walton case of November 5, 1975, left the abductee with an intense thirst and metallic taste in his mouth,[119] as did abductions in France, 1950[120] and Seattle, Washington in 1985.[121]

What does this mean? It seems unlikely that contactees and abductees are served juice in lead-lined vessels. Still, it may be a fascinating and worthwhile endeavor to check the post-experience lead levels in abductees.

Alcohol

As evidenced by Lady Wilde's account, the story of Jemmy Doyle, and the tales of the elle-maids, offers of alcoholic beverages are common in reports involving faeries. This is to be expected, as ale and wine were the most commonly consumed drinks in the Middle Ages—obtaining clean drinking water was difficult, thus transforming alcoholic beverages into staples.

As such, faeries in folklore offer alcohol with much greater frequency than milk. In one tale, two young men plowing their father's land in Germany were yearning for a distraction from the work at hand, and began to daydream of fresh-baked bread and cold ale. So intense was their desire that they could virtually smell it, and they were astonished to find at the end of their furrow a freshly baked loaf and a brace of beer tankards. Recognizing this as a gift from the *erdluitle*, or dwarfs, they fell upon the food and quickly ate it. One of the boys tossed a few coins into his stein to show appreciation, but the other scoffed and only threw in dirt, thinking the ignorant dwarfs would be none the wiser. By year's end, the latter was dead.[122]

Another story related by William of Newbridge in the 12th century told of a Yorkshire man who, coming home in an inebriated state heard voices, laughter, and the sounds of feasting coming from a nearby barrow. The man saw an open door in the side of the mound and peeked inside to behold a large banquet. One of the faerie attendants, upon seeing him without libations, handed a cup of wine to the voyeur. Despite his love of drink, the man poured out the contents but kept the cup, escaping with a vessel of "unusual colour, and of extraordinary form." Over the years, the faerie cup would pass into the possession of various English and Scottish kings.[123]

It is no secret that intoxication is central to faerie phenomenon. The Good Folk seem to love preying upon people with a few drinks in their system: cultures around the world describe the ghost lights, will-o'-the-wisp, *ignus fatuus* (foolish fire), jack-o'-lanterns, and hobby lanterns that lead astray the unwary, particularly those returning home from drinking. Becoming "fairy struck"—the sudden sense of paralysis so common to faerie encounters—was also a euphemism for someone who had partaken too freely of their libations.[124] To emphasize this point, consider that the Jemmy Doyle story concludes with the protagonist's child finding him the following morning in a field, his breath still smelling of punch.

The reason *why* faeries seem to relish harassing drunkards is up for debate. Does the alcohol actually make it easier to contact the faeries, stripping away some of the psychological barriers we erect during our alert, conscious state? Or does their love of the bottle keep a drinker's testimony safe from serious scrutiny?

Contactee George Hunt Williamson revealed in 1953's

Other Tongues—Other Flesh that any drinker makes an "excellent subject for Orion control."[125] Williamson was one of the pioneers in the field of channeling, wherein non-human intelligences communicate via a medium. Depending upon your view of both him and his methods, Williamson's observation may or may not be relevant to our discussion.

Alcohol is still a scapegoat for explaining away modern anomalous experiences. In August 1967, one British Ministry of Defence representative condescendingly commented, "We have not had many reports of UFOs, but we usually get them in the holiday season or at weekends, after the pubs close."[126] More recently, *The Economist* noted that American UFO sightings tend to be sighted during drinking hours, without any regard for the fact that very few of us have time to watch the skies while at work or while sleeping.[127]

Such sentiments are echoed in popular culture where, at least in some circles, "alien abduction" is slang for a night of black-out-level heavy drinking. The term is no doubt a reference to the post-experience sickness, dizziness, and missing time reported by abductees. It is interesting to juxtapose intoxicated faerie witnesses with the case studies of abductee and researcher Karla Turner, especially the tales she relates in *Masquerade of Angels* and *Into the Fringe*; alcohol flows freely throughout the books, though this may be more indicative of an American problem with alcoholism than something unique to abduction phenomenon.

In spite of these cursory connections, there are very few modern accounts of witnesses describing alcohol-type beverages in conjunction with alien encounters, making wine and ale almost exclusive to faerie phenomenon. Witnesses will on occasion evoke alcoholic pageantry, such as goblets or chalices (recall the young girl in Australia mentioned above), but the actual liquid itself is almost never described as alcoholic.

An exception is Enrique Mercado Orué, author of *28 Horas a Bordo de un OVNI* (*28 Hours on Board a UFO*), who claimed that on August 26, 1976, in Mexico City he was taken aboard an extraterrestrial craft by beautiful humanlike inhabitants. The entities, of varying size and clad in form-fitting metallic outfits, escorted Orué to a guest room where his hunger was sated with four "crackers" and a small glass resembling wine. He was told that this meal would keep him sustained for four days.[128]

A report detailed by Centro de Investigações e Pesquisas de Fenômenos Aéreos Não Identificados tells another rare story involving alcohol. Plínio Bragatto was working on a six pack of beer the evening of December 9, 1996, when he spotted a strange object in the Brazilian sky. Upon landing, two small beings exited and asked Bragatto aboard, an invitation he accepted because, after all, he "saw that they were good people." The beings were short and ugly, possessed of an enormous mouth, ears, and nose and hair that began growing halfway down their head. They performed a quick medical examination on Bragatto before giving him a fruit similar to a papaya (which they called a "pico") something resembling an empanada, and a beverage he equated with Campari. Ever the gracious guest, Bragatto shared one of his beers. They appeared to enjoy it, and took him to Mars for eight hours before returning him to earth.[129]

Such descriptions, though few, recall the curious case of Orfeo Angelucci. Though he never described it as alcoholic, Angelucci's books *The Secret of the Saucers* and *Son of the Sun* are practically love letters to a mysterious, bubbling, amber "nectar" first given to him May 23, 1952, in Burbank, California. Pursued by a mysterious light, Angelucci stopped his car and was told by a voice to take a "goblet" that had miraculously appeared on the fender. "It was the most delicious beverage I had ever tasted," Angelucci wrote in *The Secret of the Saucers*. "I drained the cup. Even as I was drinking a feeling of strength and well-being swept over me and all of my unpleasant symptoms vanished."[130]

Throughout his contact, entities seemed to use various forms of this nectar to initiate and terminate his encounters. In the follow-up book, *Son of the Sun*, Angelucci describes encountering a mysterious man in a diner two years after his initial encounter.

At that meeting, the man dropped an "oyster white pellet" into Angelucci's water, the resultant mixture creating his beloved nectar. When he drank it this time, Angelucci saw apparent hallucinations, including the sensation that he had been transported to a far-flung galaxy and the image of a tiny woman dancing in his glass.[131]

One working theory is that Angelucci's experience may have a purely hallucinogenic component at its core. Fortean researcher and author Nick Redfern posits that the famed "nectar" may have actually been LSD. "If you look at it from the perspective of the timeframe with MKUltra testing psychedelics and trying to get people to talk—here's Angelucci, babbling about his story—this mysterious character says, 'I want you to tell your story' and pops him a pill," Redfern said, referencing the CIA's early mind control program.

Redfern goes on to note that Angelucci noticed two military individuals in close proximity at the diner, and that there may have been some paranoia among the military that Russians were reaching out to contactees to help spread the ideals of communism. The theory is compelling: after all, many contactees described aliens living in a socialist utopia, and Twentynine Palms (the epicenter of many of Angelucci's experiences) is the home of the United States Marine Corps Air Ground Combat Center, making the presence of government agents in the vicinity a certainty. [132]

The hallucinogenic possibility is one of many angles on the case—others have noted a similarity between Angelucci's works and the visions Guy Ballard purportedly had at Mount Shasta. Regardless of its true origin, Angelucci's nectar is still worth inclusion in a survey and analysis of entity food.

CHAPTER 5
FOOD: FRUITS

Alas! the forbidden fruits were eaten,
And thereby the warm life of reason was congealed.
A grain of wheat eclipsed the sun of Adam,
Like as the Dragon's tail dulls the brightness of the moon.
                                    —Rumi, *Masnavi-I Ma'navi*

Ludovico Granchi had been investigating some peculiar lights in the woods near his Rio de Janeiro home one evening in September 1988 when he heard an unsettling buzzing noise akin to grasshoppers. Without warning, he was surrounded by five very small men dressed in uniform, each with dark-green eyes, white skin, and light hair. In their hands they held some type of lit wand—the apparent source of the mysterious lights.

The entities escorted Granchi to a nearby cave where he was laid upon a stone slab. He watched as they used their wands to examine him, all the while chirping like crickets to one another. When Granchi asked if they knew his name, however, one of the entities answered correctly in a high voice speaking perfect Portuguese. The examination concluded, Granchi was given a smooth, seedless red fruit to eat that had the texture of an apple but the taste of a plum. A nasty leg injury sustained prior to the encounter fully healed soon thereafter, although Granchi was confused and pale for a week afterward.[133]

A fruit similar to this "plum" features in "Faerie Dwelling on

Selena Moor," a legend given in *Traditions and Hearthside Stories of West Cornwall*. One Mr. Noy had disappeared after heading to a nearby inn to purchase drink, and was found asleep in a barn after three-days' time. He explained to his rescuers that he had become lost and, after traveling for a great distance in a strange land, happened upon a faerie banquet. The small people were feasting and dancing, and after a time one lady, taller than the others, left to fetch him a flagon of ale. While she was gone, another woman took Noy and spirited him away to a nearby orchard. He soon recognized her as Grace Hutchens, a former lover who had died some time earlier.

She warned him against taking anything from the people or the orchard. "For eating a tempting plum in this enchanted orchard was my undoing," she said, further explaining that the body buried in her stead was but a changeling, a shell, created by the little people. She had become lost searching for a stray sheep, and, famished, plucked "a beautiful golden plum" from one of the trees. The fruit had turned bitter in her mouth and she fainted, only to awaken as a prisoner of the faeries. She said their food was only a sham, with fruit that appears delicious but is "only sloes, hoggins (haws), and blackberries." She also told Noy they were not Christians, but actually "star-worshippers."

When her masters called for her, Noy wracked his brain how to rescue Grace. Recalling that faerie spells could be broken by turning an article of clothing inside out, he removed, reversed, and tossed his gloves to the ground, hoping to break the enchantment. Everyone, including his old flame, disappeared, and Noy was knocked unconscious by some unseen force. He awoke in the barn, where rescuers later located him. Noy lived out his days despondent.[134]

"Faerie Dwelling on Selena Moor" is notable for the way it threads together so many aspects common to modern encounters: missing time, a tall entity overseeing shorter ones, amnesia, and entity food—in this case, fruit.

Description, Taste, and Effect

After liquids, fruits are the next most commonly reported entity food, though they are a distant second. As with liquids, exact descriptions often elude witnesses, while other reports draw a direct comparison with the produce of earth. Vegetables are mentioned only on rare occasions.

The faeries of Selena Moor and Granchi's faerie-esque account notwithstanding, the exchange of edible plants tends to occur most often in encounters with aliens or Sasquatch. Warren Scott, a building superintendent from Seattle, Washington, claimed he was camping alone 30 miles northeast of Vancouver, Canada, in June 1961 when a Sasquatch kidnapped him and carried him 70 miles. When the beast finally dropped Scott into a deep cave with several of its kind, the stench was overwhelming. Scott said that the animals were a family unit. The one he identified as the "mother" brought him inedible chunks of raw meat and fresh greens, the latter of which presumably sustained him through his ordeal. He located the cave's hidden exit several days later when the beasts let their guard down.[135]

A similar tale from the late 19th century is told of a man from Briançon, France, who was purportedly taken by *homme des bois*, a hairy forest man, and kept in a cave with its family. He was sustained on berries for a time, but his hirsute captor eventually lost interest in him.[136] Both the French account and Scott's story are evocative of Albert Ostman's 1957 encounter, where he was brought "sweet roots."

Like most entity food, the fruits and vegetables offered by nonhuman beings tend to be sweet, with bitterness reported second most-often. They appear in narratives close to the encounter's end, though the correlation is not as pronounced as it is with liquids. Even more so than reports involving liquids, modern reports of alien-offered fruit are mired in bizarre symbolism and High Strangeness. As such, they are most prevalent in contactee cases, which, as previously noted, also frequently feature fruit juices.

• One witness described a story related to him by his grand-father, who grew up in Andhra Pradesh, India, in 1931. According to the story, the young witness saw a "sage" meditating under a tree and stopped to pay his respects. The sage said he was from the stars, then asked the boy to follow him to a near-by mountaintop. There they found the sage's *vimana*, an ambiguous Sanskrit word used to describe temples, vehicles and, most interestingly, mythical flying palaces or aircraft. Aboard the *vimana*, the young boy was seated in a golden chair and given some fruits to eat. The encounter concluded with a series of dire apocalyptic warnings for the distant future.[137]

• In his anthology *The Communion Letters*, Whitley Strieber reprinted correspondence from an individual who claimed to have been taken with a lifelong friend to another planet. While there, they plucked a pomegranate-like fruit from a nearby tree. "The grays said we could eat the fruit, it wouldn't hurt us," the writer explained. "We were told to scatter the seeds of the fruit when we were done."[138]

• Researcher Barbara Hudson described a case from the summer of 1955 when she awoke to find a tall being with glowing eyes in her New York City bedroom. The entity asked the witness to follow him, taking her into the living room where a gray mist had collected. They were immediately trans-ported to a metallic, elevator-like enclosure and exited into a corridor that terminated in a room bathed in bright pink light. Inside were approximately nine other beings, all tall with black hair, examining various monitors. She was eventually led to yet another area where she was given a meal consisting of wines and fruits resembling "an apple or something that looked like a melon." After finishing her meal, she was informed it was time to return home and she was taken back to her apartment via the gray mist.[139] The similarities to the 1931 Indian case are interesting: an invitation to follow and an ascent followed by a meal of fruit.

• In February 1974 two young Panamanian boys and their sister were washing their clothes in the local river when a strange woman in a brilliant blue dress appeared to them. She had white skin and long black hair. While the sister fled, the boys slowly approached the woman before she suddenly vanished. Several days later the boys returned to the river, only to disappear and return home four days later in fine condition. They explained they had been on an adventure with the mysterious lady, who this time appeared in the company of another woman and two men. The six of them took a "walk in the clouds" together where they were given fruit to eat.[140]

• On April 12, 1980 two bright lights and a shadowy figure allegedly landed on the farm of a Cuban prison, leaving behind a vast array of tropical fruit. Prisoners reported gigantic fruits resembling papayas, oranges, and apples. In an echo of the Granchi case, one of the inmates had an infected leg wound completely heal two days after eating the fruit.[141]

• A young woman named Irina from Yaroslavl, Russia, was awoken by a bright light streaming in through her window on the evening of February 10, 1997. A tall woman with white skin, black eyes, and long, straight black hair—compare to the Panama case above—materialized, saying, "I am Gelida from the planet Uta." Irina lost consciousness and awoke aboard an alien spacecraft where, among other things, she was given a lecture on how the negligence of Gelida's people had destroyed their homeworld. Irina then passed out again and came to in a beautiful green meadow, presumably the new homeworld Gelida's people had colonized. Irina's dog, Chuck, was with her, running about the meadow and feasting upon impossibly large "strawberries" with a meaty flesh. Gelida invited her guest to try the fruit, which reminded Irina of a strawberry crossed with a pineapple. The juice of the berry dribbled on her dress, and when she looked at the stain Irina realized she was back at home in bed, Chuck barking at her feet. While the entire experience is easy to write off as a dream, the stain allegedly remained on Irina's nightgown and a doctor's visit shortly thereafter revealed a high amount of leukocytes and a low amount of lymphocytes in her blood.[142]

One of the most vivid accounts of both fruits and vegetables comes from Elizabeth Klarer, a South African contactee who claimed to have met (and conceived with) Akon, a humanlike entity from the planet Meton, in the 1950s. Klarer asserts many extraordinary claims in her 1980 autobiography *Beyond the Light Barrier*, but one of the more mundane anecdotes is a dinner she recalled sharing with her alien lover:

> A golden tray laden with delicious salads and fruits appeared, literally materializing onto the white table beside the divan, along with long-stemmed crystal containers in which golden fruit juice sparkled.
>
> "The light ray placed it there for you," Akon said with a smile. "You had better have some of that sustenance before I answer your questions."
>
> I wondered about that wonderful light ray. I had felt its fleeting warmth as the tray of food appeared.
>
> The fruit juice was simply lovely, with a flavor of ripe pomegranates. The salads consisted of delicate, bright green leaves and various cut vegetables mixed with crisp nuts, flavored with almonds and spices with a creamy dressing sprinkled over. Crisp, juicy fruits like large apricots and thin slices of moist,

fresh oat bread completed the most delicious meal
I had ever had.

"We assimilate all the protein and vitamins we need
from this diet," Akon's brother told me. "There is
no need to get it secondhand through animal meat,
as people of Earth do. It is all grown here in the
spaceship. Therefore, it is always fresh. It is natural
for you to enjoy this type of food. Your body craves
it after the heavy, cooked meals prepared on Earth,
which you must not touch again."[143]

Klarer mentioned pomegranate juice served alongside her
cosmic salad—as explained earlier, pomegranate was the fruit
with which Hades trapped Persephone in the Underworld.
Pomegranate is also mentioned in Whitley Strieber's *Communion*,
where, during his first experience of missing time, he recalled "a
perfectly terrible memory of eating what I have always thought was
a rotten pomegranate, which was so bitter that it almost split my
head open" (recall the bitterness of the plum from Selena Moor).
Strieber would later reevaluate this memory in *Transformation* and
compare the flavor to a fig.[144]

Symbolism

Both the pomegranate and the fig held positions of great esteem
in ancient times. Figs were the fruit of immortality to the ancient
Egyptians;[145] as an evergreen, the pomegranate commanded similar
respect in Zoroastrian tradition, where it symbolized everlasting
life.[146]

Both fruits are also featured heavily in the Christian Bible.
Numbers 13 mentions the Brook of Eshcol, plentiful with figs
and pomegranates, as the dwelling place of the sons of Anak, the
Nephilim. Gigantic offspring of fallen angels, the Nephilim have
long been connected by Ancient Astronaut theorists to both aliens

and large hairy hominids.

Fruit is one of the few guiltless foods in existence, made to be eaten, without any need for preparation of any kind. It has long served as a symbol of knowledge, in particular the apple, which emblazons everything from laptops to elementary school logos. The fruit Adam and Eve consumed in the Garden of Eden— sometimes an apple, in other traditions a pomegranate—was forbidden because it would impart unto them knowledge of good and evil.

Inherently feminine, fruit's very existence has long suggested plenty and fertility. "Fruit similes are common in descriptions of the female body, smooth and curvaceous, rounded and firm or fleshy, luscious, juicy," writes Eve Jackson in *Food and Transformation: Imagery and Symbolism of Eating*. "Breasts like peaches, mangos; apple cheeks, cherry lips; natural, wholesome, pleasure-giving, seductive, voluptuous."[147] In some European folklore, trees could be made fruitful if a pregnant woman ate their first fruit. The fruit, with its seeds inside, is itself a symbol for the pregnant woman. These overtones dovetail with the sexual encounters sometimes reported by witnesses, which will be discussed in relation to food in a later chapter.

CHAPTER 6
FOOD: BREAD

If thou tastest a crust of bread, thou tastest all the stars and all the heavens. – Robert Browning

On July 6, 1990, Anna Dmitrievna Yerygina was herding goats down a lonesome road in Zvarykino, Belgorod, Russia when a mysterious woman appeared out of thin air. Dressed in a light-gray loose-fitting outfit with a hood, she seemed ordinary, if a bit on the tall and lean side.

The woman approached Yerygina to greet her, then asked if goats' milk was tasty. Yerygina said it was, but expressed her preference for that of cows. The woman listened, then without segue abruptly invited her on a brief excursion that would last no longer than three hours. Though initially concerned for her herd and family during any absence, Yerygina's worries evaporated when the woman touched her shoulder and said, "Do not be afraid." She felt a peculiar calm fall over her and was escorted toward a large oval craft in a nearby field. A man awaited them, ready to help the two ladies aboard.

Yerygina sat in the dimly lit interior and, the next thing she knew, was in an entirely different room with several other individuals dressed in the same grey coveralls. In spite of the lack of windows or other clues, she had the intuition that she must be on another world, a sentiment expressed to her hosts. Asked how that felt, Yerygina replied that everything seemed wonderful there, a heaven in contrast to her joyless life on earth. The entities seemed to radiate a sort of spiritual warmth and hospitality.

At some length one of the entities offered Yerygina some bread, which she described as very tasty, as well as a strange liquid. When she finished the meal her memory went blank— she recovered consciousness back in the field by her goats, the strange woman at her side. The woman told her goodbye with a smile, promising they would meet again. Yerygina went on to have several more experiences, her curious encounters reported in both the "Zarya" (Belarus) and "Leninskaya Smena" (Belgorod Oblast) newspapers.[148]

Description, Taste, and Effect

Like other examples of entity food, bread often precedes a lapse in memory. It is most commonly found in faerie folklore (recall the 1912 MacDonald case from Scotland and "The Fairy Ped" tale), although it occasionally appears from time-to-time in contactee lore. The rare appearances of bread in Sasquatch abductions are presumably the result of theft; in a 1602 French case related by Norwegian cryptozoologist Erik Knatterud, one Anthoinette Culet claimed to have been abducted by an "ugly but amorous" hairy beast that "stole and brought her baskets of bread, fruit, cheese, linen and thread." That same night the beast wandered into the village where it was shot to death, the post-mortem declaring it to be a bear, albeit one that "almost looked like a human" with "a navel like humans [sic]."[149]

Entity-offered bread is often described as delicious or sweet. Scottish lore held that any beautiful, healthy mother who allowed a faerie babe to suckle at her breast would receive delicious food tasting of "wheaten-bread, mixed with wine and honey."[150] In 1645, Anne Jeffries fell ill, afterwards possessing clairvoyance and the ability to visit the faeries; they would leave her food, which, when shared with her employer, was described as "the most delicious bread that ever I did eat, either before or since."[151]

Modern accounts explicitly mentioning bread are much harder to come by than those from faerie lore, though they are not unheard of.

- Lina Ivanova Kravets had a lengthy encounter with a trio of 11-foot tall, three-eyed "extraterrestrials" in Shtanivka, Ukraine, in August 1953. They claimed to be on a mission to rescue a missing scout team. The host and her unlikely guests discussed several issues of great importance with Kravets, including spirituality and life on their planet. Before her encounter ended, Kravets was given a piece of "bread" the size of a small coin. Breaking it open she spied something dark and odorless inside, and decided to return the gift without partaking. The tiny size of the bread evokes the aforementioned 1912 MacDonald case.[152]

- On December 31, 1989, *Moskovskaya Pravda* ran an article describing the account of "Mrs. L," a 40-something mother of two living in Protvino, Russia. On September 13 of that year, Mrs. L. was returning home from the grocery store when two tall women in tight silvery suits jumped out from behind some boulders and paralyzed her. The women, who had light blond hair, gray-green skin, and antennaed hats, took the witness to a small disc-shaped craft by the side of the road. They invited their captive for a ride, which they insisted would not last long—after some prodding, Mrs. L. hesitantly accepted. Inside were three chairs, one of which was occupied by a man with his back toward her. Mrs. L. offered some of the bread she had just purchased, but the women declined, instead offering their guest a bit of "their" bread. Without thinking, she reflexively popped it into her mouth and swallowed; she later described the taste as that of a lightly sweet rye bread. The craft ascended, flying over Protvino before dropping Mrs. L. off at her apartment. The space people told her they would meet again, much to Mrs. L.'s chagrin.[153]

Joe Simonton's Pancakes

Without a doubt the most famous entity food report of all time is the case of Joe Simonton, a chicken farmer from Eagle River, Wisconsin.

It was around 11:00 a.m. on April 18, 1961, when Simonton noticed a strange sound similar to radials on wet pavement coming from outside his farmhouse. Looking outside he noticed a peculiar silver machine descending into his yard, around thirty feet in diameter and "shaped like two inverted bowls." Simonton stepped closer and a hatch opened on the craft, revealing three dark-skinned "Italians" inside. Each was about five feet tall, dressed in dark outfits with knitted headgear.

One of the occupants held a shiny jug aloft, and the good-natured Simonton took the vessel inside to fill it with water. Upon returning to the craft he caught a glimpse of its interior, which to his eyes appeared made of wrought iron. Simonton's attention was then drawn to one of the men who was "frying food on a flameless grill of some sort." Noticing his curiosity, the man offered Simonton four flat, porous pancakes, each about three inches in diameter. The entities sealed the craft and departed, the entire exchange lasting around five minutes.[154]

Simonton's credibility was viewed by the local community and every investigator as beyond reproach, both for his reputation as an honest farmer and his lack of a motive in concocting such a ridiculous tale. His credibility was only strengthened by the pancakes, which were still in his possession. One was given to a local judge, one to J. Allen Hynek (UFO investigator for the Air Force's Project Blue Book), one to the National Investigation Committees on Aerial Phenomena, and one Simonton kept for himself.[155] He claimed they tasted like cardboard.

Although a thorough analysis was performed on one of the pancakes by the U.S. Department of Health, Education, and

Welfare, the food was determined to be made of terrestrial, if tasteless, ingredients, including hydrogenated oil and buckwheat flour. There are conflicting reports as to the exact type of grain used, and rumors circulate about "unknown grains" in the pancake—in any event, the analysis was underwhelming. The official United States Air Force explanation was that Simonton was honest but had mistakenly conflated the reality of his breakfast with his dreams.

Jacques Vallée wrote about Simonton's encounter at great length in his book *Passport to Magonia*, immediately seeing parallels between the experience and interactions with faerie folk. This is a worthy line of inquiry, and closer scrutiny yields more similarities and questions—for example, what conclusion are we to draw between inedible faerie food devoid of glamour and the blandness of Simonton's pancakes? Taking a slightly different approach, is there some connection between the missing flavor of the pancakes and the *foyson* extracted from food by faeries?

In her *Encyclopedia of Fairies in World Folklore and Mythology*, Theresa Bane describes the *oennerbanske*, a race of dwarfs native to the Netherlands' Friesland Islands prone to stealing young girls and children. The *oennerbanske* have a gentler side, however, as they are also known for helping in building construction and "assisting the farmers in the field by bringing them fresh water to drink and pancakes to eat."[156]

Other Grains

Other grains have been reported by entity food witnesses in addition to bread. Rice, a food staple for many cultures, appears in several reports, such as tale of a boy who was spirited away on September 30, 1907, in Aichi prefecture, Japan. The child was setting out white rice cakes as religious offerings for an upcoming festival when he mysteriously disappeared for several hours. After some time his family heard a loud thump in their house and visited the roof to investigate, only to find their son unconscious with white rice cake covering his mouth. When he came to, the boy claimed to have met a stranger who "walked over the tree tops" and took him into peoples' homes, eating all the cakes that had been set out. The boy became a dullard afterward, a variation on the motif of eating in fairyland and returning irreparably changed. Another Japanese tale, this one from 1814, involved a boy taken to a strange land for several days and also fed cakes, but this time to no apparent ill effect. [157]

In his out-of-print book *UFO Contact from Undersea*, the late Lt. Colonel Wendelle Stevens interviewed one "David Delmundo" who was allegedly abducted off the coast of Puerto Rico in 1972. Delmundo (a pseudonym) had been taken by a short, grey-skinned being with wraparound eyes to a secret base beneath the seafloor where he was fed a "white, creamy substance similar to cornmeal." He described the taste as neither sweet nor salty yet still "very good and satisfying," leaving one with the sensation of being nourished.[158] This sense of satisfaction is a recurring theme in cases where witnesses consume grain products—recall the crackers and wine given to Enrique Mercado Orué in 1976, which purportedly kept him sated for four days.

Symbolism

Like fruit, bread has long been associated with fertility and rebirth. Wheat dies and is reborn time-and-again, and has been tied to themes of renewal since ancient Egypt. For millennia, bakers in countless cultures have fashioned bread in the shape of moons, suns, and genitalia, representing reproduction and rebirth. This duality is well represented in the Christian Bible: the Old Testament associates bread with the fertility of the earth, mentioning it more than 20 times, while the New Testament (over 30 references) embraces bread as a central focal point of the Eucharist, offering eternal life. In short, bread symbolizes the cyclical nature of existence in all its many forms.[159] These themes of rebirth and sexuality, as touched upon in the chapter on fruit, are essential to our later discussion.

Bread's power also extended to protection against evil. In Holland stale bread in a cradle wards off disease, in Morocco it cures stuttering, in Egypt indigestion. Bread and salt have long been central to Eurasian hospitality rites.[160] As noted earlier, a bit of stale bread could safeguard against faeries and yet at the same time, along with milk, was the most common offering made to appease the Good Folk.

Bread has also, at least tangentially, been used as a means of explaining perceived paranormal phenomena. Ergot, a type of fungus known to grow on rye and other grains, can produce convulsive symptoms if consumed; some have posited that cultures suffering an outbreak of ergotism could mistake the disease for bewitchment. A similar theory gaining traction among historians is that ergot-tainted bread may have caused the lycanthropic hallucinations that lead to the extensive werewolf trials of 16th and 17th century Europe.

It was perhaps a misnomer to cite the Joe Simonton case as the most famous entity food account. Without a doubt more people are familiar with the manna that rained from heaven to feed the Israelites, sustaining them as they traversed the desert en route to the Promised Land. Scholars have banged their collective heads against the wall for centuries seeking a scientific explanation for exactly what sustained the Jewish people those four decades, but to no avail. Theories range from airborne bits of lichen to quail dung (!) to tamarisk trees, the candidate currently with the most academic cache. When attacked by insects, the tamarisk tree actually weeps a sugary sap that hardens and falls to the ground in edible pieces.[161] Of course, none of these explain how a generation could subside on such an odd, meager diet alone.

Researcher Peter Gilman suggested in 1967 that manna could have been "angel hair," the cobweb-like (or gelatinous, depending on the account) material occasionally found after UFO sightings, particularly at landing sites. There are two primary problems with this theory, however: one, angel hair tends to evaporate quickly, and as such its makeup has never been studied for any nutritional value; and two, such a theory simply explains away one mystery with another, a particularly bad habit among the paranormal community.[162]

Notions of bread as a gift from heaven go much deeper than the Old Testament tale of manna. The serendipitous crossbreeding between different species of wheat some 10,000 years ago marked a major turning point for civilization, allowing mankind to transition from a hunter-gatherer existence to an agrarian society, where large settlements were allowed to grow and flourish. In the apocryphal Christian Book of Enoch, this development is attributed to the aforementioned Nephilim, who taught mankind how to cultivate plants, a role similar to that played by the Kachinas in Hopi legends and the god Quetzalcoatl in Mesoamerican myth.

Just how lucky was this convenient hybridization? "Since the emergence of bread wheat about 10,000 years ago, the unlikely yet successful crossing of two distinct species of wheat grains has never happened again," wrote author Rita Louise. "Scientists continue to claim that nature was able to produce a series of fortunate genetic anomalies that ultimately transformed humanity, yet are still unable to explain how they occurred."[163]

It is well known that 1989-1991 saw a surge in UFO and entity reports from the former USSR, although it is unclear whether the activity was actually ramping up or if post-Soviet censorship was more lenient. Regardless, consider the fact that a substantial number of modern entity food cases explicitly featuring bread— be it given to or taken from witnesses, as we will see later—are from Slavic countries, with a window of incidence in this '89-91 timeframe. This fact is ironic when one considers that the region, in particular Ukraine, has long been regarded as the "bread basket of Europe."

Bread's association with rebirth may offer some insight into its appearance during this period. Ancient Slavs engaged in a fascinating ritual they referred to as "baking the child," where a young boy or girl was placed inside a warm stove in a symbolic parallel to the transformative baking process. Tamra Andrews writes in *Nectar & Ambrosia: An Encyclopedia of Food in World Mythology* that baking the child was "a healing ritual; the child metaphorically returned to the mother's womb to be born again healthy, transformed, and reformed by the heating fire. The Slavs performed this ritual to heal through fire, to change the unacceptable to the acceptable, just as the baking process turned raw food into cooked."[164] A hideous literal version of this ritual appears in folktales of the witch Baba Yaga and in the tale of Hansel and Gretel.

Could the cluster of reports featuring bread in the collapsing Soviet Union somehow be an expression of the country's transition and rebirth back into Russia? If we entertain the suggestion that a witness' psychology may have some bearing upon the experience—a notion supported by reports of telepathy with humanoids and UFOs responding to thought—that may well be the case.

CHAPTER 7
FOOD: PILLS

Let food be thy medicine and medicine be thy food. – Hippocrates

Recurring experiencer "Jane Murphy" related an experience in 1975 when, as a 16 year old, she awoke to find herself in a field behind her home in Yorkshire, England. Several strange entities were with her, leading Jane toward what appeared to be a large craft landed nearby. Without warning, the beings placed something over her mouth and administered an injection, causing her to black out. Jane regained consciousness in what she assumed was the alien ship, where she was placed in a human-shaped cavity and, in her estimation, somehow "cleansed" without water. She was then made to lay upon a table where one of the foul-smelling entities examined her genitalia and raped her.

Following this horrifying ordeal, Jane was placed at a table with some tasteless "coloured pills." She took one and soon found herself back in bed, a mark at the site of her injection. Afterward she was plagued by a persistent vaginal infection, which was only cleared up after spending some time as a hospital outpatient.[165]

Description, Taste, and Effect

Though not considered "food" in the strictest sense, pellets, tablets, and pills are consumed in entity food cases roughly as often as grain products. They are more or less exclusive to the surgical pageantry of alien abductions, and—perhaps because they are a relatively modern consumable—are never reported in faerie or Sasquatch cases. Like all entity food, pills tend to be administered at an encounter's end and cause amnesia, with sensations of sated appetite occasionally attributed as well. Pills are uniformly described as white or "multicolored" in entity food reports and tend to be tasteless. Given their similar size, color, shape, and effect, the possibility should be considered that reports of wafers and crackers are actually describing pills, tablets, and pellets.

Pills are rarely administered alone, most frequently appearing in conjunction with injections or liquids. Recall that the nectar drunk by Orfeo Angelucci in Twentynine Palms was created by dropping a white tablet into ordinary tap water. On December 6, 1984, the wife of Brazilian abductee Antonio Carlos Ferreira was watching television when the screen went dark and she was paralyzed. Out of nowhere a tall blond man in a white jumpsuit appeared, presenting a glass of yellow "orange juice" and a small white pill. The witness had no choice but to swallow both, and later remembered "feeling like it opened her body from the inside" before she passed out. It is notable that her husband, who had been at a neighbor's house during this encounter, claimed to have seen a strange light in the sky around the same time.[166]

The 1979 entity food experience of Miami resident Filiberto Cardenas also illustrates how pills, liquids, and injections can come together during a single experience. Cardenas was traveling with three family friends when he experienced car trouble around 6:30 p.m. and went to check under the hood. A large, luminous object immediately appeared above them, and Cardenas vanished in full view of the passengers. He was recovered by a police officer two hours later and sixteen miles away, telling a most peculiar story.

Cardenas claimed he was pulled inside the glowing object where he met three humanlike beings in tight white suits with a snake-like emblem on the chest. The entities, who were of average height and spoke fluent Spanish, took him to a tunnel beneath the ocean, all the while speaking of impending conflicts and disasters. Once in the undersea cavern, Cardenas was fed a liquid that tasted of honey and greeted by an earthling who claimed to have lived among the extraterrestrials for some time. He was escorted through a tunnel to a great city before arriving in another space where something sucked him against a wall. The surface rotated to become a table and Cardenas was run through a classic abduction examination—complete with an implant and needles—before being taken to yet another room. Here he slept, awoken by the entities from time-to-time to take some sort of tablets. Cardenas was eventually brought aboard a ship, given "something to eat," and returned to Miami. Once home he suffered from excessive sweating, extreme thirst, decreased libido, temperature fluctuations, and 108 pinpricks all over his body.[167] It is important to note the similarities between this case and the 1980 Iván Morales case mentioned earlier.

Other notable representative cases where witnesses have received pills:

• Orlando Jorge Feraudi claimed in an Argentinian newspaper that he had been taken by a very tall, pale entity in 1965 when he was just 18 years old. During Ferraudi's time he was given five "eggs," all of varying color, which he ate together with another abductee, a girl six years his junior. None of the eggs seemed to have any taste, and the pair washed the meal down with a clear, thick liquid. The fact that the eggs shared attributes with the Jane Murphy case (multi-colored) and were accompanied by a drink strongly suggests that these were in fact pills.[168]

• On August 22, 1980, one witness and her daughter were driving a desolate road in East Texas when they began having car trouble. The radio malfunctioned, the headlights dimmed, and the vehicle was suddenly lifted into a craft hovering above. Now in a bright, circular room, a voice in the mother's mind told her to exit the vehicle. When she failed to comply, a short entity with a large head and huge oval eyes appeared, its feet covered by a mist that clung to the floor. The creature opened the door, dragging them to a pair of tables. Mother and daughter were clamped down, examined, and given pills of various colors and shapes before returning to their car.[169]

• A dubious report from the November 2, 1982, issue of the *National Enquirer* described six Soviet sailors adrift in the Black Sea who were eventually rescued by 20 short humanoids aboard a cigar-shaped craft. The entities offered "food pills" to the two men who agreed to stay with them, putting them in a semi-conscious state. A similar story—or perhaps a misconstrued version of the same encounter—was alleged to have taken place in the Pacific Ocean in 1936.[170]

In 1974 oil-field worker Carl Higdon was taken by a strange being while hunting in Medicine Bow-Routt National Forest. The 41-year-old Wyoming resident had fired upon five elk when his bullet miraculously fell to the ground, apparently stopped by a six-foot-tall entity with yellow-hued skin, small eyes, and two antennae. The being raised its hand as though in a greeting, simultaneously floating a package of pills in Higdon's direction.

"He asked me if I was hungry and I said yes," Higdon said. "So he tossed me some pills and I took one. I don't know why I did it—I never take pills of any kind unless a doctor prescribes them, not even aspirin."[171] The hunter took a pill at the entity's instruction and the next thing Higdon knew, he was in a cube-shaped space along with at least one other alien and the five elk. Later, under hypnotic regression, Higdon revealed he had been taken on a miraculous journey to another world before returning to the forest. The evidence following Higdon's experience is compelling: his spent 7mm bullet was recovered, smashed as though it had hit some unseen barrier; his car was six miles from the last location he remembered; he was healed of a tubercular-type scar on his lung; and his longstanding kidney stone difficulties miraculously vanished.[172]

Note in this account that Higdon was told the pills would "last" four days, whatever that means. Recall Enrique Mercade Orué, who was told two years later that his "crackers" would keep him sustained for four days. This four day time period has cropped up in several accounts from previous chapters, including the 1759 Jacobsson case as well as in the 1974 Panamanian case involving the children who went for a "walk in the clouds."

One of the few reports describing a pill's taste comes from the case files of researcher Kriston Endre. A witness driving near Szatymaz, Hungary, in 1980 noted that, upon arriving at his destination, he had experienced some missing time. Several nights later he awoke in a domed room accompanied by a small, gray figure with bony hands and the ability to communicate telepathically. The entity and the witness had an overall pleasant "conversation," at least until the being expressed concern for its guest's health. The entity then produced several small tablets approximately 1.5 cm long.

Operating under the weak will typical of so many entity food experiencers, the witness took one of the pills. To his dismay it dissolved on his tongue before he could swallow, leaving a "disgusting" tasting sticky substance in his mouth. The entity insisted he swallow, but the witness was unable and subsequently blacked out. He awoke in bed with a horrible taste in his mouth, only slightly alleviated by a liberal helping of chewing gum. A few nights later the entity approached him once more, this time with even more pills—it was only after a third interaction that the witness was able to push past his revulsion and swallow the unpleasant tablets.[173]

Unlike most entity food, pills are almost exclusively medicinal in nature, no doubt why they appear in the examination stage of abduction reports. As such, there is a more overt implication that the food is administered to produce some sort of effect in the witness. This begs the question of whether or not we should be thinking less about the *types* of food offered by nonhuman entities and more about *why they are being offered in the first place.*

CHAPTER 8
FOOD: MISCELLANEOUS

At high tide the fish eat ants; at low tide the ants eat fish.
> – Thai proverb

If one assumes that encounters with unearthly entities are a wholly psychological phenomenon, it stands to reason that, given the prevalence of meat and candy in Western society, more entity food encounters would report these foods. Surprisingly, these types of foods are among the rarest mentioned, with only a handful of examples in the literature. This chapter covers the outliers of the entity food phenomenon: meat, candy, gelatin, salt, and some indefinable cases of true High Strangeness.

Meat

While tales of faeries occasionally mentioned mince pies and feasts of animal flesh, very few entity food accounts on the whole mention meat of any sort, particularly in the modern era. A few reports from contactees like Armando Zurbarán and Ante Jonsson mention grilled meats, but even these are few and far between. Of the few contactee cases that *do* mention meat, beef and fish are most common—there are few (if any) reports of poultry being served. In *Son of the Sun*, Orfeo Angelucci tells how Adam, the fellow who had provided him with his nectar tablet in Twentynine Palms, claimed to have consumed a synthetically-created steak with hosts from Alpha Centauri.[174] In July 1957, German contactee Martin Wiesengrün was allegedly invited to a meal primarily comprised of fruits and vegetables that also included fish,[175] while a young boy who disappeared in Brazil in 1978 claimed that he had boarded a "rocket" and eaten rice and fish during his absence, according to researcher Pablo Villarubia Mauso.[176]

Marginally more common are descriptions of Sasquatch bringing bits of raw meat to captives, usually in conjunction with fruits or vegetables. The sensational Russian newspaper *Pravda* reported in 2004 that St. Petersburg resident Oksana Terletskay was held captive by a "bigfoot" or "yeti" for over a year, where she was forced to copulate with the beast and was brought a diet of berries, nuts, mushrooms, eggs, and raw meat.[177]

The aforementioned tales of Warren Scott and Albert Ostman not withstanding, women are usually the victims of Sasquatch kidnappings and often report salacious motives for their abduction. In a 1954 article for *Liberty Magazine*, early Bigfoot researcher John W. Burns told the (perhaps apocryphal) story of Serephine Long, a Chehalis Native American girl who also claimed to have been held prisoner by a large, hairy hominid. The 17-year old Long was walking home one day when an enormous furry hand snatched her up, sealing her eyes shut with tree gum (an important detail to be addressed in a later chapter) and carrying her to a cave inhabited by a young Sasquatch and his parents. Long eventually became pregnant with the creature's child and begged to be returned to her people; her captor finally obliged, but not before reapplying the tree gum. She gave birth that evening in her village, the infant living for only a few hours.[178] During her year-long imprisonment Long said that she was "fed well," some reports indicating that her diet consisted of "roots, fish, and meat."[179]

This account is strikingly similar to the early 20th century tale of Buddhist nun Noma Dima, who was returning home and lifted bodily by a large hairy figure. During her stay with a Yeti, she was not only brought berries and other wild fruits to eat, but small frogs as well. On one occasion, the beast smashed open a bull's head and the two partook of the animal's brain. When she came forward with her account in 1968, Dima explained how the Yeti released her after siring a child with her; in a parallel to Serephine Long, mother and son returned to the village and cohabitated peacefully with its citizens for a time, at least until a series of crop failures. Aspersions were cast upon the son, thought to be cursed, and the father arrived to reclaim his child. Dima objected, and the Yeti ripped the hybrid boy to shreds.[180]

In one unique case reported by *The Lafeyette Advertiser* in 1889, a Georgia farmer noticed that his fence rails, hogs, and corn had begun to mysteriously disappear over the course of the summer. When he finally discovered huge "bear" tracks leading into the swamp, he resolved to lead a party to track down the animal. While they did not find the culprit, they did find, on a raised island in the swamp, an enormous pen constructed of the missing fence rails. Inside were the missing hogs, fattened on the stolen corn. The hogs were recovered and sold to a local butcher, who passed the cuts on to area customers. As with most entity food, the pork was sweet, so much so that an attempt was made to replicate its "juicy richness" with other hogs, to no avail.[181]

Gelatin

On rare occasions extraterrestrial witnesses will report a clear, nondescript gelatinous substance given to them to eat, a rare example of food from another realm that is truly alien and indescribable. The material is by turns referred to as jelly, jam, marmalade, or even "cottage cheese," and is—unsurprisingly—often sweet.

A startling account was related in the August 2000 "Enigmas Express" supplement of Spain's *Nacional* newspaper. A 46-year-old liberal arts professor was hunting birds with two students near Mérida when an ominous fog fell upon the forest. The group was separated and the witness, growing tired, fell asleep beneath a tree (shades of Rip van Winkle). He later awakened to the horror of a giant tentacle trying to grab his arm and immediately began trying to free himself. Before passing out, he caught a glimpse of an enormous egg-shaped object and a dark figure looming nearby.

The witness regained consciousness in a bright white room. A disembodied voice instructed him to remain calm while three reptilian beings entered, each with protruding eyes, large lips, and hands with four fingers and a claw. The entities examined him, politely answering a few questions and explaining that his experience had been a failed attempt on their part to draw blood for study. In the course of the operation, the witness' heart had failed and they were forced to intervene directly.

The entities fed him a red liquid, hot whitish "broth," and a sort of marmalade, a meal that they said would sustain him for the entire day. The beings seemed kind, speaking for a while longer before escorting the witness outside. He returned home quite late, only to collapse in front of his family the following morning—the witness was rushed to the hospital, where it was revealed that he had developed a cardiac condition. X-rays revealed a spherical object lodged in his chest but, when follow-up photography was ordered the next day, the abnormality had vanished. His remaining four years were spent in-and-out of the hospital. [182]

A story investigated by reporter Elena Potapova and researcher Alexey K. Priyma tells of Tula, Russia, resident Tatyana G. Gavrilina, a witness who purportedly ate "Martian marmalade" in November 1990. After being taken from her bed and undergoing a medical examination by humanlike aliens, Gavrilina was told that her stomach was "in bad shape." She lost consciousness and, when she came to, was presented with candy-like "marmalade" that her hosts claimed would heal her. Gavrilina and one of the female entities each took a piece of the substance and ate it, after which she was immediately stricken with debilitating stomach cramps. She passed out again and awoke in her bed, the pain gone. [183]

These oddly specific themes—a suspicious medicinal jelly shared with a woman by humanlike entities—are repeated in a handful of other Russian reports. The manner in which Gavrilina's "marmalade" alleviated her pain evokes quince jelly, used as a remedy for ailing stomachs since antiquity.

Celtic folklore tells of "fairy butter," a substance claimed by some to be a staple of the faeries. The "butter" was in actuality not butter at all, but rather a type of yellow fungus that would turn gelatinous after putrefying in the rain.[184] Variations such as troll butter and witches butter also exist, the term "butter" applied to any fungi with a gelatinous fruiting body. According to naturalist Thomas Pennant, the Welsh used the term "fairy butter" to describe petroleum jelly found in deep limestone caverns. Pennant ascribed to it a healing quality: rubbed on affected areas, this fairy butter could alleviate rheumatism.[185]

Candy

When London resident Elaine Avis and her husband were abducted from their car by owl-faced beings in the 1970s, the last thing they expected was to be offered something to eat. Yet Elaine, under hypnotic regression, distinctly recalled "pink peppermint creams" offered to her on a white tray. Wisely, she declined to eat them.[186]

The notion of an entity using candy in an encounter is unsettling for a multitude of reasons, not the least of which is how predatory it feels. Human beings are, as a species, hard-wired to enjoy sweet tastes, and it is often our youngest that are drawn to them.

Indeed, a majority of entity food cases involving candy tend to focus around children. A contributor to Whitley Strieber's website *Unknown Country* recalled visits from "little gray monkeys" who began visiting her as a child in 1958, enticing her to keep their visits secret with candies that tasted "like a cross between grape and cherry." The smell, however, "was somehow distastefully organic, like the smell of a compost heap."[187] Again we are presented with evidence that entity food may be something unpalatable masquerading as a delicacy.

Maxim Zhirkov, a boy from Toropovo, Russia, claimed that he

was pulled into a metallic object in the sky on his way home from a tennis match in 1990. Zhirkov said he met two beings, their faces obscured by antennaed helmets, who brusquely asked his name. When he replied, the boy felt the ship take off while a nearby screen began to play familiar scenes of his life back on earth. The aliens then offered him candy from something resembling a glass tube—Zhirkov disappointedly described the taste akin to "candle wax." The remainder of the boy's tale has all of the more fanciful hallmarks of a contactee story, including a visit to the aliens' homeworld before he was returned home.[188]

Villa Velha, Brazil, experienced a loss of children aged 9-15 in 1969, causing many to suspect a widespread kidnapping ring. The missing, mostly boys, were generally from poor families, ruling out the possibility of a ransom motive, and police had absolutely no leads in the investigation. In February of the following year, four of the missing children mysteriously reappeared, telling half-remembered fragments of their abductions. One child identified as "Vani" recalled being offered sweets by a stranger named "Laura" who took her to an airfield, at which point Vani raised enough hell to cause her captor to abandon the effort. Vani was given what seemed to be hush money and returned her to her village. Today's jaded reader may feel that the kidnappings could be ascribed to something prosaic albeit sinister, such as slavery, organ trafficking, or sex trafficking; noted UFO investigator John Keel, however, felt the case may have had occult origins.[189]

An odd series of encounters in France in the 1970s involved a substance akin to chocolate. For reasons unknown even to him, Paul de Brescia found himself walking toward a secluded wooden area near Grasse on August 25, 1971, when he happened upon two very tall humanoids, each wearing bluish metallic coveralls with white gloves and blond hair. They told him they were from the star system Vega, having come to Earth to convince humanity to change its ways. After conversing for a while, the entities gave de Brescia what appeared to be a piece of chocolate, which caused drowsiness upon consumption. He awoke in his apartment, only recovering his memory in full at a later date.[190]

Three years later, a witness in Origny-en-Thiérache, France, was biking in the early morning when two "cosmonauts" in helmeted space suits stopped him in his tracks. Immediately he noticed a large, dark, circular object approximately the size of two automobiles, presumably their craft, sitting in a nearby field. The witness watched dumbfounded as the two entities looked to one another, the one on the left gesturing to its companion. The other cosmonaut reached behind its back as though fishing into a pocket or pouch and produced a small brown piece of what appeared to be chocolate, gesturing with its free hand that the witness should eat it. The report indicates that the two beings waited patiently for him to consume the "candy," then promptly let him pass as soon as he was finished. The witness noted that the substance lacked any discernable taste and had a slightly softer consistency than chocolate, but he suffered no physical effects from the food he consumed.[191]

Jaime Bordas Bley also claimed to have received a dark, square candy from a strange entity, an encounter Jacques Vallée detailed at length in *Messengers of Deception*. Bley, whose name Vallée Gallicanized as "Jacques Bordas," was born in 1911 and remained an overweight, sickly boy until age 12 when he stepped out onto the family terrace and saw several metallic triangles in the sky. Three of them landed, and out came a being in a white suit and mantle. The entity knew of Bley's dream to be fit and strong, saying, "Now that we have adopted you, we will never forsake you. In the future we will come back to you again. In the meantime, as a token of friendship, take this." The boy took and ate the candy, awakening later with a tarlike taste in his mouth. By age 16, Bley was in peak physical condition, becoming an expert mountain climber and joining the circus two years later.[192]

As with so many entity food cases, the lines tend to blur between categories. It is entirely possible that these "candies" are in fact pills—after all, many medications, particularly those designed for children, are infused with sweet, pleasant tastes to make them easier to swallow.

Salt

Salt is unique because, while it occurs rarely-to-never in entity food reports, it is still very important to the subject at hand. Throughout the centuries salt has been a symbol of immortality and durability, and as such has been ascribed many magical properties.

Recall that salt is one of the preferred charms to ward off faeries. This is likely due to salt's reputation as a food preservative and its ability to ward off decay; given their established association with the dead, it is a logical extrapolation that the faeries would be averse to salt.[193] Finvarra, Irish king both of the faeries and the dead, kidnapped a mortal queen only to have her rescued by a tenacious young lord who dug his way to fairyland, covering the ground with salt to prevent any faerie tampering with his work.[194]

Indeed, salt's use as a prophylactic against evil extends far beyond faeries and the dead. One Roman legend tells of a man who suspected his wife of witchcraft and demanded he accompany her to her Sabbath. At the next banquet, the man noticed that there was no salt on any of the food and, unaware of the demonic aversion to the mineral, requested some. When it arrived he declared, "Thank God, the salt has come!" This two-fold expletive sent the Black Mass into a frenzy, and the husband suddenly found himself in Benevento, 100 miles from home. He made his way back to Rome and promptly reported his wife's transgressions.[195]

One of the rare entity food accounts involving salt comes from a letter originally published in the May 1968 edition of *Fate* magazine. Written by Rev. Albert H. Baller of Clinton, Massachusetts, the letter details how, just prior to delivering a lecture on UFOs, a dining companion offered the following anecdote:

He said that he was in the trenches near Ypres in August, 1915, when the Germans launched the first gas attack. Since it was the very first, neither he nor any of his buddies knew what it meant when they looked out over no-man's-land and saw a strange grey cloud rolling towards them. When it struck, pandemonium broke out. Men dropped all around him and the trench was in an uproar. Then, he said, a strange thing happened. Out of the mist, walking across no-man's land, came a figure. He seemed to be without special protection and he wore the uniform of the Royal Medical Corps. The engineer remembered that the stranger spoke English with what seemed to be a French accent.

On his belt the stranger from the poison cloud had a series of small hooks on which were suspended tin cups. In his hand he carried a bucket of what looked like water. As he slid down into the trench he began removing the cups, dipping them into the bucket and passing them out to the soldiers, telling them to drink quickly. The engineer was among those who received the potion. He said it was extremely salty, almost too salty to swallow. But all of the soldiers who were given the liquid did drink it, and not one of them suffered lasting effects from the gas.

When the gas cloud had blown over and things calmed down the unusual visitor was not to be found. No explanation for his visit could be given by the Royal Medical Corps—but the fact remained that thousands of soldiers died or suffered lasting effects from that grim attack, but not a single soldier who took the cup from the stranger was among the casualties.[196]

Other entity food cases detailing salt are very few, and usually of dubious provenance. Italian researcher Arcangelo Cassano investigated a 1975 case out of Bari that suggested the witness—who claimed to have drunk a white, milky liquid that tasted like saltwater—had actually been in a lucid dream rather than experiencing a waking encounter.[197] A similar case long-circulated on the internet from Russia, involving a Red Army member given "salted lemonade," is no less problematic; investigator Patrick Gross, after failing to locate the individuals involved or the purported locale, declared the case "invented by UFOlogists."[198]

On the other end of the spectrum, saltless food fell from the heavens in 1949 in the Dominican Republic. A female witness was leaving home when she noticed a brilliant object in the sky with what appeared to be beings inside. She called her neighbors, and the UFO dropped food to the ground that, when tasted, had a strong flavor, but lacked salt. One cannot rule out misidentification of a terrestrial craft on a humanitarian mission—possibly a helicopter, which was a relatively new sight in the 1940s.[199]

The Indefinable

"In the palm of his hand, the boy had something that looked like sand granules, which he began picking at with his other hand and eating from it," recalls Anibal Perez. "And at the same time making gestures, offering some of the stuff to us. He wanted us to eat some of it."

The year was 1982 and Perez, then 14, had been enjoying the waters of Media Luna Beach, Vieques, Puerto Rico, with his nephew when something extraordinary happened. In the distance, a dark form emerged from the water and approached the pair—it was a Caucasian boy around their age in tight white shorts, "emitting weird sounds similar to the ones dolphins make." The strange lad was affable, seemingly wanting to make friends. He would submerge for minutes at a time before popping up from the bottom with his peculiar snack.

Perez and his nephew declined the offer, then began splashing the boy away, only to be mimicked in turn. At last he swam out toward deeper water, but returned once more, this time with seaweed from the ocean floor. He ate some of the plant material and made an offer, again to the same result.

The witnesses tried to communicate, eventually getting the boy to gesture and repeat some of their words. At last Perez's nephew asked him what country he was from. "He just stared at us for a moment as if thinking of what he was going to say, and then he said, 'Sea... bottom... country,'" Perez remembers. "He then pointed down to the deep with his finger." The strange boy bade his new friends goodbye, never to appear again and leaving Perez to contemplate the experience to this day.[200]

It is actually quite surprising that there are not more accounts detailing food of unearthly description. One would think that anything eaten in a foreign realm would be so wholly bizarre as to defy comparison with any element in a human diet, and yet most seem rather mundane.

Still, there are a few cases where witnesses have received something very strange. Reports have included pulsating orange spheres, strange cones, and "oil-like medicine," all intended for consumption. Twenty-eight-year-old Joaquina Nogueira de Sousa of Pacajus, Brazil, was returning home one night in 1994 when she noticed "a weird light, very powerful, lighting up an entire grove of cashew nut trees." She had stopped to watch when two tall "luminous beings," one male and one female, appeared in her path. The man, well muscled and possessed of large, pointed ears, said to her "Don't be afraid. We are not going to do you any harm. We don't want anything from you. Keep calm." He identified himself as "Karran" while his companion pulled what appeared to be a communicator from her belt and brought it to her ear.

According to an article written by Reginaldo de Athyayde for the November-December 1994 issue of Brazil's *UFO* magazine, Karran gave Joaquina something from his belt, which he gestured for her to eat. The girl described whatever it was as sour, her mouth filling with saliva. Though nauseous and spitting to rid herself of what she thought might be poison, Joaquina felt herself entranced by Karran's gaze. The being seemed to place something in the girl's ear just as her brother, José de Arimatéia, stumbled upon the scene and dashed to her rescue.

Arimatéia attested to the fact that the two beings quickly pulled the device from her ear and vanished.[201] Curiously, Herminio and Bianca Reis, another Brazilian couple, claimed to have had interactions with a "tropical Aryan" named Karran in the 1970s. Mr. and Mrs. Reis were allegedly given a viscous, bitter liquid to drink, one that put them to sleep.[202]

The Nogueira account is reminiscent of the surreal 1990 encounters alleged by a young Ukrainian college student named Darya. She was waiting for the bus one day in August when a peculiar yellow globe about the size of a tangerine floated toward her. Though she was not alone, no one else seemed to notice the glowing sphere as she took it in her hands, feeling a "painless burning sensation." The ball reappeared later in her backyard, this time accompanied by a male and female humanoid who fed her a strange—but tasty—yellow food. Four months later the pair again visited Darya and presented the same yellow food, though Darya found this batch disagreeable. It was apparently some kind of substance to facilitate interstellar travel, so this time she was able to accompany her tall visitors to their homeworld.[203]

The abrupt change in taste noted by Darya suggests that the attributes of whatever she consumed were not fixed, while its color evokes the fairy butter mentioned earlier. Note also the manner in which the food given to Darya expressly facilitated travel, as it did with Ante Jonsson. This is a minor motif in entity food cases—the bookending of the experience with the administration of food.

Vague descriptions of food can be frustrating to researchers, leaving one to wonder if they are the result of amnesia or simply food that is too alien to articulate. One American woman appeared at a sheriff's office in 1973 after being reported missing several days earlier, claiming that she was driving home from college when she had car trouble and got out to check the engine. The woman was seized by three creatures with masklike white faces, two large eyes set close to the side of the head, and three-clawed hands. She then floated up toward a disc-shaped object in a nearby field where she was stripped, strapped to a table, and examined. Needles were inserted into her arms and abdomen, and electrodes attached during some sort of interrogation before she was offered food, which she did not consume, and water, which she did. She fell asleep only to wake up later, still in the entities' custody, and was offered more food. She ate it this time, but said it was "tasteless, like chewing a wad of paper." The woman fell asleep one final time and awoke in a cornfield.[204]

As usual, the waters are muddied by the propensity of such encounters to not always be what they seem. While searching for a gas station near Crater Lake, Oregon one night in the early 1950s, a mother and children happened upon a large, brightly lit "restaurant," circular in shape with a mirrored exterior. They parked alongside several other cars and entered, where they ordered food from one of several blonde, 4.5-foot-tall servers. They wore silvery clothing emblazoned with some sort of logo, their voices soft and musical. After eating, everyone piled back into the car, which would not start until it coasted back onto the highway. The witnesses soon found that no locals knew of this restaurant, that they had no less money from paying for the meal, and—most convincingly—the building was gone when they returned to the site.[205]

The mother's memory sharpened around 15 years later, and she was convinced that they had indeed not visited a restaurant, and instead had been made to believe they had. This revelation of a "screen memory" brings all of the imagery—including the presence of food—into question, and raises at least two very important questions. First, why choose a screen memory that involves food? And secondly, if this is indeed a screen memory, are we *ever* actually dealing with physical food in *any* entity food cases?

Though this qualitative analysis gives us a better handle on entity food than ever before, establishing what individuals eat during encounters with humanoids is only one aspect of a much more complex phenomenon. To truly grasp the nuances of our culinary relationship with such entities we must also take a closer look at the opposite side of these exchanges: in particular, what we offer them.

CHAPTER 9
RELATIONSHIPS: GIVING & TAKING

*An elder in my church knew a woman who was accustomed, in
milking her cows, to offer libations to the fairies. The woman was later
converted to Christ and gave up the practice, and as a result one of her
cows was taken by the fairies. Then she revived the practice.*
– Scottish Protestant minister, speaking to W.Y. Evans-Wentz
in *Fairy-Faith in the Celtic Countries*

In *Inhumanoids: Real Encounters with Beings That Can't Exist*,
B.M. Nunnelly tells an unsettling story about one family who got
more than they bargained for while vacationing in an Oregon cabin
in July 1997. Early in their trip the youngest daughter, 8-year-old
Violet Bredlow, disappeared in the forest. When they found her,
she claimed to have been carried through the air by some unseen
friends.

That evening, Violet prepared two plates of leftovers, telling
her family that if "they" weren't fed they would become angry and
force the family to leave. The mother was informed that the friends
who had carried Violet through the forest were actually two little
people, and had requested that they receive the family scraps in the
storage room of the cabin. The girl said that the men refused to eat
while anyone was watching, so after she had placed the plates on
the floor she and her mother left, the door slamming shut of its
own accord behind them. Startled, the mother immediately went
to look inside but only saw two rats feasting on the leftovers. Violet

contended that they were not rats but tiny men with wrinkled faces who were talking inside her head.

Violet's evening ritual continued until the father set out a rat trap. The mother was shocked to hear the snap of metal one evening and screams from her daughter, who claimed that her mental link with the little people made her feel their pain. The mother rushed to the sprung trap in the storage room and saw, to her amazement, a small man in green trying to free the foot of another tiny entity. The mother pried the rattrap open and the man took off, cursing, "If it's rats he wants, it's rats he gets!" The cabin was immediately overrun with dozens of rats, the vermin successfully driving the Bredlows out of the cabin.[206]

In all honesty, the subject of nonhuman entities receiving mortal food could take up a whole book unto itself. Stories of alien diners, for example, where strange individuals enter an establishment only to be bewildered by the menu and the simple act of eating, are legion. One humorous case from 1970 featured a peculiar diminutive "family" which entered a St. Louis hotel restaurant for dinner, asking the origins of every menu item before eating peas one-by-one with a knife.[207] For all their ominous threats to UFO witness, the Men in Black (MIB) tend to have a particularly difficult time with Jell-O; one, who identified himself as Major Richard French, visited a Minnesotan witness in 1967 and tried to drink it,[208] while another tried to do the exact same thing in a northern California diner in 1976.[209]

While these tales are fascinating in their own right, at present we will focus less on case studies and more on the relationships they point to—how humans have offered their food to beings from other realms since the beginning of time.

Offerings and Consequences

Disciples of every spiritual discipline have sought to supplicate supernatural entities with offerings since time immemorial. Animal sacrifice has existed in nearly every ancient culture, including the

Egyptians, Hebrews, Greeks, Romans, Yoruba, and Aztecs, often complimented by non-blood sacrifices such as grain, honey, fruit, and vegetables, particularly in the Hindu tradition. Often, offerings to appease the gods would be set on fire to release the essence of the sacrifice to the heavens. In some sense, these offerings even extend to denominations of modern Christianity, which frame the Eucharist as a continuation of Christ's sacrifice on the cross.

Offerings are not only made to deities but to the dead as well, with foodstuffs either given to those on the cusp of death or placed in the presence of the lifeless body. Those dying in Ireland were given *lón báis*, or death sustenance, to sustain them on their journey into the afterlife,[210] while other inhabitants of the British Isles would consume bread, salt, or beer in the departed's presence as "sin-eaters," taking on the transgressions of the deceased and allowing their safe passage into heaven.[211] Having at last reached their final destination to heaven, the dead in rural Greece are exhumed five years after their passing and doused by a priest with red wine in the shape of a cross.[212] In Mexican Catholic tradition, *Día de los Muertos* celebrations (October 31 – November 2) still include offerings of food and drink at the graves of departed family members, the souls extracting the food's essence in a fashion that recalls earlier discussions of faerie *foyson*.[213]

Given this worldwide affinity for leaving food for the dead, it is little surprise that faeries, so often associated with the deceased, are frequent recipients of similar offerings. Each of the Good Folk have very specific demands: French *follet* ask for grain, Italian *massariol* love macaroni, Mediterranean *nereides* prefer honey, Russian *vodyany* delight in fattened horses dumped through a hole in the ice. Pixies of Cornwall are fond of milk in particular, and any farmer so ill-natured as to spread salt around a cow to keep them away would be led astray by the faeries at the first opportunity.[214]

Offerings were not always just for the faeries, however. Food was occasionally left out for those stolen by the Good Folk so that they would not have to partake of faerie food and be lost forever. "In a poignant Irish lullaby, a young woman refuses to eat the food of the fairies, declaring: 'I have eaten no bit nor supped no drink of theirs / But cold mashed potatoes on my father's dresser!'" writes Purkiss in *Troublesome Things: A History of Fairies and Fairy Stories*. "This fairy-taken woman desperately revisits her home to eat their leftovers, and the food she eats symbolizes her status as an outsider with nothing of her own." [215]

Anyone who took good care of their local faeries would expect to have a bountiful crop that ripened on time, a clean hearth, and good fortune. In Scotland, brewers would pour malt from each new batch of beer into a "Brownie's stone," and in turn the faeries would "hasten the brewing process and improve the flavour of the home brew." [216] In *Devon Traditions and Fairy-Tales*, J.R.W. Coxhead tells of several faeries who took up residence in a farmer's barn, shucking his corn—and stealing corn from his neighbors— in exchange for offerings of bread and cheese. [217]

The *kornböcke* of Eastern Europe, closely associated with the folkloric Krampus of Christmas, lived within the grain and helped it to ripen. After the last sheaf of the harvest was taken, the *kornböcke* would hibernate in the farmer's home for the winter and, if not fed enough, would "spill the beer in the cellar, throw weevils into the flour, and make the grain rot." [218] Indeed, offerings assured protection as much as prosperity—any faerie that did not receive its offerings was a dangerous thing. Denied that which was owed them, some faeries would go so far as to take horses or cows in recompense, or worse. Evans-Wentz collected the following folktale from Dinah Moore, a Celtic woman of Glen Meay:

> At night the fairies came into a house in Glen Rushen to bake. The family had put no water out for them; and a beggar-man who had been left lodging on the sofa downstairs heard the fairies say, "We have no water, so we'll take blood out of the toe of the servant who forgot our water." And from the girl's blood they mixed their dough. Then they baked their cakes, ate most of them, and poked

pieces up under the thatched roof. The next day the servant-girl fell ill, and was ill until the old beggar-man returned to the house and cured her with a bit of the cake which he took from under the thatch.[219]

There has been much discussion in recent years about Sasquatch "habituation," an interaction that seems to directly parallel faerie offerings of the past. The term is used to describe the practice of acclimating a Sasquatch or family of Sasquatch to one's presence, forming a trust or bond with the witness that leads to multiple interactions over time. This is commonly accomplished by setting out food as "gifts" for the entities, much in the same way faeries are left offerings overnight. Such snacks are quick to disappear, a "mystery" more often than not attributable to native wildlife, though there are at times extenuating circumstances that suggest otherwise (e.g. food left in a container requiring the dexterity of a primate to open, food suspended vertically in a tree requiring excessive height to reach, etc.). From time-to-time these offerings may be reciprocated by Sasquatch, with smooth stones, feathers, or even other dead animals appearing in the place of the missing food.

The reverence and respect in which the Celts hold the faeries is sometimes echoed among Sasquatch habituators. "This food is not in the same areas as the critters' food," said one Native American from Oklahoma who claimed frequent visits in the summer of 2007. "I separate the food out of respect. I would not serve a guest food from the dog dish nor will I share snacks for the children of the Shadow People with the raccoons on the ground."[220]

Individuals claiming habituation make themselves very easy targets for cynics, perhaps rightly so, given their ample opportunities to collect concrete proof of the existence of large hairy hominids. Indeed, some alleged habituators claim to have tried to collect video or photographic evidence but are constantly stymied, either by equipment malfunctions or the fact that whatever has taken their offering fails to appear on camera.

While there don't seem to be any benefits *per se* to giving
Sasquatch food beyond the occasional river stone or bird feather
left in kind, it is worthwhile to compare the wrath of spurned
faeries to the repercussions of abruptly halting Sasquatch
offerings. Mississippi Sasquatch researcher Jim "Bear" Grant told
one habituator's highly sensational story on the February 23, 2014,
edition of *Bigfoot Hotspot Radio*:

> My buddy gets sent to Kuwait [in Desert Storm].
> While he's in Kuwait, his grandfather assumes his
> [habituation] responsibility and is continuously
> feeding these things [Sasquatch]... His grandfather
> had eighty-something goats on his property with
> five dogs. His grandfather—while my friend was
> in Kuwait—[had] a severe heart attack. They had to
> put him in the hospital. Even my friend in Kuwait
> could not get leave from the Army to come back
> and take care of his grandfather. Thank God his
> grandfather recovered... somebody figured out
> that somebody needs to go out there and feed his
> livestock, and this was something like a week later...
> they drive out there to the countryside, and when
> they get there all the goats are dead. Something
> had ripped them to pieces. Then, all the dogs, all
> five dogs, were ripped to pieces.[221]

In one Scottish legend from the island of Inch, this is the exact
course of action a scorned Brownie took when a family failed to
leave out milk.[222]

Though it may seem germane to our discussion, we will *not* be
discussing the subject of unexplained livestock mutilation beyond
noting the above anecdote and drawing a handful of parallels. It is
simply too large and complex a topic to broach in this setting. There
is ample evidence for livestock mutilations to be tied to a bevy of
phenomena both anomalous and mundane: UFOs, misidentified

scavenger activity, government monitoring of radiation levels, and even Sasquatch have all been accused. It is suggested that anyone wishing to further explore the literature look to the work of researcher Christopher O'Brien and his book *Stalking the Herd*.

That being said, it is not an uncommon theme for mutilated livestock to remain untouched by scavengers in much the same manner that animals avoid *foyson*-deprived food. In the folktale "The Tacksman of Auchriachan," a prize ox is "stolen" by a host of faeries who have not received their fair share of the owner's profits. The farmer overhears the entities' plan while hiding in their abode and immediately returns home. His prize ox is still there, never touched under his son's watchful eye, but the father nonetheless declares the animal a sham, now deprived of its *foyson*. He kills the beast, and "neither cat nor dog would put a tooth in either of them." The motifs of this story—not only the disinterest of scavengers in the corpse, but also the manner in which the animal was attacked without anyone noticing—repeat themselves time-and-again in livestock mutilation cases.[223]

Regardless of whether or not mutilations are tied to any phenomenon that is truly unexplained, they are not the only form of retaliation allegedly visited upon livestock by the supernatural. One Welsh story tells how a farmer near Festiniog offended the faeries and had his entire herd driven into a lake.[224] The relocation of livestock continues in the modern era: in 1977, a dairy herd of 100 cattle near Haverfordwest, Wales, escaped their locked paddock no less than six times, often appearing in locations too distant to reach themselves. The herdsman had spotted strange lights in the sky several days before, and of course faeries escaped the blame, the culprits identified instead as omnipresent extraterrestrials with obscure motives.[225] In their book *Hunt for the Skinwalker*, Colm Kelleher and George Knapp tell of an incident where four cattle missing from a Utah ranch were found inside a locked trailer that the owner had not opened in years.[226]

Though not as formalized as in antiquity, witnesses to this day still offer foodstuffs to strange entities, often of the very nature once accepted by faeries.

• *La Razón*, a newspaper out of Buenos Aires, reported that on June 15, 1964, two fair-skinned "men" descended from the sky in a strange machine and asked Rafael Aguirre Donoso for water in a mixture of English and Spanish. Donoso took some out of his car radiator, which the entities took back to their craft before disappearing into the heavens.[227]

• An entity in Brazil asked a witness for water once more when Dona Maria, a resident of the Clemente Ferreira Sanatorium in Lins, was awakened by a strange noise early one morning in 1968. Upon opening her eyes, Maria beheld a strange woman in "light-coloured clothes" who spoke an unknown language. Eventually Maria worked out that the being wanted water, as it was holding a mug and an elaborately engraved glass water bottle. Maria took the bottle to the nearest drinking fountain (by the hospital entrance) and began to fill the vessel, all the while noticing that the visitor was staring outside. The bottle filled, Maria was beginning to fill the mug when the woman put a hand on her shoulder and repeated "Rempaua" over and over again. The two then walked out the front door where, to her shock, Maria saw a pear-shaped craft hovering just above the ground about 25 yards away. The woman took her water and walked toward the craft, meeting another being—too distant to discern sex—and waving goodbye before entering the craft, which climbed into the sky in a slow spiral.[228]

• On the morning of January 4, 1979, Mrs. Jean Hingley was waving her husband goodbye outside her home in Rowley Regis, England, when she noticed a peculiar glow emanating from the carport. When she went to look, the light was gone, having moved instead to the garden. Puzzled, she returned to the back door and opened it, only to have three small figures rush inside. In Hingley's words, they were dressed in "silvery-green tunics" and fishbowl helmets, each around 3.5 feet tall, with black eyes, white faces, no noses, small mouths, and... beautiful, multicolored wings. Hingley, albeit paralyzed, managed to initiate a pleasant conversation with the intruders, discussing the recent Christmas season, and soon the entities were floating around the apartment, picking up anything they could get their hands on. Regaining her motor control, Hingley offered them a drink, to which they asked for water. She obliged—though Hingley did not see them consume it, each being returned an empty glass. The entities steered the conversation toward religion before their host fetched some mince pies. The beings took the treats but were soon frightened away when Hingley tried to demonstrate how to smoke a cigarette. The aliens fled, pies still in-hand, back outside toward a large, orange object waiting in the garden. The ground displayed burn marks afterward, and several electrical items in the house were ruined.[229]

• Hermie Orieno, fourth grade faculty advisor at Rizal Elementary School in the Philippines, sent several students outside to clean up the schoolyard one January morning in 2004 when something astounding happened. As they neared one of the property's acacia trees, several students noticed two tiny dwarves dressed in green and blue. The creatures—whose names were Wendy and Wendell—began to speak with the children, assuring them that they meant no harm and were merely on the property to help keep clean the schoolyard. Three other students, including witnesses Divine Grace Castillo, Myrna Salaver, and Charmaine Clarin, approached and saw the short entities as well. One of the children, Sandy (last name withheld) offered the dwarfs a biscuit, which they graciously accepted and ate. It was at that moment that a young boy, Kent Grey, saw the commotion and approached the crowd—he could not see the dwarfs and began hitting the ground with a stick in anger. According to Sandy, Kent hit one of the beings, causing others to flee from their hiding places. "Their master, who had a long beard and wore black clothes, was very angry at what happened," wrote Jaime T. Licauco in *Dwarves and Other Nature Spirits*. "Mrs. Orieno, though she could not see anything, apologized to the dwarves for what happened and asked not to retaliate to Kent because he could not see them."[230]

Also recall Joe Simonton's water-for-pancakes trade; there are many such cases. Milk was gladly received by several green, large-eyed entities treating an injured comrade at the home of a woman in Yaroslavl Oblast, Russia, in 1937.[231] More recently, a woman in Minnesota answered her door to find three "little men," each under 26 inches tall with large heads and eyes, pointing at their mouths—she offered them bread, butter, and sausage, each of which was well-received, and hot coffee, which was spit out.[232]

A more explicit parallel between the rewarded faerie offerings of old and gifts to entities today can be seen in the activity that allegedly took place in Zasmushchalsya, Russia. In 1976 a farmer with the pseudonym Nikolai Kirselev claimed that he and his peers observed disc-like objects in the summer sky. The sightings escalated until several yellow-skinned beings in gray jumpsuits landed near a local beekeeper to ask for one of his hives. This act set off a reciprocal relationship where the visitors would fix broken farm equipment in exchange for food staples and permission to utilize the local crops for research purposes, resulting in broad crop circles throughout the fields.[233] Unfortunately, the source for this account is the *Megapolis-Express*, a rather sensationalist newspaper operating in post-Soviet Russia, and as such should be viewed with suspicion.

Witnesses of the airship waves of the late 19th century were often asked by the crafts' occupants for food staples. On April 17, 1897, an Indiana farmer reported that he had seen a large airship land near his property, from which a man stepped out and asked for a full pail of milk. As soon as the pail was collected, the man hopped back aboard and took off into the sky.[234] That same month, a similar airship was reported in Pine Lake, Michigan, its occupants waking William Megiveron from his sleep to ask for "four-dozen egg sandwiches and a kettle of coffee."[235] Again, skepticism is advised.

Regardless of the veracity of every report, there is a clear trend to be seen here. Offerings from witnesses tend to be predictable and have remained relatively unchanged for centuries: unlike the Reese's Pieces offered to the alien in Steven Spielberg's film *E.T. the Extra-Terrestrial*, milk, bread, eggs, and butter would all be perfectly at home on a plate left for the faeries.

Theft

Most entities also have a penchant for taking foodstuffs that do not belong to them. It can be overt, as when a Sasquatch raids a camp of its provisions, or it can be subtler, as when a faerie blight causes a crop failure.

European tradition listed numerous ways by which entities could rob the innocent. Lady Gregory, an associate of William Butler Yeats, wrote that, "For their feasts [faeries] choose the best of all sorts, taking it from the solid world, leaving some worthless likeness in its place; when they rob the potatoes from the ridges, the diggers find but rottenness and decay; they take the strength from the meat in the pot, so that when put on the plates it does not nourish."[236] The Joint-Eater, or *Alp-Luachra*, of Irish folklore sits beside a victim and consumes the *foyson* of every meal so that the unsuspecting host never gains weight.[237] This food theft can be particularly oblique, such as when faeries prevent milk from transforming into butter by stealing the butterfat, often in the guise of persistent butterflies that hover nearby during the churning process.[238]

These foods are not always to the faeries' liking, however. One Moravian folktale circa 1600 says that a baker's daughter, sent on an errand to the castle Prostějov in the modern Czech Republic, was delivering milk rolls when a small gnome appeared. He snatched the three rolls in her hand, taking a mouthful of each one before spitting them out with revulsion. He retreated into the woods, and shortly thereafter the daughter saw a fireball ascend to the clouds.[239]

A particularly astonishing rash of thefts purportedly took place in 1932 in Russia. After a craft landed in a nearby potato field, seven short entities and their taller leader more or less acted like they owned the small town, taking food from homes (in particular bread) and unleashing doglike "pets" which seemed to have an affinity for milk, eggs, chicken, and geese. These uninvited guests eventually departed, though not before ransacking the town and causing many residents to flee. Such a story strains credulity and is obviously not included here for its air of authenticity; rather, it is mentioned for its glimmer of truth in a folkloric sense. So much of the aliens' impish behavior in this tale could easily describe typical faerie mischief: the creatures fouled supplies of livestock feed, mutilated sheep, pilfered grain and potatoes in the fields, and siphoned massive amounts of grain from local silos.[240]

It is fascinating that, from antiquity through the modern era, the victims of these thefts have, by-and-large, been farmers. In *Uninvited Visitors*, Ivan T. Sanderson tells of a farmer's wife who lost a bushel of produce to six "brats... all dressed in funny gray uniforms [with] silly Buck Rogers space helmets on their heads, and toy pistols hanging from their belts." After pulling up onions, lettuce, and other vegetables from the garden, the interlopers fled to the forest, from which a loud hum could be heard. The entities reappeared the next day and were spotted by a young lady on the farm, who also reported a "saucer" about 20 feet in diameter that disappeared in a mist.[241] This case bears similarities to a 1954 case noted in *Passport to Magonia* where an Italian farmer was paralyzed and forced to watch as his rabbits were stolen by mischievous dwarfs.[242]

Sasquatch have been known to opportunistically seize any food left out in the open. In Latin America, a handful of cases mention raids on fruit plantations by hirsute thieves; in North America, Sasquatch enjoy opportunistically stealing newly-felled game. J. Robert Alley's *Raincoast Sasquatch* details several highly suggestive stories, such as the tale of one Alaskan hunter who recalled how, in 1989, a buck shot "in the chest at 200 yards with a .300-caliber round" simply disappeared after going down. "Sometimes you miss a shot or hit it badly you know, but this deer was hit well, went down well and there was nothing there," he recalled in a 1998 interview. "It was just like something walked out of the trees back there and made off with it." Even more compelling is the testimony of two hunters in the region who reported that *something* took their kill during a 1998 bear hunt, placed it in a depression in the ground, and covered it with moss in an attempt to conceal the body.[243]

Sasquatch and their ilk seem to have a love of milk as well. In the middle ages, gigantic, shaggy "wild men" allegedly roamed Europe, sometimes assisting with herding but more often than not stealing milk and abducting children.[244] An elderly Acehnese hunter reported in 1935 that he often saw the Orang Pendek, a hairy hominid from the island of Sumatra that he referred to as "kukuman," steal buffalo milk if left unattended.[245] On the North American continent, one Bigfoot researcher claimed to have heard the second-hand story of a farmer from Polk County, Arkansas, who investigated a milk cow's cries late at night... upon entering the barn, he was shocked to see a large, hairy manlike figure atop the animal, sucking at the cow's udder.[246]

This strong interest in procuring milk seems to extend to all entities. Faeries are particularly apt, including the Italian *salvanel*, famous for stealing the milk of farmers.[247] If libations of milk are not left for the *loireag* of the Hebrides, the entity attacks the nearest herd of cows or sheep and sucks every last drop from them.[248] Some attributed this affinity for milk to its richness,[249] though it seems more likely to be because of the faeries' inability to produce milk—recall the rewards for any comely lady who allowed a faerie child to suckle at her breast.[250]

In *The Secret Commonwealth of Elves, Fauns & Fairies*, Robert

Kirk says of the faeries' methods:

> ... these subterraneans eat but little in their dwellings; their food being exactly clean, and served up by pleasant children like enchanted Puppets. What food they extract from us is conveyed to their homes by secret paths, as some skillful women do the pith and milk from their neighbours' cows into their own cheese-hold through a hair-tether, at a great distance by art, magic, or by drawing a spigot fastened to a post, which will bring milk as far off as a bull will be heard to roar. The cheese made of the remaining milk of a cow thus strained will swim in water like a cork. The method they take to recover their milk is bitter chiding of the suspected enchanters, charging them by a counter-charm to give them back their own in God or their master's name. But a little of the mother's dung smeared on the calves mouth before it suck any does prevent this theft.[251]

The magic Kirk refers to is the uncanny ability of the faeries to siphon off milk or its essence from a distance. Such abilities are frequently attributed to faeries, including their High King Dagda, who used his abilities in wartime to shunt both grain and milk production on human farms.[252] Milk is still "taken" in this nonphysical manner in modern accounts—the aforementioned herd in Wales, for example, had a decreased milk yield following their relocation.[253]

• A farmer in the Catskill Mountains of New York had just set out milk for his cats when he heard "a shrill, whining sound, like a dynamo" and witnessed "two holes in the sky, as white as snow... perfectly round." The next morning he found the milk untouched by the cats ("unusual," according to the witness).[254] Recall earlier how cats would become sick after drinking *foyson*-less milk.

• Utah rancher Lennis Gines saw blue and yellow lights near her home on the Provo River in fall 1972. The time was around 4:30 a.m., and her son, Sam, had risen to milk the cows but stopped to watch the lights with his mother as they played along the river for 45 minutes. By the time Sam went to round up the cows, he said the animals "were nervous and didn't give the milk they usually gave."[255]

• In 1978, 62-year old Tommy Gibson saw two silvery grey ovals above Currochtrie Farm in Llanerchymedd, North Wales, each approximately 30 feet across. The objects went out to sea before returning two minutes later, this time humming noisily and frightening his cattle. The herd stampeded and rushed into the cowshed, after which the animals refused to give any milk whatsoever. Bill Gibbons and Jenny Randles later remarked at how unusual this was, as "the cattle sit quite content all day long as jet aircraft from nearby RAF West Freeugh scream overhead on low flying exercises!"[256]

• In late 2004 participants in a Russian military exercise observed several metallic discs over Belarus, and a female resident of the area soon after reported a dramatic underproduction of her cows' milk immediately thereafter.[257]

These examples may all have a prosaic explanation—frightened animals could easily be uncooperative enough to diminish milk production—but the net effect of "lost" milk is the same.

All this being said, not every UFO occupant finds miraculous evaporation to be the most efficient means of procuring milk. Researcher Pablo Villarrubia Mauso claimed that in 1990 Flores de Mamani was herding her goats in Los Zazos, Argentina, when she and the animals froze in their tracks. Two beings in brown diver's suits floated to the ground from a mysterious sphere in the sky, and one set to drawing blood from the witness while the other milked one of the herd.[258]

Conventional UFOlogical wisdom would hold that these beings are intergalactic scientists, collecting samples from earth for some arcane reason. This may well be the case, but it seems just as likely that what is desired by these intelligences isn't material at all, but is rather the witness interaction itself. The further we proceed down the rabbit hole, the more and more apparent it becomes that whatever is behind the UFO phenomenon prefers symbolism and mythology as the currency of conversation, leading one to wonder whether this penchant for milk—long held by cultures worldwide as a revered "elixir of life"—says more about their desires, or ours.

CHAPTER 10
CONNECTIONS: *SATTVIC* DIET

As you eat, so is your mind; As is the food, so is your mind.
          – Harish Johari, *Ayurvedic Healing Cuisine*

"The same [UFO] description rarely appears again in another report," the late great John Keel wrote in 1970. "The descriptions are as varied as the reports themselves. Correlations are difficult."[259] It is indeed impossible to draw solid, airtight conclusions with any Fortean phenomenon: one hundred different researchers will reach one hundred different conclusions. The task is rendered no easier when examining entity food reports, whose variety makes trends tenuous at best.

There are no conclusions to be made here—only connections.

While the identity of foods exchanged *from* humans *to* entities is clear, the exact nature of foods exchanged *to* humans *from* entities is still up for debate. Though it would seem unlikely for these beings to offer witnesses mundane mortal food, that is nonetheless the manner in which entity food is constantly described, with few exceptions. Our only real choice is to work from a place of strength regarding these cases and what they *appear* to involve; actual samples are nonexistent, Joe Simonton's pancakes notwithstanding. Thus we can safely say that faeries, aliens, and Sasquatch at the very least offer simulacra of earthly food, which may provide a clue as to its purpose.

All this said, the preceding chapters illustrate a few broad strokes when viewed in aggregate. More to the point, the food exchanged between entities and humans can be grouped into three predominant categories: liquids (especially juices and milk), fruits & vegetables, and bread. Is there a real-world equivalent to this diet?

Taken at face value, the foods involved in entity food cases correspond to a lacto vegetarian diet, i.e. a plant-based food regimen that incorporates dairy products such as milk, cheese, and butter. Such diets have their roots in ancient India and are today most commonly practiced by followers of Eastern religions, particularly those in the Hindu tradition.[260] *Ayurveda*, the Hindu discipline of traditional medicine, refers to certain lacto vegetarian diets as *sattvic*.

The Sattvic Diet

The *sattvic* diet is closely tied to the notion of *gunas*, the three basic tendencies used to describe all behavior and natural phenomena in the *Bhagavad Gita,* a 700-verse Hindu scripture. Of the three *gunas, tamas* is the darkest and most negative, skewing toward lethargy and entropy; *rajas* is associated with change and action; and *sattva* is the purest, associated with balance and order.[261] The *gunas* not only represent a continuum from ignorance to enlightenment, but also a trifecta of qualities existing simultaneously in all things. For this reason, some *ayurvedic* philosophers refer to the *gunas* as "a tricolored braid," three dimensions of one single reality; indeed, the word *guna* means "single thread of a cord."

Concepts similar to the *gunas* are found throughout the world in a variety of cultures, where "hot" and "cold" foods are used to keep humors, internal substances which directly influence one's temperament, in balance. In *ayurvedic* tradition, eating certain foods leads the mind and body to associate with the corresponding *guna*. An individual who eats *tamasic* foods will become pessimistic, lazy, and their health will suffer, whereas an individual consuming *rajasic* food will become passionate, egotistic, and moved to action.

Those consuming *sattvic* foods are peaceful and serene, and find themselves in good health. A study that appeared in the April 2007 edition of *Current Science*, India's leading interdisciplinary science journal, found a statistically significant correlation between foods associated with the three *gunas* and the consumer's corresponding state of mental health.[262]

Though *ayurvedic* scholars may differ on the finer points of categorization due to certain regional preferences and disciplines, *tamasic, rajasic,* and *sattvic* foods are generally grouped in the following manner:

Guna	Corresponding foods	Tastes
Tamas	Pork, beef, non-scaly fish, potatoes, peanuts, onions, eggplants, drugs/alcohol, as well as leftovers, processed, canned, frozen, or decaying food. In some traditions, all meats, eggs, and garlic.	Unpleasant, strong
Rajas	Scaly fish, eggs, goat, sheep, chicken, fried foods, candies, small amounts of alcohol, or tea/coffee. In some traditions, garlic.	Bitter, sour, salty
Sattva	Sweet fruits and their juices, dairy products, honey, grains (especially wheat and barley), most nuts and seeds, vegetables (esp. beans, peas, rice, leafy greens, squash), fresh nuts & seeds, carrots, sweet potatoes, beets	Fresh, sweet, tasty

What separates the *sattvic* diet from a generic lacto vegetarian regimen is the emphasis placed on certain foods, e.g. the *tamasic* category contains plenty of foods that are in line with a lacto vegetarian diet but are not deemed *sattvic*. Entity food corresponds not only to the broader lacto vegetarian definition but also, curiously enough, adheres rather faithfully to the narrowly defined *sattvic* classification.

Juice, milk, fruits & vegetables, and bread may be staples in any lacto vegetarian lifestyle but are absolutely central to the *sattvic* diet. According to *ayurvedic* scholar Harish Johari, fruits and "fresh juices from sweet, ripe fruits are the best *sattvic* foods,"[263] a claim that fits nicely with the frequency of fruit juice in entity food cases. Milk from any animal is also highly *sattvic*. Bread of wheat or barley, not unlike that given by faeries, is *sattvic*. It is worthwhile to note that the tastes said to be most *sattvic*—"sweet" and "tasty"—are the most commonly reported flavors in eyewitness descriptions, even when there is no real-world analogue to what is eaten.[264]

While *tamasic* foods rarely appear in entity food reports, *rajasic* foods and the bitter taste profile do crop up from time to time, such as the alcohol offered in faerie encounters. These outliers are not directly contrary to the overall *sattvic* trend, however—Johari notes that "we need a certain amount of *rajasic* energy to survive" and accomplish the technical needs of day-to-day life.

Since spoiled or old foods are considered *tamasic*, it comes as little surprise that *sattva* has a temporal component. It can be lost. Milk, for example, becomes *rajasic* four hours after leaving the cow.[265] The concept that foods can lose their *sattvic* attributes reinforces the intangibility of *sattva* itself, bringing to mind obvious comparisons with *foyson*. Do faeries steal milk instantaneously, direct from-the-source in order to circumvent this loss of *sattva* over time?

The question, however unlikely, arises: are *sattva* and *foyson* one-and-the-same?

Alleged Effects of a *Sattvic* Diet

Advocates of *ayurvedic* cuisine claim that a diet high in *sattvic* foods not only leads to a sense of balance and well-being, but can also result in clairvoyance. When *sattva* dominates an individual, they are more likely to become a seer or holy man, developing psychic abilities.[266]

None of this may seem relevant to our discussion on first glance. In truth, an astounding number of individuals who have encountered the paranormal live with psychic phenomena throughout their lives. Recall Anne Jeffries, whose ability to commune with the faeries went hand-in-hand with clairvoyance and a steady diet of faerie food. Rarely discussed is the fact that famous abductee Betty Hill claimed to have dreams throughout her life that accurately predicted the fatal car accidents of multiple friends.[267] Experiencer Mike Clelland, who has a longstanding interest in the psychic-UFO connection, continues to this day to be bombarded with synchronicities, those profoundly meaningful coincidences that seem outside the realm of chance. Clelland describes his feeling upon noticing the trend:

> I felt all high and mighty and I wrote a little essay on this. I felt like I was Mr. Smarty-Pants. I was making this connection. Then this close friend of mine, I said, "Hey, UFO Abductees have more synchronicities than the statistical norm," and she rolled her eyes and said, "Anyone on a spiritual path will have more synchronicities." Which is true. So there is an element of this contact experience, there's the New Age-y side to it where it's very obvious, where it feels like a spiritual path. I think that's the very definition of a spiritual path, in a way, is to be wrestling with these grander questions.[268]

Alien abduction as a spiritual path? It is tempting to write off all such accounts as New Age bunk, but there is an established link between paranormal experiences and witnesses developing a newfound spiritual-psychic disposition. Thomas Bullard noted this trend in his seminal 1987 catalogue *UFO Abductions: The Measure of a Mystery*, saying abductees had experienced "extrasensory experiences," including clairvoyance, precognition, or "visions of the future" in 20 of the 270 cases he collected.[269]

We must proceed carefully here. Many paranormal witnesses—including Clelland and Hill, ironically enough—never claim to have been offered food, while still others are extremely, profoundly traumatized by the experience. None of this is to suggest that every witness receives a glass of fruit juice and sets upon a spiritual quest. This is only an attempt to highlight two facts: first, that when foods appear in entity encounters, they tend to correspond to the *sattvic* diet; and second, that both a *sattvic* diet and entity encounters can lead to self-reported spiritual enlightenment.

Even conceding this connection, there are other ways in which the unexplained and the *sattvic* diet collide. It is not uncommon for paranormal experiencers to alter their diet, or develop a new outlook on what they eat. In medieval times someone returning from the faerie realm might be wise to incorporate a more *sattvic* approach to nutrition—as already mentioned in passing, many of those who came back are said to have crumbled into dust after resuming their normal meals. Following their 1977 abduction, Elaine Avis and her husband eschewed alcohol, tobacco, "food with any preservatives, colourings, flavouring, or anything else unnatural," and meat, which they in turn encouraged others to give up.[270]

While under hypnotic regression, Karla Turner recalled one incident where she was accompanied to her kitchen by four gray, shadowy figures. Once there, she set about preparing dinner but experienced intense emotions of thankfulness upon seeing her pot roast. "Something died for that," Turner said during her session. "It's so important. I feel like I've got to pray or give something back." This reverence for beef is hard to come by in Western society, but such respect is one of the main reasons the *sattvic* diet does not include meat.[271]

The eating habits of witness are also influenced by more direct means. Some faeries explicitly disapprove of the consumption of strong ale,[272] while contactee Elizabeth Klarer was explicitly told by her host that the human body craved a vegetarian diet, not the heavy meats and processed foods of Western culture.[273] Even though Enrique Mercado Orué was given a wine-like substance in his 1976 encounter, he had been approached seven years earlier in a Mexico City bar by one of his recurring alien contacts and explicitly instructed not to drink whiskey, nor to eat meat; the latter, he was informed, made one cold, ill, and fatigued.[274]

A sizeable portion of Whitley Strieber's *Transformation* is dedicated to the author's struggle with addiction to—of all things—sugar. Strieber recalls visits in 1985 from an angelic being who warned, "Your metabolism has been altered. If you continue to eat sweets, you cannot hope to live long, and if you eat chocolate you will die."

Later that year, Strieber's wife had a dream of him dropping dead after eating a candy bar. He tried to give up this addiction, adopting a largely vegetarian lifestyle that abstained from caffeine, but continued to fall off the wagon where sweets were concerned. Eventually word reached Strieber of an old friend's mother who had awakened to find "half a dozen little men in her room; men wearing broad-brimmed hats like Asian farmers' hats." Her ensuing lapse into a hypoglycemic coma and death were attributed to severe diabetes, and Strieber felt this was his wake up call. He finally kicked the habit after several more nighttime visits from the entities. Compare the previously cited observations of Mike Clelland to Strieber's final thoughts in the book:

> I sat eating my unsweetened pancakes and wondering if they realized just how hard this was going to be for me. And at once I felt like an idiot. Obviously that must be perfectly clear to them. That was the whole damned point, wasn't it?[275]

CHAPTER 11
CONNECTIONS: SLEEP PARALYSIS

You may be an undigested bit of beef, a blot of mustard, a crumb of cheese, a fragment of underdone potato. There's more of gravy than of grave about you, whatever you are!
— Charles Dickens, *A Christmas Carol*

Sleep Paralysis

For many people, the scenario is all-too familiar: you awake in the middle of the night, unable to move. A paralysis has seized you, caused by a great heaviness weighing upon your chest, and somewhere in your bedroom, lurking on the periphery, is... something. A malign intellect that means you harm, a presence that you can feel skulking in the shadows. A dark shape looms above you....

Suddenly you can move again, and the intruder is gone.

Sleep paralysis is a surprisingly common phenomenon characterized by the sensation of being awake coupled with the inability to move; it is often accompanied by a sensation of intense pressure on the chest. Though seemingly supernatural, it is in actuality a transitional (hypnagogic) phase between sleep and wakefulness, when the mind is alert but the body is still in a state of rest. Episodes are often quite brief, around one minute, though they may last much, much longer in some individuals. To this day, its root causes are poorly understood—in some individuals it is a frequent occurrence, while others may only experience it once in a lifetime, if at all.

Practically every culture has at least one explanation for the phenomenon, usually involving a spirit sitting upon one's chest. It is believed that sleep paralysis is the inspiration for tales of the incubus and succubus, demons who prowl into bedrooms at night to rape their paralyzed victims. In Scandinavian culture, this entity is referred to as a *mare*, a belief that spawned the term "nightmare." Sleep paralysis is sometimes referred to as "Old Hag Syndrome" today.

Scientific thought on sleep paralysis has come full circle. What was once attributed to paranormal experiences is now seen as an explanation for them, particularly in the case of alien abduction accounts. Certainly, the generic symptoms—awakening at night, an inability to move, a malicious presence in the room—correlate nicely, but fail to account for the later stages of the phenomenon. Scientists have contorted themselves into knots trying to introduce hallucinations into the scenario as an attempt to explain the actual abduction itself. In the meantime, some researchers walk the line between both schools of thought, proposing that perhaps the very real, very scientific hypnagogic state might somehow allow access to the very subjective, very spiritual paranormal state.

Is there a link between sleep paralysis and food? The ancient Greeks felt so. Early physicians accused a host of gastric offenders, including indigestible food, binge eating, or too much alcohol.[276] Such beliefs persist through the modern record, with Robert Burton's *The Anatomy of Melancholy* linking sleep paralysis to the consumption of "black meat" (e.g. game such as hare or venison) in the 17th century.[277]

Claims of the connection between sleep paralysis and diet were particularly strong in the 19th century, as evidenced by the writings of John Waller, a surgeon in Britain's Royal Navy who claimed that "he could produce an attack of incubus at any time by eating avocados."[278] Perhaps most famously, in Charles Dickens' *A*

Christmas Carol Ebenezer Scrooge tells the ghost of Jacob Marley that "a slight disorder of the stomach" could be the cause of his apparition.

New research may indicate some truth to the link. A 2001 study from the *Journal of Scientific Exploration* suggests that an imbalance of electrolytes, minerals in the blood that carry electric charges to regulate body function, might interfere with deep sleep and cause a hypnagogic reaction.[279] One of the most common electrolytes found in food is, of course, sodium. Could the folklore of salt repelling faeries be grounded in a much more pragmatic solution for avoiding sleep paralysis?

Entity Food and the Dream State

There is at least one story where entity food is the implied source of a nighttime apparition. In *Passport to Magonia*, Jacques Vallée retells a story from *De delictis et poenis*, a compilation of sinful acts collected by Franciscan priest Father Sinistrari. In the tale, Sinistrari tells of a virtuous lady of Pavia named Hieronyma:

> One day, Hieronyma prepared some bread and brought it to the baker's to have it baked. He brought it back to her, and at the same time he brought her a large pancake of a very peculiar shape, made with butter and Venetian pastes, such as they used to make cakes in that city. She refused it, saying she had not prepared anything like it.

> "But," said the baker, "I have not had any bread to bake today but yours. The pancake must come from your house too; your memory probably fails you."

> The good lady allowed herself to be convinced; she took the pancake and ate it with her husband, her three-year old daughter, and a servant girl.

During the following night, while she was in bed with her husband and both were asleep, she found herself awakened by an extremely fine voice, somewhat like a high-pitched whistling sound. It was softly saying in her ear some very clear words: "How did you like the cake?" In fear, our good lady began to use the sign of the cross and to invoke in succession the names of Jesus and Mary.

"Fear naught," said the voice. "I mean no harm to you. On the contrary, there is nothing I would not do in order to please you. I am in love with your beauty, and my greatest desire is to enjoy your embraces."

At the same time, she felt that someone was kissing her cheeks, but so softly and gently that she might have thought it was only the finest cotton down touching her. She resisted, without answering anything, only repeating many times the names of Jesus and Mary and making the sign of the cross. The temptation lasted thus about half an hour, after which time the tempter went away.[280]

The nighttime visitor was, of course, an incubus.

The Yoruba of southwestern Nigeria draw a direct connection between sleep paralysis and entity food. They believe that anyone suffering from sleep paralysis is the victim of *ogun oru* (nocturnal warfare), a sort of sorcery brought about by consuming cursed food in their dreams. Victims are most vulnerable between 3:00 and 4:00 a.m. The food is offered by an angry spirit who wishes to claim the victim as its mate, though many do not recall the dream due to "spiritual concealment." The curse is only removable through prayer and spiritual intercession.[281]

It would be easy to lump *ogun oru* in with superstition if so much of it didn't ring true. The belief incorporates a plethora of aspects seen across the paranormal: entity food, supernatural beings, sleep paralysis, demonic possession, sexuality, amnesia. Even the time frame is significant: there is a persistent belief in paranormal circles that supernatural phenomena are most active between 3:00 and 4:00 a.m. Consider also that food is the trigger for *ogun oru*, just as entity food tends to bookend encounters with paranormal beings. In both cases, the food is used to initiate a change—be it physical or mental—in the percipient.

During the course of researching his book *Magic, Mysticism, & the Molecule*, author Micah Hanks frequently experienced dreams in which he was offered various psychotropic substances. "I began finding myself in bizarre scenarios within my dreams nearly every night, in which people, or sometimes other weird beings like robots and aliens, would hand me little 'samples' of the very substances about which I would read during my waking hours," he writes. "In a sense, I could liken this to the feeling that someone, or maybe *something*, had been trying to encourage me to experiment with these substances, perhaps taunting me subtly from someplace outside my own consciousness."[282]

Hanks alludes to the fact that he would never have accepted the substances offered to him in real life, yet he did in his dreams; this is exactly what happens in entity food cases, where individuals such as Carl Higdon take food that they normally would avoid. Is there an altered state of consciousness at play in these reports, something akin to when we sleep?

Andrew Paquette is an artist, writer, and self-proclaimed prophetic dreamer, who, if his stories are to be believed, has an incredible track record of dream-induced clairvoyance. Paquette reports numerous out-of-body experiences during his symbolically oblique dreams, often in the presence of *servo spiritii* ("watching" or "protective spirits"). One such entity—appearing in the guise of a kindly old lady—would always offer him a drink prior to each excursion into the *mundus alo*, the spirit world. The beverage always appeared to be some type of tea, only once taking a different form (in this case, the Japanese alcoholic beverage *sake*). "On each occasion, I wasn't aware that I was in the *mundus alo* until I had the drink," Paquette wrote. "The drink itself operated like a post-hypnotic suggestion by causing me to wake up within the dream." By taking the drink of the *servo spiritus*, Paquette was able to see his situation more clearly, shifting his dream into a lucid state where he realized he was asleep and could interact with the spirits around him.[283]

Paquette's encounters with the *servo spiritus* are important because they introduce a key concept to our discussion: the possibility that the symbolism of nonphysical food may somehow trigger a reaction in the consciousness of the witness. We must acknowledge the possibility that, just as in dreams, entity food may not be food at all—and may not even be physical.

CHAPTER 12
CONNECTIONS: SEXUALITY

Food, far more than sex, is the great leveler. Just as every king, prophet, warrior, and saint has a mother, so every Napoleon, every Einstein, every Jesus has to eat. – Betty Fussell, *My Kitchen Wars*

Food and sex have a tangled history in religion, tradition, and mythology. Both are pleasures of the flesh, provide instant gratification, and are essential to survival, be it as an individual or as a species. There is a reason that both gluttony and lust are regarded as Deadly Sins. In some cultures, such as parts of Mongolia, sex is as much a part of hospitality as food, the host hoping that his guest may be a god in disguise and bestow a demigod to his wife.[284]

Judeo-Christian belief tells of the Forbidden Fruit—usually an apple or pomegranate, though other candidates exist— which caused Adam and Eve to recognize their nakedness and feel shame. Gunnlöð, a lonely female troll from Norse mythology, guarded the magical Mead of Poetry coveted by Odin; attempting to steal the brew, he was instead seduced by her.[285] Women in Greek mythology wandering the woods might be taken by a satyr, a drunken man-goat hybrid whose antics bear some resemblance to modern tales of Sasquatch abduction. Satyrs were companions of Dionysus, the god of revelry, the grape harvest, and wine.

It was Dionysus who put a sleeping potion into the well of the androgynous Greco-Roman deity Agdistis. After the drug had taken affect, Dionysus tied Agdistis' foot to his penis with a rope that, predictably enough, led to his castration when the potion wore off. According to legend, the blood that spilled fertilized the ground, and a pomegranate tree grew in its place.[286]

In the ancient world, any Buddhist who encountered a dangerous spirit was encouraged to coax the demon into a tantric vow, a sort of pact that not only avoided conflict but also assured a mutual allegiance. "The vows are administered by means of a sacramental drop of sexual fluids," writes Jacob P. Dalton in *The Taming of the Demons: Violence and Liberation in Tibetan Buddhism*, adding that perfumed water was an acceptable substitute. "After the sacrament is swallowed, it works its way into one's heart, where it remains for the rest of one's life." While the vow would protect the consumer if honored, a broken vow would turn the liquid to poison.[287]

Sexuality, as referenced in previous chapters, often plays a role whenever individuals are abducted by humanoids. The sexual component has become part of the alien abduction meme, from the "anal probe" so humorously mentioned in pop-culture to the genetic hybridization program that many researchers believe to be the keystone of extraterrestrial interaction. Lesser known are cases of faeries taking human women as wives, and practically absent from public discourse are Sasquatch abductions, where women are taken for breeding purposes.

Thus it comes as little surprise that the most often reported entity foods, in particular fruit and bread, are loaded with reproductive meaning.

Entity Food in Close Proximity to Intercourse

Reports of food in proximity to sex are rare to nonexistent in Sasquatch abductions, outside of cases such as Serephine Long's ordeal. In these instances there seems to be no apparent cause-and-effect correlation between the foraged meals brought by the beasts and the sexual advances they make, other than to sustain their captive.

When food appears in conjunction with sex in faerie lore, it is often part of some sort of an agreement. One troubling variation on the story of Snow White features a direct exchange of food for sex. While trying to find her way out of a forest, a young servant girl happened upon a cottage inhabited by seven dwarfs. The dwarfs, who were all brothers, offered her a meal and a room for the night if she agreed to bed down with one of them. She slept with the eldest of the seven brothers, and when she returned her community ostracized her.[288]

Faeries seem to view the exchange of food as a means by which sexual contracts and marriages can be held binding. In the oldest Irish versions of the Loathly Lady tale, a faerie queen disguised as an old hag rescues a young knight, demanding his hand in marriage as recompense; after sharing a ceremonial drink signifying the knight's agreement to the union, the Loathly Lady reveals her true beauty.[289] Another story outlines how a young man baked a "fairy cake" and turned away two faerie suitors before at last being approached by "a beautiful lady in green" who took his cake, ate it, and bound herself to him.[290] On the other hand, a young British man failed to court a Lady of the Lake because the bread he offered was by turns too hard and underdone.[291]

Aliens are less bothered by the notion of consent. Carl R. and his wife Dagmar had noticed strange happenings around their Iowa farm in August 1982 before awakening in the middle of the night to find a greenish-glowing disc hovering above the orchard. A stairwell descended, the couple entered, and short entities with round heads and large eyes separated the two. Dagmar was taken to a medical examination, while Carl was approached by two of the entities carrying "a green vial filled with a liquid that appeared to be swirling of its own volition in its container." Communicating with the beings telepathically and convinced they meant him no harm, he downed the beverage and almost immediately found himself with an uncontrollable erection. A mechanical device was clamped around his penis, inducing orgasm moments later and collecting his semen. Carl and Dagmar awoke in bed, thinking they had overslept until they began to recall the incident several days later.[292]

Another couple, hypnotically regressed under the supervision of UFOCCI (UFO Contact Center International) Director Aileen Garouette, was driving in British Columbia when they noticed two hours of missing time. Their regression revealed that both had been taken by strange beings, given some sort of drink, and had intercourse with their captors.[293]

The late researcher Karla Turner encountered numerous occasions where a drink was given in close proximity to sexual intercourse. Her 1992 book *Into the Fringe* describes the experiences of Casey, an abductee who was taken aboard a ship and given a "cinnamon-smelling liquid" before being seduced by a white-haired woman. The entire interaction was watched by a wizened being he referred to as the Old One.[294]

One of—if not, to be frank, *the*—most salacious and disturbing incident featuring entity food in close proximity to sex is an account from another Karla Turner book, *Masquerade of Angels*. Lifetime abductee Ted Rice related a horrifying evening in his youth when, while sleeping with his grandmother, a reptilian humanoid entered the room and forcibly dropped a "clear, maybe slightly yellow" liquid upon their tongues. Rice's deceased grandfather entered the room and had sexual intercourse with his widow, only to dismount and reveal himself as another reptilian. Rice was then forced to perform oral sex on the alien while several of its comrades had sex with the grandmother as well. The event ended with Rice being anally raped. Rice speculated that the liquid might have had aphrodisiac qualities, though he recalled no sexual stimulation.[295]

Pregnancy

Cause undoubtedly spawns effect, and one has to ask about the repercussions of such liaisons. What of pregnancies? According to many, a sinister hybrid program is the centerpiece of the opaque alien agenda, and indeed many repeat abductees report meetings with these beings throughout their lives. Female alien abductees experience reproductive difficulties with near-universal regularity, and some of the assertions are incredibly disturbing if true. Female abductees have claimed unexplained pregnancies without intercourse or in spite of contraception, as well as pregnancies mysteriously terminating with no fetus to be found. Stories abound of doctors accusing their patients of receiving abortions when the victim has taken no such action. Such horrifying accounts have already been mentioned for the way in which they parallel faeries' predilection for abducting children—if anyone is interested in this darker aspect of UFO lore, there is no shortage of literature to choose from.

Not all sexual activity with entities ends in pregnancy. One wonders if the pills taken by Jane Murphy in 1975 were perhaps some form of abortifacient, for though she suffered from a persistent infection, there was never any sign of pregnancy to speak of. It is possible that any pre- or post-coitus food may serve this purpose.

If Murphy's pills were to prevent pregnancy, they would be the diametric opposite of what was given to Isabel, one of the participants studied by the late John Mack. Isabel claimed to be the recipient of a type of in vitro fertilization from her alien abductees, and was routinely given a bitter fluid to drink. She strongly believed that the beverage was a medicinal "supervitamin" to help her and the hybrid child remain healthy.[296]

The Psychological Angle: Oral Humiliation

Encounters such as Ted Rice's horrific rape form the foundation for the argument that alien abductions may actually represent repressed memories of sexual abuse. The parallels are obvious, in particular the sense of pain and helplessness reported by so many abductees. Rice recalled the beings laughing during his rape, an example of the sexual humiliation felt in so many encounters—could entity food also be some form of oral humiliation?

Recall that men outnumber women approximately 2:1 in

entity food cases. According to a 1996 article in *Psychological Inquiry*, male masochistic fantasies feature "more severe pain, oral humiliation, partner infidelity, and active participation by third persons" than those of females. The authors, Leonard S. Newman and Roy F. Baumeister, determined that, while oral humiliation was a "low-frequency category" in the whole of alien abduction accounts, "there is some resemblance between the apparent sex differences in masochistic scripts and the sex differences in UFO abduction accounts."[297]

Chapter 13
Connections: Absorption, Ointment, & The Entity Diet

Is there any absolute impossibility in supposing man to be destined for a similar change; to imagine him no longer dining, with unwieldy paraphernalia of servants and plates, upon food queerly dyed and distorted, but nourishing himself in elegant simplicity by immersion in a tub of nutritive fluid? – H.G. Wells, "Of a Book Unwritten: The Man of the Year Million"

The subject of entity diet was briefly broached in earlier chapters, where a great deal of focus was given to the faerie diet, i.e. their consumption of the essence, or *foyson,* of food. Trying to establish the diet of aliens and Sasquatch, however, has the potential to lead us down a rabbit hole that, in all honesty, could prove just as lengthy as this survey of entity food. The primary focus of this book is the *exchange* of food between entities and humans, and an in-depth study trying to reconcile nonhuman biology with current scientific understanding is beyond our scope. This being said, let us take a cursory view of the evidence, as there is at least one line of inquiry that may prove particularly fruitful to explaining cases where food is exchanged.

Theories on Sasquatch's appetite are straightforward and comparatively mundane. "Based on the numerous accounts that mention feeding or carrying food, the Sasquatch diet seems to span the wide spectrum of a generalized omnivore," writes Dr. Jeffrey Meldrum in *Sasquatch: Legend Meets Science*. "Eyewitnesses have reported everything from roots and berries to deer and elk."[298] Native Americans have long held that these creatures prey upon human beings as well, though the authenticity of such claims is hotly debated. Ample evidence does suggest that large hairy hominids are opportunistic scavengers of human refuse sites, as quite a few witnesses have caught Sasquatch with their torsos half-buried in a dumpster.

Of course, this information is only useful if one subscribes to the notion of a flesh-and-blood animal. There is a vocal minority among believers who feel Sasquatch is paranormal or at the very least interdimensional, thus having no need for earthly sustenance. Among disbelievers, many skeptics have a difficult time believing that any ecosystem in proximity to a human settlement, particularly in North America, could sustain the immense caloric needs of a 7-to-10-foot-tall primate.

By now it should be clear that Sasquatch are outliers in our discussion, only tangentially intersecting with the greater trends seen in entity food reports. For this reason—coupled with how thoroughly we have outlined the concept of *foyson* in faerie lore—a majority of this chapter will only focus on trying to establish what proposed extraterrestrial diet is supported by fact, and how that changes our perception of entity food interactions.

Navigating theories on extraterrestrial cuisine is a tricky undertaking, with many conflicting tales. Insofar as conventional diets, they run the gamut. Some are diets indistinguishable from terrestrial food. Elizabeth Klarer's companions were vegetarians, as are a great many entities in contactee cases. The reptilian beings encountered by channeler Joy D'Light in 1961 were herbivores,[299] and the aliens encountered by Armando Zurbarán drank "plant milk." All-liquid diets are mentioned in accounts as well, though not with the frequency one would expect given the great number of beverages reported.

More abstract means of consumption, wholly alien, appear a good deal. Predictably enough, these usually describe synthetic foodstuffs such as artificially grown proteins. Some are a bit more peculiar: on April 21, 1897, a West Virginia man claimed to have met eight 12-foot-tall entities with large heads who visited for an hour, all the while eating small pills and "drinking air."[300] One 1998 Costa Rican witness described beings who, instead of eating, absorbed the entire spectrum of light energy,[301] while one of the abductees in John Mack's *Abduction: Human Encounters with Aliens* was told that "to liberate latent powers, we have to 'levitate our body' and live without eating."[302] Such ideas are reminiscent of esoteric Ayurvedic beliefs that have since devolved into New Age concepts like "breatharianism," the notion of surviving on air and sunlight alone.

That being said, aliens self-report on the nature of their diet in most of these examples. Why should they be trusted? Everything about our experiences with the unknown suggests that these entities deal in deception, theater, and metaphor. In truth, there is more than sufficient evidence to suggest that our little green friends are not entirely forthcoming on the finer points of their diet.

The Absorption Theory

Like Sasquatch, many have ascribed anthropophagic tendencies to aliens, perhaps most famously in a widely circulated (yet poorly referenced) tale from Valdamar Valerian's *Matrix II*. According to the report, an abductee saw "a vat full of red liquid and body parts of humans and animals... she could see Greys bobbing up and down, almost swimming."

While abduction research does not overtly suggest that aliens are harvesting people for consumption, there may be a grain of truth to the report. "Nourishment is ingested by smearing a soupy mixture of biologicals [sic] on the epidermis," the report says of the Greys. "Food sources [include] Bovine cattle [and human] parts... distilled into a high protein broth."[303]

The notion that aliens might absorb nutrition through their skin is not a recent one. A November 10, 2005, *Magonia* editorial by Martin S. Kottmeyer provided an excellent overview of the concept's history, tracing it from 1988's *The Krill Report*, a suspect document of the early internet, through the work of Dr. David Jacobs.[304] Jacobs, a staunch proponent of the Extraterrestrial Hypothesis (ETH), proclaimed in his 1998 book *The Threat* that "we now know that the aliens obtain fuel differently from humans, that their skin has a unique function, and that they convert 'food' to energy very differently."[305]

Casting aside the dubious claim that we can "know" *anything* about these alien intelligences, the Absorption Theory (as Jacobs dubbed it) has been at play in the field of UFOlogy for some time. There is plenty of anecdotal evidence in support of the notion, much of it noted in Kottmeyer's editorial.

Witnesses are a constant source of oblique confirmation. One anonymous abductee from Texas was allegedly escorted out of her bedroom and into a flying saucer by two short, brown, mouthless entities on June 1, 1962. During the ensuing examination, she asked a taller, more human entity how the creatures ate. His reply: "Differently from us—don't worry about it."[306] A seeming answer to this question was provided by "Joe," another abductee studied by Mack, who recalled watching as alien infants were sponged with a green liquid "as if to put energy into their bodies."[307]

Additional corroborating behavior is detailed in Brad Steiger's *The UFO Abductors*. A Colorado forest ranger was investigating the lights of what he assumed was a stranded truck in 1982 when he encountered a short, large-headed, large-eyed dwarf. Accompanying the being was a beautiful blonde woman who remained behind when her diminutive companion disappeared. The ranger, ostensibly "rescuing" the lady, took her back to his cabin and prepared a cup of coffee for her. "She sipped at the cup slowly, looking at the contents as if she had never before seen coffee," Steiger wrote. "[The ranger] caught her putting her finger in to test the brew as if she could somehow pick up the liquid with her fingertips and drink it that way." One thing led to another and the woman revisited him eighteen months later, this time with a child in tow.[308]

Government informants of varying repute have stepped forward with much more explicit information. On December 29, 1987, John Lear—son of the inventor of the Lear Jet, an experienced aviator with close government ties, and a future UFO researcher—claimed to have learned that aliens possessed an atrophied digestive system and consumed their food through a hormonal/enzyme solution "mixed with hydrogen peroxide and applied to the skin by spreading or dipping parts of their bodies in the solution. The body absorbs the solution, then excretes the waste back through the skin."[309]

In 1997's *The Day After Roswell*, published one year before the death of the author, United States Army Colonel Philip J. Corso, military doctors are described examining the occupants of the famously crashed craft, only to be perplexed by their biology: "… if an exchange of nutrients and waste occurred within their systems, that exchange could only have taken place through the creature's skin or the outer protective covering they wore because there were no digestive or waste systems."[310]

Further evidence for the Absorption Hypothesis can be seen in descriptions of the aliens themselves, which are almost always reported as having tiny, slit like mouths (or no mouth at all). This is more common in descriptions of Grey aliens, who usually lack genitalia and an anus as well. Ernie Sears, a recurring abductee from Southampton, England, told the *Southern Daily Echo*, "They have no mouth, just a thin slip of skin and hardly any nose. They don't ingest food like we do."[311] Researcher Leonard Stringfield noted in the November 1978 issue of *Flying Saucer Review* that the extraterrestrial mouth "appears not to function as a means of communication or as an orifice for food ingestion," at least in a majority of reports.[312]

A purely biological-evolutionary point-of-view implies that these orifices have atrophied or disappeared from lack of use. If one takes a more psychological-symbolic outlook, one can find a parallel in religious iconography, which often depicts holy figures with small mouths, representative of their disinterest in the base pleasures of earth.[313]

Jacobs adopted the Absorption Theory after listening to testimony from several hypnotically regressed abductees, some of whom were directly informed of this method by their alien captors. Even if one does not ascribe to the ETH as Jacobs does, it must be admitted that the Absorption Theory is quite attractive. It dovetails nicely not only with a great deal of direct eyewitness testimony, but also agrees with the entities' well-established propensity to offer liquids to those in their custody.

Astonishingly, the Absorption Theory mirrors the concept of *foyson*, a similarity noted by Kevin Aspinall in the summer 1995 edition of *Flying Saucer Review*. Aspinall points out the manner in which Robert Kirk wrote of faerie consumption:

> The pith and spirits only of women's milk feed their children, being artificially conveyed (as air and oil sink into our bodies) to make them vigorous and fresh. And this shorter way of conveying a pure ailment (without the usual digestions), by transfusing it and transpiring through the pores into the veins, arteries, and vessels that supply the body, is nothing more absurd than an infant's being fed by the navel before it is born, or than a plant which growth by attracting a lively juice from the earth through many small roots and tendons....[314]

Kirk suggested that this transfusion is only possible because faerie bodies are so "spongious, thin, and delicate."[315] Though there is no evidence to suggest as much—and, to be honest, plenty of evidence to the contrary—the notion of Sasquatch eating *foyson* would handily eliminate the immense dietary needs mentioned earlier.

There are parallels in faerie lore to the small and nonexistent mouths spotted in modern alien accounts. Every mill in the

British Isles is said to house a *killmoulis*, a grotesque faerie with an enormous nose and no mouth. It was said that he ingested food through his nose, although some have proposed it was his subsistence on *foyson* that allowed him to bypass traditional consumption entirely.[316] If not via his nose, perhaps the avenue of ingestion was a hole in his back, a feature attributed to many faeries. In one folk tale from Corsica, a Lady of the Lake married a mortal and refused to sup at the dinner table, instead taking her food back to her room each night. Spying through her keyhole one evening, the husband watched as his wife dumped the food into an empty hole at her back.[317]

Supernatural entities commonly eschew natural means of consumption, especially those who live farther up in the stratosphere. British Air Force pilots in World War II blamed faulty equipment on "gremlins" and often sighted balls of light outside their aircraft, which they referred to as "foo fighters." In folklore, gremlins—a race of faerie folk—have no need of food or water.[318] Similarly, Homer claimed in the *Iliad* that the gods "eat no bread" nor drink wine, in direct contrast to bread-eating humans.[319] A perverse old English belief held that witches abducted unbaptized children to boil into a jelly, part of which they drank and the other half they smeared on their bodies, all in an effort to acquire magical powers.[320]

Ointments

If we consider the implications of the Absorption Theory, we are faced with something of a quandary. Quite a few alien encounters feature liquids, gels, and ointments smeared over the abductee's naked body, a fact begging the question: if aliens consume via their skin, does this make any abduction involving ointment an entity food case?

Pursuing this line of inquiry broadens our pool of entity food reports considerably, as the number of ointment cases nearly equals the number of beverage reports (and, in a sense, could be viewed as a natural subset of the larger "liquid" category). There certainly is evidence to suggest that these full-body immersions possess a nutritive component. When Mário Restier was taken aboard an alien craft in 1949, he was placed—clothing and all—into a tub full of liquid that he was told would "eliminate the discomfort of large accelerations and also nourish the body."[321]

Such substances are usually reported by abductees as clear, thick, and odorless, their alleged effects ranging from disinfection to protecting the human form from the stresses of interstellar travel. In the rare cases where it is not applied to the entire body, alien ointment is rubbed on the abductee's lips—Miguel Freitas of Argentina was taken aboard a craft by an unidentified humanoid and submitted to rigorous "questioning," part of which included an injection and a grayish material "smeared on his mouth."[322] This mouth-smearing scenario has been repeated throughout several Eurasian cases investigated by Ukrainian researcher Anton Anfalov, each of which involved strange "pastes" that the entities claimed would facilitate travel. This idea has such currency that *Fire In the Sky*, the highly fictionalized 1993 film depicting Travis Walton's abduction, also features a type of jelly smeared on the victim's mouth during a pivotal examination scene.

It is quite common for ointments to appear in conjunction with travel preparation. Brazilian abductee Arturo Berlet claimed to have visited Mars in a liquid container,[323] while Betty Andreasson recalled gel-filled "chairs" in one of her famous recurring journeys. When East Texas resident Meagan Elliott was taken in 1980, she experienced "a sense of acceleration" while "some sort of liquid wetted her."[324]

At this point it should come as no surprise that this scenario—wherein a witness is taken by an entity, anointed with a topical substance, and shown an environment hitherto "invisible"—has ties to both faerie and Sasquatch lore. Because the concept is often traditionally tied to the concept of glamour, however, there is one important distinction: alien abductions feature full-body application, whereas faerie and Sasquatch legends focus on ointment applied to the eye.

The nature of faerie ointment is open to debate. In some traditions, the water from boiled eggs forms the substance's foundation, while others contend that it is a simple jelly or jam.[325] The most famous story of faerie ointment is "Midwife to the Fairies," first told in the 13th-century writings of Gervase of Tilbury. In the tale, a human midwife is fetched in the dark of night to a strange house and charged with looking after a faerie infant. Part of this charge involves a special ointment that she is instructed to rub on the baby's eyes at regular intervals. Depending on the story's telling the midwife either accidentally or deliberately anointed one of her own eyes, whereupon she could perceive the entire hidden faerie world around her. The faeries later discovered her newfound ability and blinded her for her insolence.[326]

Another tale was related by Edwin Sidney Hartland in his 1890 book, *The Science of Fairy Tales: An Inquiry into Fairy Mythology*. According to legend, a faerie mother from Scotland took her infant's wet-nurse on a visit to fairyland as a means of showing thanks. The human was only able to enter the magical world after her guide "dropped three drops of a precious dew on the nurse's left eyelid, and they were admitted to a beautiful land watered with meandering rivulets and yellow with corn, where the trees were laden with fruits which dropped honey."[327] Compare this act to the oft-mentioned drops remembered in Whitley Strieber's encounters.

In western culture such tales are easy to write off as inspired by the Christian Bible, where Jesus of Nazareth cures blindness by applying dirt and spittle to the eyes of the afflicted. Unfortunately for those offering such prosaic explanations, reports where entities administer eye ointment are widespread throughout the non-Christian world as well. As an example, consider the *asamanukpai* of West African folklore, small dwarfs who are said to inhabit the forests of Ghana. They gladly receive offerings of trinkets, rum, fruit, and water, and grant powers of clairvoyance and fortune-telling by "squeezing magical fairy-fruit juice into the eyes" of those lucky enough to win their favor.[328] This folklore agrees nicely with the propensity for entities to offer fruit juice to witnesses, as noted earlier.

Some Native American traditions also claim that Sasquatch smear the eyes of those they abduct. Recall the tale of Serephine Long, who could neither visit nor leave the Sasquatch's lair without having a sticky substance applied to her eyes. This was not an isolated incident: such behavior has long been attributed to the *Tsonoqua* in Kwakiutl and Tlingit lore, where the giantess would snatch up young children, slap tree gum on their eyes, and take them away to be eaten.[329]

Sexual Preparation

There is an oddly specific trend within ointment reports that should be addressed, worthy enough of its own section: Brazilian abductees who are covered in a kind of "stimulating" oil or liquid prior to intercourse with alien women. Such a bizarre, narrow category might be humorous if the stories weren't so fundamentally upsetting.

The most famous of this curious subset is the case of Antônio Vilas-Boas. Vilas-Boas was plowing a field in Minas Gerais, Brazil, on the evening of October 16, 1957, when he saw a glowing red craft descend from above. After attempting to flee the frightening scene both on his tractor and on foot, Vilas-Boas was apprehended by a short humanoid in grey coveralls.[330] The being, which spoke in a strange barking fashion, was joined by three of its comrades who helped drag their captive into the landed craft.

Once inside the entities stripped Vilas-Boas naked. "Then one of the men approached me with something in his hand," he later recalled. "It seemed to be a sort of wet sponge, and with it he began to spread a liquid all over my skin... The liquid was clear as water, but quite thick, and without smell. I thought it was some sort of oil, but was wrong, for my skin did not become greasy or oily."

The beings took several blood samples in a separate room

before leading Vilas-Boas to a third space where he waited for what felt like over half an hour. After a time he was—in his estimation—gassed with a noxious vapor that made him vomit. Another interminable period of time passed, and a nude woman greeted him.[331]

"Her body was much more beautiful than that of any woman I have ever known," Vilas-Boas later reminisced. She proceeded to make her carnal intentions quite clear to him, and he "began to get excited... This seems incredible in the situation in which I found myself. I think that the liquid that they had rubbed on my skin was the cause of this. They must have done it purposely. All I know is that I became uncontrollably excited...."

It is interesting to note how Vilas-Boas seemed to be a slave to his captors' wishes. Just as Carl Higdon surprised himself by taking his abductor's pills, Vilas-Boas seemed equally astonished by his own actions. The ensuing sex act proceeded as any earthly coupling would, with the exception of a few animalistic grunts issued by his intergalactic partner. After the dismount, she rubbed her belly and gestured upwards, as if to inform him of their future child's home. Vilas-Boas was then taken on a tour of the craft, given his clothing, and summarily returned home. He stuck to his story for the rest of his life.[332]

Anyone would expect this bizarre scenario to be a one-time anomaly, highly unlikely to repeat itself, and yet its salient aspects were duplicated over two decades later. Jose Ignacio Alvaro, a student living in Rio Grande do Sul, was walking home at 8:00 p.m. when the town was plunged into a power outage. When he looked up, Alvaro saw a floating sphere that shot a blue beam of light at him, causing him to pass out. According to testimony recovered under hypnosis, Alvaro was escorted into the craft by a nondescript entity who told him he had a very important task to accomplish. Once inside the ship Alvaro met "a tall, nude woman with protuberant eyes" who "rubbed him down with a sponge." She then seduced him, and Alvaro awoke under the stars some distance from his original location with the words, "The task is accomplished" reverberating in his head. [333]

The next year would see *yet another* Brazilian case with the same main points, this time as part of the famous Mirassol UFO Incident. In addition to receiving juice-type drinks and multiple injections, Antonio Carlos Ferreira was stripped naked by short beings with slanted eyes on June 27, 1979, and covered in a "thin yellowish oil" that researchers later speculated to be a kind of disinfectant. Unlike the lady encountered by Boas, Ferreira described his partner as hideous, and it was only after some effort on his captors' part that he was able to consummate the act. [334]

Less explicit but highly suggestive of this pattern is the November 29, 1982, encounter of João Valério da Silva. While standing by an outdoor sink, da Silva heard a strange ticking noise behind him and turned, only to be blinded by a bright light coming from what appeared to be a type of platform or elevator descending to the ground. A short figure in a full-body coverall forced da Silva inside where another entity was waiting and the three ascended into a sort of "vestibule." It was here that a beautiful naked woman—appearing wholly human— approached da Silva and touched his cheek, causing him to lose consciousness. Over four hours later da Silva's wife and 21-year-old daughter found him outside by the sink, completely nude, covered in "some kind of oil" and sporting "a circular mark on his left breast with strange lesions within it." His shirt, found nearby, was also soaked in the substance, and his watch had stopped forty minutes earlier. [335]

Why does such an odd scenario keep repeating itself in Brazil? It is frustrating that there are no clear reasons why such a consistent trend would take place. It may be possible that lubed-up sex fiends from Zeta Reticuli are traveling to Brazil for breeding stock, but why wouldn't this scenario be equally prevalent in other regions around the globe? Abductions where ointment is rubbed on the skin prior to sex are rare outside of Brazil, one of the few exceptions being the May 2, 1968, Shane Kurz encounter (which involved a female witness, something not seen in the Brazilian cases). [336]

Perhaps the takeaway should be that, just as entity food tends to end an encounter, ointments from aliens, faeries, and Sasquatch tend to facilitate experiences: revealing an unseen world, allowing travel, or instigating sexual relations.

Religious Symbolism

The spreading of oils and ointments on the body has long held a place in religion. The title "Christ" actually means "anointed," and as applied to Jesus of Nazareth references His identity as the messiah, a king or priest anointed with holy oil. Baptisms and Christenings, where candidates are immersed in Holy Water and admitted into the Christian church, are an outgrowth of anointment beliefs. Unction was also central to Hebraic tradition where, like food, it was tied to customs regarding hospitality (Jesus, for example, was anointed in the house of the Pharisee in Luke 7:39-46).

Anointing in the early days of Judaism may have involved oils full of potent hallucinogens. In Exodus 30:22-23, the Lord says to Moses, "Take the following fine spices: 500 shekels of liquid myrrh, half as much of fragrant cinnamon, 250 shekels of q'aneh-bosm, 500 shekels of cassia—all according to the sanctuary shekel—and a hind of olive oil. Make these into a sacred anointing oil, a fragrant blend, the work of a perfumer. It will be the sacred anointing oil." Readers may recognize "q'aneh-bosm" in its more modern form: cannabis, or marijuana.[337]

This herb in essence transformed the sacred anointing oil of early Jews into an *entheogen*, a term coined by professor Carl P. Ruck to describe hallucinogenic substances used in shamanic and religious ritual to "release the god." *Soma*—mentioned before in conjunction with the Great Ocean of milk from Hindu tradition—is a substance that, while lost to time, was believed to be an entheogen as well.

Ruck says of the Hebrews' anointing oil, "There can be little doubt about a role for cannabis in Judaic religion....There is no way that so important a plant as a fiber source for textiles and nutritive oils and one so easy to grow would have gone unnoticed... the mere harvesting of it would have induced an entheogenic reaction."[338]

This potent dose of THC (tetrahydrocannabinol, the active ingredient in cannabis) would undoubtedly have changed the consciousness of the user, perhaps allowing them to see supernatural entities and perceive "invisible realms," as with faerie ointment. Please do not misunderstand this comparison: no one is suggesting that faeries, aliens, and Sasquatch are roaming around waiting for the right moment to slather unsuspecting victims with marijuana oil. Rather, attention is brought to these connections only to highlight the similarity between hallucinogenic anointing oil in early Judaism and the ointments smeared on witnesses' bodies during entity encounters. These connections apply to other entheogens throughout world culture, and this association will be the central subject of the next chapter.

Anointing is integral in Eastern traditions as well, particularly in the Hindu belief system where it features as a blessing. *Pancāmirtam*, a jellylike substance comprised of various fruits, honey, and sugar, is spread twice annually on an icon of the god Murukan̲ at his temple in Palani. Bits of these "washings of the god" are combined with other amounts of *pancāmirtam* not utilized in the ritual before being sold for consumption. The substance, pungent and sweet, is said to restore health with miraculous results. As such, this ritual sits at the crossroads of the supernatural, food, ointment, and offerings—coincidentally enough, *pancāmirtam* is also closely associated with the Hindu "elixir of life": *Soma*.[339]

Implications to Understanding

Suffice to say, our entire discussion becomes even more difficult once the Absorption Theory is introduced. This controversial hypothesis blurs the boundaries of what is and isn't food, forcing us to examine cases involving ointment and—even more problematic—raising doubts about why these beings seem to administer earthly, culture-appropriate consumables.

To wit: for beings that don't eat physical food through conventional means, they certainly seem to have a good deal of it lying about to distribute.

The Absorption Theory makes it apparent that regardless of whatever aliens and faeries consume, the food given to witnesses is not on-hand for their own consumption. The assertion that extraterrestrial food might somehow be compatible with the human digestive system (and vice versa) is illogical at a very basic level. In their 1980 book *Life Beyond Earth: The Intelligent Earthling's Guide to Life in the Universe*, Gerald Feinberg and Robert Shapiro handily deconstruct the notion, noting that even the smallest molecular changes can render an edible substance like starch into something wholly indigestible, such as wood. The composition of extraterrestrial food, even if minutely different from terrestrial fare, could be fundamentally inedible, if not downright dangerous. "The effect of munching an extraterrestrial 'carrot' could be approximated by sampling the contents of a chemistry lab at random," they wrote.[340]

The argument could be made that perhaps these meals are prepared for humans and humans alone. While it is conceivable that entities may stockpile "treats" to toss our way (akin to an animal trainer), this is such an anthropomorphic line of thought that it feels incongruous with the other, more bizarre aspects of unexplained phenomena. Is this the answer—that these beings can enter our world from another realm, tap into our mind, communicate telepathically, control our actions, and evade detection by modern man, yet are forced to dole out dog biscuits?

These are the hoops we must jump through to accommodate the exchange of physical, earthly food between entities and humans. Even for those of us operating in an already unbelievable field, such mental gymnastics strain believability.

To summarize: entities have been known to offer witnesses food and drink that resembles earthly fare. Logical deduction makes entity consumption of actual earth food unlikely from a scientific standpoint (incompatibility), a folkloric approach (*foyson*), or when incorporating eyewitness testimony (the Absorption Theory). By extension, the presence of actual earthly food in any of these encounters seems dubious at best.

Where does all of this leave us?

Perhaps entity encounters are mired in more theater and deception than previously thought. Returning to the question of whether entity food is physical at all, recall that faerie food is only detritus *made to look* like appetizing food and drink. Aliens and faeries—and in some accounts, Sasquatch—are all attributed the ability to control witness motor function and communicate via telepathy. How difficult would it be to create a "food mirage" in the mind of the witness, a simulacrum of something familiar, presented as a symbolic vehicle to facilitate interaction with nonhuman intelligences? Such an explanation goes a long way to explain the absurdity of a great many encounters, and simultaneously addresses why entities offer earthly foodstuffs in spite of their alien means of consumption.

Even if this is the answer to the entity food riddle, more questions must still be answered. While we may have a working hypothesis for *what* entity food is, we are still at a loss as to *how* this is accomplished or—most importantly—*why*. What is the desired effect of these food simulacra?

If we are to gain any additional insight we must take a detour not into the deepest depths of interstellar space, nor the darkest corners of the wild forest, but rather into the vast expanse of the human mind.

CHAPTER 14
CONNECTIONS: ENTHEOGENS

KERMIT: Uh, you will note that the, uh, Spooble is composed almost entirely of, uh... <ahem> liquid.
SPOOBLE: You betcha! Or, as they say on Koozbane, we Spoobles are all wet!   *– The Muppet Show,* Episode 223

For millennia shamans, witch doctors, holy men, and seers have employed substances to facilitate interaction with the spirit world. As noted in the previous chapter, these substances are called entheogens—many in Western society would pejoratively refer to them simply as "psychedelics"—and are the keystone for a vast array of native spiritual traditions across the globe. Most frequently these chemical compounds are found in plants and fungi (the aforementioned cannabis, iboga, magic mushrooms, kava, etc.) but may also be found in animals, such as the Colorado River toad. They are consumed in the same manner that any substance can be administered—orally, through the skin, or inhaled.

Mescaline, ibogaine, and dimethyltryptamine are just a few of the psychoactive constituents that produce entheogenic effects. Individuals under the influence of these chemicals report altered states of consciousness, out-of-body experiences, profound spiritual insights, and otherworldly visions, often of deities and similar nonhuman intelligences. Users also report strange humming sounds, bringing to mind the buzzing noises in alien abduction accounts. Modern science, obsessed with materialism, claims that such auditory and visual stimuli are simple hallucinations caused by these chemicals, imagery produced in the mind by the firing of synapses and lacking any basis in reality.

There is ample anecdotal evidence, however, that this might not entirely be the case. For example, those taking entheogens have reported learning real-world knowledge to which they should have no access, such as another individual's whereabouts. Often a particular substance will produce consistent visions between multiple users, suggesting that the experience is not "in the eye of the beholder" as conventional science would have us believe. Such persistent claims may mean that there is a type of validity to psychedelic revelations.

Our understanding of consciousness is tenuous. Science is still unable to pin down exactly *what it is*. While some claim that consciousness is just an epiphenomenon of brain activity—akin to digestion and the intestines—most spiritual traditions are adamant that it is separate and non-local, that it is its own entity. Peer-reviewed near-death experience research has begun to provide support for such claims.

Gaining traction is the notion that human consciousness may be similar to a television channel, with the brain (the television) interpreting an incoming signal. Damage the receiver, and the channel doesn't disappear, it is merely garbled. Extending this metaphor, the human brain may be able to access other "channels," ethereal at first blush yet no less real.

If consciousness is a channel and your brain a T.V., what if entheogens are a remote control? As psychologist and philosopher William James said, "our normal waking consciousness, rational consciousness as we call it, is but one special type of consciousness, whilst all about it, parted from it by the flimsiest of screens, there lie potential forms of consciousness entirely different. "[341]

It is entirely appropriate to ask what all of this has to do with our discussion of entity food. Rest assured, the connections are plentiful. Witnesses of the paranormal occasionally feel and act as though they are in an altered state—trances, for example, are explicitly mentioned in faerie lore. Nearly every person offered entity food accepts it, something very few individuals would do in an alert, discriminating state of mind. Users of psychedelics have reported strange beings offering them food and drink while under the influence, not unlike Micah Hanks' dreams (dreams themselves are an altered state we all experience). Lastly, many traditions claim that entheogens are gifts from other intelligences, given to allow us access to their realm.

In short, these substances are the ultimate entity food, tangible and readily available. They can be examined, studied, and replicated in scientific surroundings. They have been quietly winding their way through our entire discussion, behind the scenes.

And they just might be the final piece of the entity food puzzle.

Shamanism

In order to truly grasp the nature of entheogens, we must first establish a working knowledge of shamanism. While many people use psychedelics for illicit and recreational purposes, entheogens were first and foremost implemented to produce the divine from within oneself, always in a religious context.

"Shaman" is the preferred nomenclature for yesteryear's terms "medicine man" and "witch doctor." The medical allusions of old were accurate, however, as shamans are often called upon to provide spiritual healing to their tribal community. They function as emissaries between our physical existence and the spiritual plane. In addition to treating otherworldly illness, shamans also serve as purveyors or thieves of luck, doing magical favors for their constituents; psychopomps, those tasked with escorting the souls of the dead to the afterlife; and sacrificial officiants.[342] Another important role in shamanic tradition is that of divination, the act of seeing the future through supernatural means. "Divinatory ceremonies, in fact, can sometimes prove the main activities of a shaman, ones that are greatly valued by the larger community," writes anthropologist Thomas A. Dubois of the University of

Wisconsin in *An Introduction to Shamanism.*[343]

Rarely do shamans choose their lifestyle. More often than not, they are struck ill at an early age, a period of disease bringing them close to death. This proximity to the ethereal realm allows spirits to make contact, offering their services for healing and assistance. Shamans are called, then compelled to accept this path, which usually involves a lengthy, intense, and often painful period of spiritual transformation—sometimes experiencing visions of dismemberment and reassembly—before coming into their own.

These trials behind them, the shaman gives his or her life to the community. To fulfill the spiritual needs of their people, shamans must contact the spirit world, usually via trance. Multiple means can be used to achieve such a state, including singing, dancing, fasting, or the consumption of various substances. Particularly effective is the use of entheogens. Once in this altered state, the shaman is able to parse meaning from chaos, foresee the future, or call upon spirit helpers to intercede in the affairs of the living.

We have known for quite some time about the similarities between shamans and alien abductees. Thomas Bullard wrote in the April 1989 edition of *The Journal of American Folklore* that the attributes of shamanic initiation in Siberian tradition "bear striking similarities with abduction reports: The experience may begin when the shaman-to-be enters a deathlike trance or coma, two helpful spirits may provide an escort, friendly spirits may help while unfriendly spirits harm the candidate, dismemberment may occur in a rounded cave with uniform lighting, the head or brain may be removed and the eyes torn out." As part of the experience, the shaman may receive a crystal or other type of transmitter, usually inserted into the head. The entire experience culminates in a rebirth (more on this later).[344]

Like shamans, abductees often live with the fallout from their experiences for the rest of their lives; they do not volunteer, and are instead chosen; they encounter strange entities during trance-like states (entheogen-induced in the past, driving and sleep-induced in modern cases); they have out-of-body experiences;

they travel between supernatural realms; and they may experience moments of clairvoyance. Recall that prophets in Vedic tradition eat *sattvic* diets, foods of the same kind offered by entities. Just as there is often a sexual component in alien, faerie, and Sasquatch abductions, Dubois notes that "the shaman may experience sexual encounters with a spirit and may come to view the relationship as a kind of marriage."[345]

Soma and *Ayahuasca*

Though there are a wide variety of entheogens in existence, we shall focus on the ones most germane to our discussion, *Soma* and *ayahuasca*. For the moment, our attention turns to the former.

Soma is unique in that its identity remains a mystery. What we know for certain is that it was a drink derived from a plant of the same name, which was of great spiritual importance to early Zoroastrian and, later, Vedic traditions. The Hindu Rigveda contains more than a hundred hymns to the substance, singing the praises of its inebriating qualities. It was ritualistically consumed by priests and Vedic initiates.

Like the Christian concept of the Holy Trinity, *Soma* was three-in-one: drink, plant, and god. It was divine and treated with respect. While not explicitly deemed an entheogen, there is almost universal belief among scholars that it was, given that Rigveda 8.48.3 says "We have drunk *Soma* and become immortal; we have attained the light, the Gods discovered."

R. Gordon Wasson compellingly proposed in *Soma: Divine Mushroom of Immortality* that the drink's active ingredient was *Amanita muscaria* (Fly Agaric), a particularly potent mushroom commonly used in Eurasian shamanism. Descriptions of the *Soma* plant do not mention a root system, seeds, or stems, supporting the notion of a mushroom, while a Vedic excerpt mentioning men urinating *Soma* seems to echo Siberian tradition, wherein the urine of those under the influence is recycled to additional psychedelic effect.[346]

To make the mushroom's milky juice palatable, it must be mixed with some other liquid. In Siberian tradition, the flavor was cut with berry juice. Wasson saw another connection here, for in Vedic tradition *Soma* was also mixed, albeit with *sattvic* foods such as milk, curds, barley water, or honey.[347]

As mentioned previously, Hindus believe that *Soma* was originally coaxed out of a great sea of milk by the moon god, Chandra. Because of this, *Soma* is forever synonymous with *amrita*, the nectar of the gods represented by lunar light (*amrita* is also the thematic equivalent of *ambrosia* in Greek mythology, the sweet liquid food of the gods which bestowed longevity upon those who consumed it). This light—itself a gift from the sun—was believed to "drip" onto the earth below and rejuvenate the world and its inhabitants. A waning moon meant that the entire Hindu pantheon was drinking the *amrita* to rejuvenate their immortality.[348]

Soma's creation parallels the mythic origin of another entheogen: *ayahuasca*. Psychologist Ralph Metzner writes in *Ayahuasca: Hallucinogens, Consciousness, and the Spirit of Nature*:

> The Tukano people of the Vaupés region of Colombia say that the first people came from the sky in a serpent canoe, and Father Sun had promised them a magical drink that would connect them with the radiant powers of the heavens. While men were in the "House of the Waters," attempting to make this drink, the first woman went into the forest to give birth. She came back with a boy radiating light, whose body she rubbed with leaves. This luminous boy-child was the vine, and each of the men cut off a piece of this living being which became his piece of the vine lineage. In a variation of this myth from the Desana, the serpent canoe came from the Milky Way, bringing a man, a woman and three plants for the people—cassava, coca and caapi. They also regarded it as a gift from the Sun, a kind

of container for the yellow-gold light of the Sun,
that provided for the first people the rules on how
to live and how to speak.[349]

Ayahuasca is in many respects the world's most celebrated
entheogen. The beverage is quite the vogue subject, and for
good reason—for more than four millennia over 70 indigenous
Amazonian cultures have used variations on the recipe, combining
various plants depending on regional preference. All formulae,
however, utilize the bark of *Banisteriopsis caapi* or its cousin *B.
inebrians*, a type of South American vine, combined with the shrub
Psychotria viridis, to create a dark, starchy, pungent brew.[350] When
consumed in the proper setting—participants in an *ayahuasca*
ceremony do so with the help of a shaman who administers proper
dosages, guides them through the experience, and observes physical
side effects—*ayahuasca* can produce profound spiritual revelations
via vivid visual and aural hallucinations.

From a physical standpoint, the experience is anything but
pleasurable. Journalist-turned-alternative-historian Graham
Hancock described the drink as "amongst the most horrible tastes
and smells on the planet—a mixture of foot-rot, raw sewage, battery
acid, sulfur and just a hint of chocolate." *Ayahuasca* is a purgative,
laxative in effect, and within an hour drinkers void themselves via
diarrhea and vomiting, all while in the throes of severe nausea.
Shamans take the view that this is negativity being forced from
the body, a central part of the experience.[351]

Those who have participated in *ayahuasca* ceremonies often
claim that the unpleasantness is worth it. The effects have the
potential to be life altering under the right circumstances, bringing
about positive personality change in certain individuals. Benefits
can include but are not limited to the treatment of depression,
anxiety, and addiction; Hancock himself attributes sessions during
October 2011 with helping him reign in his excessive marijuana
use. [352] Such changes are often brought about through a life
review, where one can see all the pain they have inflicted upon

others throughout their life. Other users report epiphanies about the beauty and harmony of the universe, seeing at last the inner workings of existence and their place within the cosmos.

Among researchers, *ayahuasca* has gained a great amount of attention for its reputation to purportedly grant users temporary psychic powers. There are numerous accounts of individuals drinking the brew and describing distant, never-visited cities in perfect detail, or predicting deaths. In one particularly compelling case, anthropologist Kenneth Kensinger was informed by six *ayahuasca* drinkers that his maternal grandmother had died, a fact confirmed via radio two days later.[353]

Also notable is the startling consistency of *ayahuasca* visions. Users report seeing jaguars and other jungle imagery, even when drinking in an urban setting. A 1972 letter from doctor and naturopath Andrew Weil spoke of rumors that "when Eskimos are given *yagé* [*ayahuasca*] in a laboratory, they see visions of huge house cats since they have never seen tigers," and that Chilean patients given the active ingredients saw jungles and jaguars in spite of having never left the city.[354]

The *Ayahuasca* Experience and Entity Food

In addition to jungles and cats, the snake is a commonly reported image during *ayahuasca* sessions. References to serpents appear in most of the *ayahuasca* origin stories, visions varying in size from ordinary serpents to the giant "cosmic snake" of Cashinahua mythology, Yube. More often than not these anthropomorphized serpents are benevolent, representing maternal nature spirits.

On occasion, however, the entities are more sinister. Anthropologist Michael Harner recalled a particularly intense *ayahuasca* session where he experienced a vision of planet Earth, still in its infancy, overwhelmed by "large, shiny, black creatures with stubby pterodactyl-like wings and huge whale bodies" that he referred to as "dragons." These dragons informed Harner that they were "the true masters of the world," having spawned humanity for their own Lovecraftian motives.

Harner passed this experience on to a shaman, who casually dismissed the entities' nihilistic claims. "Oh, they're always saying that," the old man grinned. "But they are only the Masters of Outer Darkness." Harner, an atheist, was later shocked at the parallels between his visions and the Book of Revelations, with which he had not been intimately familiar.[355]

Those who take *ayahuasca* also report short entities such as dwarfs or elves. Often these beings will dismember the user as if to make internal repairs, then reassemble them before the experience ends, a common theme of shamanic visions. Psychologist Raoul Adamson recalled meeting little green "jungle elves" that took his body apart in order to bestow upon him "an improved, more flexible, more comfortable body-mind." Upon expressing his initial distress, the beings "replied cheerfully, 'Not to worry, we'll put you back together, you're fine.'"[356]

It must be noted that while *ayahuasca* sessions often include similar imagery, it is not *identical* imagery. No two experiences are alike. To that end, there are also reports of users experiencing what are essentially offers of entity food while under the effects of the brew. During the sessions where he was trying to kick his cannabis habit, Graham Hancock was approached by intelligences presenting entity food. "On the fifth session, after the traumas of the fourth, I took a very small cup of Ayahuasca," he wrote in 2013. "I was approached by entities offering me food and drink but I remembered the rule expressed in many ancient cultures that one should never eat food in the Underworld (witness, for example, the story of Demeter and Persephone) so I refused and opened my eyes to stop the vision."[357]

Similarly Fernando Payaguaje, the last shaman-chief of the Ecuadorian Secoya tribe, claimed to have met God on several separate occasions, all while under the influence of *ayahuasca*. He recalls his first time meeting the supreme deity:

I kept my distance, of course, because you don't get

close to where God is unless you're an angel or a person of the sky who lives there. But I heard how God addressed me, "You are going to be a healer. You will have the power to heal. To do that, you should love people and do good, not evil."

That's what God said, and later, "Drink this so that you can cure any illness."

And he gave me a little packet of salt stones. The angels brought it, repeating, "Don't get too close."

…That's how it was. Do you know why we become healers? Because God, once you finally meet him, washes out your mouth, gives it a rinse. At that moment, you truly become a healer. He washed mine with salt, symbol of healings. My saliva sounded like music and turned to shining gold. And, what's happened now? My people have become evangelicals. Well, I have no idea who their God is, but mine has red shoes and lives in his own house. When he said goodbye, he told me, "My son, now you, too, are God."

There is quite a bit to unpack in Payaguaje's statements. As with most encounters of this type, his experience ended shortly after taking the substance he was offered, although its salty nature does not agree with the bulk of entity food reports. It is interesting to contrast the encounter in God's house to Payaguaje's advice when visiting the "place of the dead"—he warns that, though dead women may offer you black corn *chicha*, "it's not wise to finish the cup…just taste a mouthful."[358]

There seems to be an awareness of the food taboo among South American shamans, as evidenced in the account of Dan Perriam. Perriam was in the middle of a 2010 *ayahuasca* session in Cusco, Peru, when he suddenly became aware of several short, leprechaun-like entities and a set of stairs leading below ground. From the stairway Perriam could hear what he described as "a very lively party... I mentally descended the stairs guided by two or three elves who were laughing and continuously encouraging me to join them and 'have a drink.'"

The bottom of the stairway led to a large wooden door. The elves, now "giddy" and seemingly full of mischief, had just begun to open the door when Perriam's supervising shaman started yelling for his return. "His concern was palpable," said Perriam. "I am still very confident that he knew exactly what was transpiring, however, and was driven to intervene."[359]

The connections and questions do not end there. Is there a correlation between the frequency of men in entity food cases and the fact that women are discouraged from becoming *ayahuasca* shamans?[360] What does it mean that *ayahuasca* is administered at the beginning of an otherworldly experience and entity food is administered at an encounter's end? Why do individuals from every culture around the world take entheogens and see dwarves, elves, and faeries, such as the Siona shamanic apprentice who claimed to have met "very short people" who encouraged him to keep drinking *yagé* and complete his spiritual transformation?[361]

There is even a *sattvic* component to the *ayahuasca* experience. South American *ayahuasqueros* advise their charges to abstain from salt, lard, and sweets—foods that are either *tamasic* or *rajasic* in Vedic tradition—prior to their sessions.[362] Recall that *ayahuasca* can assist addicts in their recovery, then compare those findings to the manner in which Whitley Strieber's experiences took him away from his unhealthy obsession with sugar.

The spiritual profundity of some alien abductions, an aspect central to a majority of *ayahuasca* experiences, has already been discussed. This is paralleled in some faerie lore, such as Milk White Milch Cow's milk and Gunnlöð the Troll's mead, each of which bestow the user with a sense of enlightenment. An argument could even be made that *Tsonoqua's* Water of Life accomplishes something similar, though that prowess is purportedly more physical than mental or spiritual.

Setting aside the subjective aspects of the experience, the physical aftermath of entity encounters—feelings of nausea, intoxication, and regurgitation—echo the experiences of many entheogen users, particularly those who have taken *ayahuasca*. Alien abductees report feeling dizzy and disoriented, accompanied by splitting headaches and vomiting. Continuing this line of thought, faeries such as West Yorkshire's Churn Milk Peg would bloat unruly children with stomach cramps, and Sasquatch are often reported to smell so foul that they cause nausea as well.

In Wichita, Kansas, on October 1, 2005, Angela Vaughn-Hausinger, a recurring abductee, allegedly witnessed something similar to an *ayahuasca* session, albeit involving a roomful of abductees and Grey aliens. Vaughn-Hausinger found herself in a room with several abductees and watched as a tall Grey alien tended to two men on separate tables, apparently father and son. The entity tilted the father's head to the side and a black, shiny tar-like fluid began oozing out of his mouth. The being repeated this procedure with the son as well, and Angela recalls being told this was "because they had something wrong with their stomachs.[363]

It takes little imagination to place the Grey alien in the role of a supervising shaman, tending to a room full of patients. Recall how the purging during the *ayahuasca* experience is claimed to be negativity leaving the body; this vomit is often dark, just like the vomit so often reported by abductees.

In her book *Coronado: The President, the Secret Service, and Alien Abductions*, hypnotherapist Yvonne R. Smith tells the story of Laci, a recurring abductee who experienced a particularly unsettling experience on March 25, 1994. Under regression, Laci recalled being stripped naked by three brownish entities before being forced to consume a dark, mudlike substance that tasted "like shit." The beings told her that she must swallow the liquid because they "needed to clean out her body." The ordeal calls to mind both *ayahuasca*'s unpleasant taste and its purgative "cleansing" qualities.[364]

Even more explicitly reminiscent of the *ayahuasca* experience is a memory from Ted Rice, the main subject of Karla Turner's *Masquerade of Angels*. He was taken one evening in the late 1980s by a strange, red-headed woman and several Grey aliens. Rice recalls the exchange:

> The woman returned from the counter area with a glass in her hand. It was filled with a green liquid, and Teddy was amazed by the way the liquid glowed in the dimly lit room.
>
> "Drink it," she communicated, holding out the glass.
>
> "No," Teddy shook his head. "I want to go home."
>
> "Drink it now," she insisted, "or you cannot go home. If you want to go home, you must mind me as you do your mother."
>
> "You're not my mother," he thought back at her, but she was unmoved.
>
> "After you drink this," she continued, "you can go home."
>
> No emotion came from the woman, but Teddy was scared into submission. Without another word, he took the glass and drank the glowing liquid. Immediately he became sick, nauseated, and pain flared up as if his insides were on fire. He lay back on the table, growing sicker, until he vomited. Tendrils of green liquid dribbled down his mouth and chin, still glowing, but at least he no longer felt ill.

And then, as if he were standing a few feet away from the table, Teddy could see his body lying there motionless.

"Am I dead?" he wondered.

Something cloudy and formless began to rise up from the small body. Teddy was amazed as he watched this mass slowly coalesce into a beautiful image of himself, and he saw that it was attached by a bottom tendril to drops of the green liquid on his face.

"It's my soul!" he thought in amazement.

The miniature image turned toward the red-headed woman and looked at her. Teddy could feel great emotion coming from this form. He felt it was showing pure love and total, instant forgiveness toward her, although he didn't understand why.[365]

The guiding female entity, pain, vomiting, ensuing out-of-body experience, and overwhelming sensation of love are all hallmarks of the *ayahuasca* experience.

It is tempting to conclude that entity food must somehow be entheogenic. This assumption must be carefully avoided, as there is no evidence to support such a claim. Still, the established comparisons between paranormal and psychedelic events are so strong and compelling that they make it obvious the two experiences are somehow linked, and the active ingredient in *ayahuasca* may show us how.

DMT: Dimethyltryptamine

Of the vast amount of chemical compounds produced in your body, only one is regulated: dimethyltryptamine. And of the 155,000 species of flora in the Amazon jungle, native tribes were able to find the one vine—*B. caapi*—that allows it to become orally active.

Dubbed "the spirit molecule," N,N-Dimethyltryptamine (DMT) acts as a neurotransmitter in mammals and can be powerfully hallucinogenic in high doses, such as those found in *Psychotria viridis, ayahuasca*'s chief ingredient. Simple oral ingestion of DMT does not cause any psychedelic effects, however, due to the ease with which monoamine oxidase, a type of enzyme, is able to break down the compound. Enter *B. caapi*, the vine additive so revered by Amazonian tribes, which just so happens to contain a monoamine oxidase inhibitor. By combining it with *P. viridis* or a similar species, the DMT is protected from the enzyme. [366]

"Was it purely happenstance, purely accident, that led some early, experiment-minded shaman to combine the *ayahuasca* vine and the chacruna leaf, to make the tea that raised the curtain on the 'invisible landscape' for the first time?" asked ethnopharmacologist Dennis McKenna. "It seems unlikely, since neither of the key ingredients are particularly inviting as food, and yet what else could it have been? The *ayahuasqueros* themselves will simply tell you that 'the vine calls.'"[367]

Because of its production in the human brain, many have speculated that an endogenous (internally arising) release of DMT may be responsible for a host of paranormal and religious experiences. The pioneering work of Dr. Rick Strassman at the University of New Mexico is responsible for this notion, and anyone seeking to explore the subject further is advised to read Strassman's excellent book *DMT: The Spirit Molecule*.[368]

DMT can produce intense psychedelic sensations including vibrant visions, euphoric effects, and intense hallucinations. Individuals taking DMT often have visions similar to those of *ayahuasca* experiences, albeit with a more industrialized bent— Terence McKenna, late brother of the aforementioned ethnopharmacologist Dennis McKenna, would often use the term "machine elves" to describe the constantly-transforming entities he encountered. Not surprisingly, these descriptions are quite consistent across multiple users, with reports of bodily disassembly, time dilation, and profound spiritual revelation.

DMT is in the same tryptamine family as its cousin melatonin, a chemical used in the body to regulate sleep. It is no coincidence that those taking melatonin as a supplement are more likely to experience hyper-vivid dreams. Our diet, in particular the consumption of tryptophan, has a large role to play in the production of both compounds.[369]

While we are all aware that tryptophan can be found in the Thanksgiving turkey, it is also found in nearly all plant proteins, and is especially high in a few vegetables such as sesame seeds, soybeans, oats, and chickpeas. In fact, many *sattvic* foods are high in tryptophan, including wheat, bananas, milk, and rice, though it should be noted that meats contain consistently higher amounts of the compound.[370] Nevertheless, the high incidence of tryptophan in the *sattvic* diet represents a compelling—if small—connection between entity food and DMT.

Recreational consumption of DMT is illegal. The substance is produced in laboratories and distributed on the black market, but unlike many illegal drugs is unlikely to cause physical or even psychological addiction. Because DMT is normally not orally active, it is commonly injected or, more popularly, inhaled. The ensuing high is quite fast (circa ten minutes) and extremely intense. In an interesting parallel to alien abductions, too much DMT may cause amnesia of the experience.

Those consuming DMT occasionally receive food from entities, or see substances similar to the ones they have just ingested. In *Contact: Them or Us*, user Dan Oshea shared his experience after using 5-MEO-DMT derived from Acacia tree root bark:

My expectation of physical bliss and a light show is soon forgotten as I am shot out of this space, more portal type imagery, and find myself on another planet, I am in the presence of others, and I seem to be underground. Getting my bearings, I realize that I am in a mine. That praying mantis creature over there is mining 'spice,' the same spice I used to get here, and that very martial looking lizardman is guarding him, or the 'spice' which is universally valuable. We all get over the shock of being aware of each other's appearance. Even though we are aware of the conscious presence of each other, accompanied by visual data, it is like remote viewing in a sense, there is no concern of physical interaction.[371]

Let us take a moment to recall that the schoolyard dwarfs seen in the Philippines were standing by an acacia tree. Though it is impossible that the tree produced a psychoactive effect in the students, one has to wonder if the connection is wholly coincidental.

Since DMT is still a Schedule I drug in the United States and remains illegal in most of the western world, users have been relegated to sharing their experiences anonymously in the dark corners of the internet.

• One DMT user's trip began with an out-of-body experience before he found himself surrounded by vague alien beings. He was on some sort of hospital bed and from this vantage point he could see a rectangular shape approaching. Once it reached him, it opened, revealing over a dozen rainbow-colored snakes swaying like grass in the wind. In addition to the serpents, the box also contained a round, long-necked flask. His attention was fixed on the vessel as it floated toward his lips. "Suddenly and involuntarily, I began to swallow, again and again, drinking what felt like pure energy... I realized with a start that I was drinking DNA." What followed was a psychedelic experience within a psychedelic experience as he morphed into all manner of life on Earth and experienced an epiphany that DNA is "written and directed by something much greater, much more pervasive, and much more subtle than we've ever till now supposed." After coming back to his mortal body, he claimed to visit the bathroom with great frequency, even though he had not drunk anything more than normal in the physical world.

•   Another account adds the sexual component to the mix. A user quickly slipped into his trip and saw several faeries "lewdly playing with themselves and each other" before huddling by a nearby flower. "They seemed to be adding to some liquid which they were creating inside one of the flowers," the user wrote. "Soon enough they were done, and from the flower head they produced a shiny looking capsule. They told me to eat it, and I felt that it had been prepared with love and that I should eat it." Before eating the capsule he believed he must be approaching the end of his DMT trip, but suddenly realized that this capsule might actually extend the experience. The final leg of his journey involved sexual contact with the faeries, after which he regained normal consciousness. All told, the experience had lasted 17 minutes.[372]

If this anecdote is true, it is of extreme importance to the entity food conundrum. Like the drink from Andrew Paquette's *servo spiritus*, the user was given a simulacrum of food and his consciousness was altered, in this case allowing him to stay in contact with the spirit world for longer than usual.

Symbolic-cause and physical-effect experiences are not without precedent, at least anecdotally speaking. According to a tale related to lucid dream researcher Robert Waggoner, a man in Holland had sworn off all recreational substances ten years prior to a particularly vivid dream in which he was offered marijuana aboard an airplane. Realizing he was asleep, the dreamer saw no harm in partaking and decided to smoke away, experiencing a pleasant high within the dream state. He was perplexed when, upon awakening, he continued to feel the "marijuana's" effects for an additional 2-3 hours.[373]

Regardless of whether or not you believe that the Dutch dreamer and the DMT user were interacting with real intelligences, it is difficult to deny that the effects they experienced were directly facilitated by these offerings—their objective "existence" notwithstanding, both the capsule and marijuana had an affect upon the users. The symbol of the food, the "food mirage" as it were, produced a reaction in their minds.

What if this is one of entity food's primary functions—to somehow produce a shift in consciousness? What if the purpose is to control the duration of the encounter by initiating, prolonging, or ending the experience?

The Snake

Taking *ayahuasca* is first and foremost understood as a spiritual journey; there is very little about the experience to encourage recreational use, particularly the taste. In order to get the most insight from a session, one must surrender wholly and completely to the power of the brew. If a user is particularly blessed, they will be visited by the soul of *ayahuasca* herself.

Graham Hancock describes Mother Ayahuasca as "a very powerful, tough love kind of lady who reveals to you the truth about yourself."[374] In a 2010 lecture entitled "Elves, Aliens, Angels, and Ayahuasca," Hancock spoke of this loving, maternal figure:

> ...the Spirit of *Ayahuasca*... is an entity, a being, a person... always regarded as female. [She] sometimes appears in the form of a human woman, sometimes appears in the form of a serpent, sometimes appears in the form of a jaguar...

There was one time when I was going through a very low patch in my life and for some reason I was filled with self-hatred, and I went down to Brazil and had five sessions of *ayahuasca* there. And during one of those sessions I was visited by the Spirit of *Ayahuasca* in the form of a huge serpent. You sensed coming from her love, and power, and what went through my mind as she wrapped her coils around my body, and rested this huge head on my shoulders and just looked into my eyes was...

"Her business is the planet, but she has time for *me*." It was extraordinary, I felt incredible waves of love coming out, and what those waves of love were saying was, "Actually you *can* like yourself, you *can* love yourself, you need to do that first of all." And I emerged from that healed in extraordinary ways which have had a huge impact on my life, subsequently.[375]

This serpentine quality is part of the reason that, like *Soma*, Mother Ayahuasca is at once deity, plant, and drink. According to anthropologist Elsje Maria Lagrou, the snake in Amazonian mythology is "the master of all liquids, from rain to menstrual blood to *ayahuasca*, the brew of transformation."[376]

The idea of the snake is also central to the physical effects of *ayahuasca*. Those drinking the brew often compare the ensuing intestinal difficulties as akin to having a serpent in their belly, a sensation occasionally accompanied by an explicit vision of such. Raoul Adamson reported a vision of a snake that entered his mouth, traversed his stomach, and became lodged in his intestines, cleansing and teaching his body.[377] Shyloh Ravenswood, another psychologist, said that drinking *ayahuasca* felt as though he "had swallowed a live boa who was inching through the acidic labyrinth of my guts, pausing to squeeze them tight in sequential spasms."[378]

This compares closely to abductees who describe unpleasant wriggling sensations in their stomachs. A man in Merseyside, England was on his evening jog in January 2011 when he noticed some odd lights and a peculiar humming sound coming from the tree line. Drawing closer he saw a large saucer-shaped object floating in the air. This was the last thing he remembered—what followed were vague impressions culminating in the memory of sinister, tall green beings forcing a feeding tube down his throat and pumping something into his stomach. He regained consciousness two nights later on a nearby beach, an unpleasant wriggling sensation in his gut. He vomited, producing several pints of a thick, black substance. His wife reported that he had been missing for two nights, and though the witness claimed to have been incredibly skeptical of abductee accounts until this encounter, he is now a believer.[379]

Snakes are associated with other entheogens as well. Some challenge the notion that the Forbidden Fruit in Judeo-Christian tradition was an apple, instead suggesting that the mushroom, with its mind-opening psychedelic revelations, is a better candidate. While traditionalists may scoff at the idea, consider that France's Abbaye de Plaincourault houses a Romanesque fresco that, instead of depicting the traditional Tree of Knowledge, shows the serpent wrapped around what appears to be an immense fly-agaric mushroom.[380] Anyone arguing that the mushroom shape is coincidental should note that, outside of the British Isles, it is not the toad that is associated with fungus but rather the snake.[381]

The snake is also connected to entheogens in Eastern philosophy. Vasuki, the great serpent (*naga*) of Hindu tradition, was said to have contributed to *Soma*'s creation by churning the ocean of milk with his body;[382] his semen is said to be molten lead.[383] Perhaps coincidentally, some South American cultures regard *ayahuasca* as the semen of the vine.[384] We have already noted the possibility of lead poisoning in conjunction with entity food—fruit juices, to be exact, one of the most common drinks offered to witnesses. The other liquid offered (thick, white "milk") is sexually symbolic in a way that speaks for itself.

To further complicate these connections, some ancient alien theorists have long equated Vasuki and the *nagas*, as well as other religious depictions of serpents, with alien visitors. In nearly every religious tradition, the serpent is a phallic symbol (correlating with the sexuality of abduction reports) and is the bringer of knowledge (echoing the role some feel aliens have played in human development).

Like the snake in South American mythology, today's aliens could be viewed as "the master of all liquids." We have already established their fondness for administering drinks and anointing witnesses, which, in conjunction with the Absorption Theory, should give researchers pause. There is a very strong connection between these entities and fluids—just as *Soma* and *ayahuasca* are at once entities and liquids, is there some value in viewing these beings through a similar lens?

Liquid ETs?

One would be hard-pressed to choose a more fitting substance than liquid to serve as a metaphor for the UFO phenomenon. Like UFOs, liquids are mutable, changeable, and adaptable. They conform to their environment, with fixed volume but no consistent shape, similar to the "fluid" rules UFOs abide by. They are literal "shape-shifters." Liquid exists in the liminal zone between solids— our rigid, earthly reality—and gas, the invisible, ephemeral realm. How much sense would it make if we found out some day that paranormal phenomena could navigate these "phase transitions of reality," similar to the manner in which water can be frozen or boiled?

The symbolic liquid-UFO link is not without precedent. In his book *Flying Saucers: A Modern Myth of Things Seen in the Skies*, famed psychiatrist Carl Jung analyzed a patient's dream where she saw a drop-shaped "flying saucer."

A UFO appears, having the form of a drop. A fluid body assumes the form of a drop when it is about to fall, from which it is clear that the UFO is conceived as a liquid falling from the sky, like rain. This surprising drop-form of the UFO and the analogy with a fluid occur in the literature. Presumably it is meant to express the commonly reported changeability of the UFO's shape. This "heavenly" fluid must be of a mysterious nature and is probably a conception similar to that of the alchemical *aqua permanens*, the "permanent water," which was also called "Heaven" in sixteenth-century alchemy, the wonderful solvent, the word *solution* being used equally for a chemical solution and for the solution of a problem.[385]

Jung proceeds to equate the appearance of the UFO with the dreamer's need to find a solution to life's problems. Terence McKenna would echo this interpretation years later, describing the UFO phenomenon as "very mercurial, very watery... when you reach out toward them, there is nothing there."[386]

In 1971 Brian Scott claimed to have been abducted by aliens while camping near Apache Junction, Arizona. At around 9:00 p.m. on the evening of March 14 Scott and his friend Eric noticed a bright object approaching from across the desert. Scott shined his flashlight at the anomaly, which quickly moved above their heads and bathed them in a purple light. Their next memory was returning home two hours later. Under hypnosis it was revealed that the two had levitated into an open doorway in the object where they were greeted by tall, "ugly humanoids with large heads, large mouths and ears, and crocodile-like skin." The tallest of the beings (an imposing 9 feet) separated the men, removed Scott's clothes, and took him to a dimly lit, foul-smelling room covered in fog. Here he was examined, an experience during which Scott recalled his hips being "separated," a wet sensation about his stomach, and a brief out-of-body vision.

Scott returned to the site around a week later where he was taken once more. This time he noticed several other beings floating in large cylinders of jellylike fluid, cables attached to their heads and bodies. The aliens released him after a second examination and promised to return, a vow fulfilled when he awoke in the middle of the night two months later and was given instructions to get two tattoos on his body. The patterns he received were of a jaguar and a spider. [387]

To summarize: Scott was taken apart and reassembled by reptiles that "emerged from" a liquid and gave him visions of a jaguar. Sound familiar?

Cases like Scott's highlight the *ayahuasca*-alien-liquid connection. Is the Absorption Theory correct, the aliens' immersion being merely a means of ingestion? Or are the aliens, in returning to vats of fluid, rejoining the true element of their composition? Is there something to be made of the fact that aliens' skin color—often white, grey, or green—loosely corresponds to that of the liquids they offer? Why is it that abductees unfailingly describe alien eyes as "liquid" and "teardrop-shaped"?

From time-to-time these coincidences are even more explicit. A handful of cases describe aliens who appear to be liquid in the literal sense. In 1963, a young girl in England claimed to have awoken in the middle of the night when a "plate-sized circle of light" entered her room and began to spill a blue liquid that slowly took the form of a man. [388] In the well-known 1992 "A70 Incident," the witness recalled a skeletal creature manifesting itself out of a hole in the floor filled with sticky fluid. [389]

In another famous case from the late 1970s, Brazilian abductee Antonio La Rubia was made to watch a type of slide show depicting various rural images. One of the final pictures his robotic captors displayed was that of a large, angry dog snarling and trying to apprehend one of the beings. "Then the dog gave out 4 or 5 barks," La Rubia said. "At this point, the being started to melt, from top to bottom, like porridge." [390]

Some UFO researchers have long posited that our planet's oceans may harbor extraterrestrial bases or even be the source of origin for these intelligences, as postulated by Ivan T. Sanderson in his 1970 book *Invisible Residents*. So often are unexplained craft witnessed in, emerging from, and diving into water that a discreet classification deemed "USO" (Unexplained Submerged Objects) has been created to account for this phenomenon. Perhaps the connection between these intelligences and liquid is more intimate than first suspected.

This close association between entities and liquid is not limited to aliens. Folklore describes a great host of aquatic faeries undoubtedly familiar to the reader, from the Arthurian Lady of the Lake to mermaids and kelpies, as well as lesser-known water hags like Peg Powler and Jenny Greenteeth. Selkies, faeries reportedly found throughout the Orkney and Shetland islands, were capable of transforming into seals. In Hans Christian Andersen's *The Little Mermaid,* the eponymous heroine is threatened with the fate of disintegrating into sea foam.

There are also a surprising amount of accounts where Sasquatch is seen swimming. This is a surprisingly un-apelike behavior, as the animals usually have a severe phobia of water. Many Sasquatch researchers have noted that the beasts can often be spotted along (or wading through) streams and creeks. This relationship is particularly pronounced in Alaskan folklore, where Sasquatch referred to as *kushtakaas*, or "land otter men," have been sighted swimming offshore in a particularly adept fashion. A 1960 Ketchikan account, which was related to Bigfoot researcher John Green, details a boy who saw a Sasquatch halfway between his docked boat and the shore:

> When the boy unfroze, he screamed bloody murder and ran blindly, over the tied up boats, back up the ladder and toward the shack, still yelling his head off. The men came running, some with lights, and about thirty of them saw the thing. They shone

several lights on it as it dived under the water and swam away. They could see it under water swimming like a frog, arms forward over its head but not doing a crawl stroke. The legs kicked, the best description was like a frog. The men could see legs and arms as it swam out of sight. Nobody in the crowd had ever seen anything like it.[391]

Such technique is unheard of in apes and does not agree particularly well with our current understanding of primate locomotion. In the year 1200 the British monk Ralph of Coggeshall wrote in *Chronicon Anglicanum* of a sort of wildman captured not in the woods, but rather in the sea. A handful of fishermen had been working the shoreline when they discovered in their nets a shaggy beast that "was naked and was like a man in all his members, covered with hair and with a long shaggy beard." The creature was held captive until, upon another visit to the shore, it broke loose and took again to the sea, "never seen again."[392]

It is important to take a step back and look at the absurdity of this discussion. Are we to believe that we are being visited by liquid creatures from another realm? Is Sasquatch an aquatic elemental? Are we at last faced with the long-feared invasion of Koozbanian Spoobles? Highly unlikely.

Much has already been written about the psychological aspect of the unexplained, wherein the witness influences the type of experience they observe. If we are to accept this notion of co-creation, then it becomes even more likely that there is deep-tissue symbolism at work in modern entity encounters. Perhaps these liquid comparisons exist because our minds have no way of interpreting the unfixed mutability of what we are seeing. Maybe modern witnesses never see aliens, faeries, or Sasquatch, and instead only see the *medium* in which they manifest.

The concept is abstract, but easily demonstrable. For example: you can't see any of the thoughts written in this book. Sure, you can see the words, the sentences, the paragraphs, all of which string together to form cogent ideas—hopefully—but those ideas are firmly inside your head. You can only see the book itself, the medium, not the actual message. Your mind is at work filtering these sentences into abstract thought. While this book has a large role in forming these thoughts, a majority of what you see in your mind's eye—such as the exact portrayal of Brian Scott's aliens—is entirely dependent upon you.

Terence McKenna put the concept more succinctly: "My voice speaking is a monkey's mouth, making little mouth-noises, that are carrying agreed-upon meaning... without the *meaning*, you only have little mouth noises, the *meaning* is a crude form of telepathy, because as you listen to my voice, my thoughts become your thoughts, and we compare them, and there is what's called communication, understanding."[393]

Entertaining this idea, perhaps nonhuman intelligences reside in different realms separate from our own, yet are always with us just "behind the veil." When we enter altered states of consciousness we can interact with these intelligences but, because of how alien and foreign they are, our minds cannot comprehend them in their true form. They are unknowable, and we instead graft existing imagery onto the experience—in the late 1800s we saw airships piloted by humans, in the 1950s flying saucers and robots, today black triangles and Greys. In this model, an alien and its spaceship are both composed of the same medium. Its jumpsuit, the same medium. Its instruments, the same medium.

The beverage it offers—the same medium. One-and-the-same.

Like *ayahuasca* and *Soma*, they are the paradox of entity and drink, together. Perhaps the spiritual logic behind these entheogens— where the god is consumed—can be extended to entity food cases. What if, by accepting liquid from an entity, witnesses are symbolically accepting an extension of the entity itself?

If this is the case, what would be expected of eating an alien? Or a faerie? A Sasquatch?

We will never know. After all, no one has eaten an alien...

Right?

CHAPTER 15
CONNECTIONS: EATING THE GOD & REBIRTH

On the night he was handed over to suffering and death, our Lord Jesus Christ took bread; and when he had given thanks to you, he broke it, and gave it to his disciples, and said, "Take, eat: This is my Body, which is given for you. Do this for the remembrance of me."
– The Holy Eucharist: Rite Two, *The Book of Common Prayer*

A tale from the Cashinahua people of South America explains the origins of *ayahuasca*. A hunter spied an anaconda that rose out of a lake and transformed into a woman. Taken with her beauty, he abandoned his wife and made love to her the next day. Afterwards, the anaconda woman squeezed leaf sap into his eyes and took him with her into her home in the lake. He lived there among the snake people but was warned to never drink their *nixi pae* (*ayahuasca*)— of course he did take some after a time and was horrified when the visions of serpents appeared.

In his fear, he shouted that the snakes would consume him. The anaconda people were insulted by these accusations and, sensing their hostility, the man wished to return to his mortal family. One of the fish from the lake assisted in his escape, putting leaf juice in his eyes, and he was allowed to return to his original wife, with whom he sired a child. A year later, his reptilian family caught and wounded him. He returned to the human village and revealed the *nixi pae* recipe to his family before dying. From his corpse sprang the *B. caapi* vine, which is used in *ayahuasca* ceremonies today.[394]

Again, *ayahuasca* is framed as the ultimate entity food, and once more we have the common themes seen time-and-again: snakes, beings emerging from liquid, ointment in the eyes, the sexual component, and the food taboo. The vines growing out of the corpse add another motif, one that was briefly touched upon in the previous chapter: eating the god.

Eating the God

"Eating the god" is a very old, very widespread tradition. At its core, it is related to the undoubtedly familiar concept that consuming a vanquished enemy would bestow their abilities upon the eater; the logic extends that, if a piece of a god was eaten, godlike abilities (including access to other planes of existence) would be conveyed upon the eater.

Aztecs made edible effigies of their deities out of grain, throwing them into the streets so that the masses might partake of the gods' "strength and virtue."[395] Ancient Greeks consumed the raw flesh of a bull meant to represent Dionysus,[396] just as the Ainu of Japan and Russia fatted a cub for the sole purpose of consuming the bear god.[397] In Indonesian folklore the dismembered corpse of Hainuwele ("Coconut Girl") grew into plants that have since become the islanders' staples.[398] It is obvious how such themes represent themselves in *Soma* and *ayahuasca*, where god, plant, and drink are one.

The Christian communion, with its feast of Christ's body (bread) and blood (wine), is the perfect example in which modern society has sublimated such concepts (wine, it should be noted, could also be argued to possess quasi-entheogenic qualities). Variations on this cultural theme of eating the god also include the consumption of anything growing out of a god, as in the Cashinahua myth, or consuming a deity's bodily fluids—in some tribes, *ayahuasca* is said to be the actual blood (*nawa himi*) and urine (*dunuc isun*) of the great cosmic serpent Yube.[399]

For his 1999 book *Passport to the Cosmos*, John Mack selected several accounts that came from experiencers who self-identified as "recurring abductees." One of these individuals was a *sangoma* (healer) from South African named Vusamazulu Credo Mutwa. The son of a Zulu mother and a Christian father, Mutwa grew up in a world where strange spirits and extraterrestrials were common. As a result, he felt "caught between, on the one hand, Western thought, including the Christian religion, and African thought, which accepts these things without question." Mutwa spoke to Mack of the *Mantindane*, beings identical to Grey aliens whom he had encountered many times before. In traditional lore, these beings would come from the sky, abduct, traumatize, torture, and impregnate humans.[400]

Pertinent to our conversation is the interview Mutwa gave in the October 5, 1999, edition of *Spectrum* magazine, where he claimed that "the Grey aliens, sir, are edible." Mutwa claimed to have heard of several individuals who had eaten the "sky gods," but it wasn't until a friend in Lesotho gave him "a small lump of grey, rather dry stuff, which he said was the flesh" that he believed the tales. After sharing in their gruesome sacrament, Mutwa and his friend awoke the next day to find their tongues swollen and their skin broken out in hives. They were unable to walk and began leaking blood out of their orifices, coming close to death.

Eventually they recovered and their skin began to peel. A sort of dementia set in:

> We started laughing like real loony tunes. It was ha-ha-ha-ha-ha-ha, day after day—for the slightest things we started laughing our heads off, for hours, until you were nearly exhausted.

> And then the laughing went away; and then a strange thing happened, a thing which my friend said was the goal which those who ate the flesh of a *Mantindane* wanted to achieve.

It was as if we had ingested a strange substance, a drug, and a drug like no other on this Earth. Suddenly, our feelings were heightened.

When you drank water, it was as if you had drunk a wine of some kind. Water became as delicious as a man-made drink. Food began to taste amazingly. Every feeling was heightened, and it's indescribable—it was as if I was one with the very heart of the universe. I cannot describe it any other way.

And this feeling of amazing intensity of feeling lasted for over 2 months. When I listened to music, it was as if there was music behind the music, behind the music. When I painted pictures—which is what I do for a living—and when I was holding a particular color on the tip of my brush, it was as if there were other colors in that color. It was an indescribable thing, sir. Even now I cannot describe it.[401]

The simplest explanation is to assume that Mutwa was drugged with some sort of hallucinogenic plant, a conclusion he admitted to have initially come to as well. But Mutwa claimed that the flesh tasted "coppery" and had the exact same smell he would associate with the *Mantindane* in later encounters.

Needless to say, the likelihood that Mutwa has actually eaten a Grey alien is astronomically low. Even Mack himself noted that Mutwa, "like other indigenous people with whom I have discussed these matters, does not sharply distinguish material or literal reality from mythic truths."[402]

It is nevertheless impossible to deny the fact that the types of sensations Mutwa claimed to have experienced—tastes he had never tasted, colors he had never seen, a sense of oneness with all creation—are incredibly evocative of the things seen under the influence of psychedelics. Just as in consuming *ayahuasca* or *Soma*, eating an alien "god" allows access to a hidden reality.

Mutwa isn't alone in the Entity Supper Club, though there aren't a lot of members. On July 23, 1992, Peter Khoury, an Australian abductee with recurring experiences, was roused from sleep by two beautiful but odd-looking nude women. One was over six feet tall, with blonde hair and enormous eyes, the other shorter and "looked Asian—but too extreme." The blonde grabbed Khoury and pulled him forcefully to her breast, in spite of his protests (recall the tale of the Scandinavian faerie who invited her victim to suckle). The third time she tried, he bit off the tip of her nipple, which became stuck in his throat. Khoury said the entire experience was unnatural, and "felt like biting a plastic dummy." There wasn't any blood, and Khoury began to cough violently to bring the nipple up. When he stopped, both women were gone.[403]

The fallout from this case was also quite peculiar. The nipple stayed in his throat for three days before his coughing finally subsided, and he noticed his genitals were painful. Upon close examination, he found a woman's hair beneath his foreskin that, when removed, allowed the pain to subside. Khoury presented the hair for genetic analysis. And the results were confounding: while the shaft was of Chinese Mongoloid ancestry, analysis of the root yielded a rare Basque-Gaelic mitochondrial DNA.[404]

Feasting upon flesh ties into the sexual aspect so often noted in the unexplained, as it has long been a common metaphor for sexuality. The Biblical Song of Songs (aka Song of Solomon) is laden with such metaphors, in particular equating the body with fruit and drink. Today we are less eloquent but still have a desire to "eat up" our partners.

Inverse consumption of flesh appears in altered states as well, a variation upon the aforementioned sensation of dismemberment. It is not uncommon for shamans to be consumed in their visions—consider the Hebrew tale of Jonah, who is consumed by the whale only to emerge with the commandment that he must prophesy in Nineveh. Returning once more to the *ayahuasca* sessions of Raoul Adamson, we find an experience that fully reverses "eating the god"—Adamson had the revelation that "If I am eaten by the serpent, I acquire its power and knowledge. Allow someone to eat you and you gain their power." This was just before he was devoured by a gigantic serpent-dragon, one that took his body apart inside its gut.[405]

Such action is also evocative of transformation. Jonah emerged from the whale a changed man, and Horus-Ra entered the mouth of the great Egyptian cow of the sky, Hathor-Nut, only to be reborn at dawn. And, on occasion, those who eat entity food are reborn.

Rebirth

The cyclicality of eating and being eaten is clear in the Greek *ourobouros*, the image of a snake consuming itself. We are once more drawn to the image of the serpent, this time eating its own tail and becoming a circle. Jung also felt the circular *ourobouros* was symbolic of alchemy and the Eastern mandala—a symbol which he in turn felt was behind the flying saucer phenomenon, at least in part. Most fruit (the second most common entity food) is round as well, and as such "indicates the completeness of the beginning and the completeness of the end, the perfect sphere of the self," according to Jungian analyst Eve Jackson.[406]

This completeness touches upon another theme common to both shamanism and the paranormal: eternal renewal. Recall how Jaime Bordas Bley's health took a drastic turn for the better following the consumption of alien "chocolate," or abductee Iván Morales, who reported that after being given a bitter yellow drink by aliens in 1980, his un-diagnosable chronic illness simply vanished.[407] Many self-identified alien abductees report similar changes, not only physically but also psychologically, psychically, and artistically.

"Any trauma may carry with it the possibility of personal transformation and growth," wrote Mack. "But the alien abduction experiences seem different to me because of their specific capacity to shatter the boundaries of the psyche and to open consciousness to a wider sense of existence and connection in the universe."[408]

Once more, it should be emphasized that not all entity food cases result in regeneration and rebirth. The tragic 2000 death of the professor from Mérida, Spain, is illustrative enough of the dangers of UFO contact. Still others find their lives thrown into turmoil over their experiences, and the seriousness of such negative impacts cannot be overstated.

Nonetheless, the majority of entity food cases detailing a subsequent change in health or consciousness are positive. On occasion, this rebirth is symbolic and not individual-specific. As previously mentioned, Russian reports of entity-given bread—representative of transformation and new life—increased in close temporal proximity to the fall of the Soviet Union. Themes of healing and rebirth are not exclusive to alien encounters, either; Evans-Wentz dedicated an entire chapter of *Fairy-Faith in the Celtic Countries* to themes of rebirth and the interplay between faeries and the underworld.

Even prosaic explanations for the abduction experience are embedded in the concept of birth. One popular psychological model suggests that alien abductions are in fact repressed birth memories. In the case of abductees snatched from their beds, a bright light appears; they are yanked from a warm, safe environment; placed in a sterile clinical setting; and approached by a being who comes close to the face and projects love (genuine or not) toward the abductee. Ointments and the Absorption Theory could be construed as a reflection of memories in utero, while the frequency of entity food to be liquid ties into this model as well, since breast-feeding is one of the first acts a newborn experiences.

Still, there is simply too much universal symbolism to write the entire experience off as a birth memory. Paranormal encounters are too consistent across too many diverse cultures, and as such *must* have some type of objective component.

Consider nepenthe, the mythic draft so often invoked in entity cases where drinks cause amnesia. Timothy Freke and Peter Gandy explain its role in rebirth in *The Jesus Mysteries: Was the "Original Jesus" A Pagan God?*:

> Plato tells us that the dead have the choice of drinking from the "Spring of Memory" and walking the right-hand path towards heaven or drinking from the "Cup of Forgetting" and walking the left-hand path towards reincarnation. The Gnostic *Book of the Saviour* teaches the same doctrine, explaining that a righteous man will be born into his next life without forgetting the wisdom he has learned in this life because he will not be given the "Draught of Oblivion" before his next birth. Rather he will receive "a cup full of intuition and wisdom" which will cause the soul not to fall asleep and forget, but to "seek after the Mysteries of Light, until it hath found them."[409]

CHAPTER 16

ENTITY FOOD: A WORKING MODEL OF MEANING & THOUGHT

It is in the admission of ignorance and the admission of uncertainty that there is a hope for the continuous motion of human beings in some direction that doesn't get confined, permanently blocked, as it has so many times before in various periods in the history of man.
— Richard P. Feynman

On his website *Numinous Intrusions*, blogger Brian Short recalled a thrilling incident in the summer of 1988 when, on the way to the cinema, he and his friends saw a strange, orange object in the sky. The exact description of the shape eluded him until years later, when he was waiting in line for coffee.

"I saw on a point-of-purchase display these neat little cellophane packages with single cookies inside, hung from the wire rack," Short wrote. "I thought excitedly, *that's exactly what it looked like!*" The cookie was a madeleine, a small, French cake with a distinctive tapered-scallop shape.[410]

When describing the strange craft they see in the sky, witnesses are quick to draw upon food vocabulary: they see craft shaped like eggs, croissants, mushrooms, burritos, hot dog buns, coffee cans, saucers, teacups, and—even though not technically food—cigars, another consumable. One 1971 account even described the craft as "like a great lump of meat on a plate."[411] The alleged occupants of such craft are described no differently. Their heads are pear-shaped, their eyes almonds. It is actually something of a fun game to leaf through a stack of old reports and try to find cases that *don't* invoke food imagery.

Mike Clelland draws comparisons between Short's experience and the work of French author Marcel Proust. In his novel *In Search of Lost Time*, Proust examines the theme of involuntary memory, where sensations spontaneously make long-forgotten events pop into one's mind. The most famous episode from the novel involves a madeleine, which when tasted causes a flood of memories to wash over the narrator: Sunday mornings in Combray, his aunt Léonie, feelings of love.

It is curious that both Proust's protagonist and Short revived their dormant memories after seeing the same treat. Like the narrator from *In Search of Lost Time*, abductees typically also have repressed memories; even the title of the book calls to mind Budd Hopkins' *Missing Time*, one of the seminal studies of the abduction phenomenon.

The comparison of Short's account to Proust's work brings together the unexplained, synchronicity, and the power of food to act upon our minds. In any form, food can be a powerful agent of psychological and physical change, helping us recall past events as in Proust's book, evoking incredibly complex memories, thoughts, images, and feelings. Zoologist J.Z. Young called food "about the most important influence in determining the organization of the brain and the behavior that the brain organization dictates."[412]

Food can be "a symbol calling forth diverse associations that carry with them patterns of emotions, attitudes, ideas, and beliefs, characterized by an overall aura of pleasantness or unpleasantness," wrote Bernard Lyman in *A Psychology of Food: More than a Matter of Taste*. "Thus, the food is a symbol-stimulus for pleasant or unpleasant associations and for the moods or sense of well-being which they engender."[413]

I know this feeling all too well. The first time I ever tried peanut butter pie was also the first time I watched 1968's *Planet of the Apes*. To this day I can still recall the moment when George Taylor (Charlton Heston) is being interrogated by Dr. Zaius (Maurice

Evans), when the dawning realization of the film's nihilistic undercurrent latched onto the peanut flavor in my mouth and the two became inseparable. In spite of my profound love for peanut butter pie, I have never been able to separate its flavor from the anxiety associated with that cinematic gut punch I received as a child. The exact moment is locked in my memory.

This anecdote's first-person narrative is deliberate. For this last chapter of my book, I am adopting a personal tone, mainly because what follows are my own personal thoughts on the meaning of entity food, and no one should in any way accept these as established fact. Remember—there are no conclusions to be made, only connections.

Are we maybe dealing with intelligences at the boundaries of the internal and external, the physical and non-physical? Entities so intelligent and foreign to us that they can only effectively communicate to us through symbolism and mythology? Certainly the family dog must consider the bulk of its owners' behavior illogical and magical.

Modern science would write off such a notion as highly unlikely, and with good reason. It is fantastic. The easiest course of action is for us to fold and admit that the phenomenon is wholly psychological.

If one is honest and examines the data, however, such a conclusion is difficult to admit. Given the number of cases involving multiple witnesses and the strong consistency of these phenomena across the world, something else seems to be at play. People of wildly different cultures, some without any interest in the unexplained, or access to the appropriate literature, nonetheless agree upon the broad strokes of any given paranormal experience, often with details specific to their encounter (e.g. hairy hominids smell bad, aliens perform examinations, etc.). At least some aspect *must* be external. Jung himself admitted that, in spite of their psycho-symbolic import, it is "an established fact" that flying saucers also have a physical component.[414]

Think back for a moment to the Crater Lake, Oregon, case,

where the witnesses were made to believe they were eating at a diner. Why were they given a screen memory invoking the pageantry of dining? What reaction was that intended to elicit?

Anyone researching these topics weaves a tangled web of connections, a web whose center we have at last reached. The facts surrounding unexplained phenomena touch each other with so much frequency in such a complex fashion that it is sometimes impossible to arrange the data in a clear and concise manner and yet, for all the undeniable trends and coincidences, we are so often left with nothing to show for it—nothing besides the nagging feeling that one more book, one more report, might somehow blow the lid off of everything and reveal the true nature of things. Now, at the end of this study, I have no more concrete answers than those I began with.

Your guess, as they say, is as good as mine.

All this being said, I personally feel as though this study strongly supports the following statements:

1. Entities—particularly aliens and faeries—give food on a semi-regular basis in encounters.
2. The food taboo, which claims that eating entity food results in imprisonment, is more symbolic than literal.
3. Entity food causes amnesia. Eating or drinking it is often the final act described by witnesses. On the rare occasion that it does not mark the end of an encounter, entity food instead is administered at the very beginning of the experience, explicitly facilitating the interaction.
4. The appearance of entity food roughly corresponds to that of foods considered *sattvic* in *ayurvedic* tradition. This is the diet preferred by Vedic mystics and clairvoyants.
5. Entities tend to give liquids more often than any other food.
6. These entities are closely associated with liquid. This association is sometimes metaphoric and, in a handful of cases, sometimes literal. This connection is reinforced by how of-

ten drinks are given to witnesses by entities.

7. There is a strong indication that entities do not consume in a normal terrestrial fashion via the mouth. While no one theory may be correct, the Absorption Theory, the concept of *foyson*, and the manner in which faerie food is revealed to be debris cloaked in *glamour* all support this claim.

8. Because they do not seem to consume in an earthly manner, it seems unlikely that these entities are offering actual food and more likely that they are offering some sort of simulacra, "food mirages," if you will.

Let us couple these points with a few facts:

1. The psychedelic compound Dimethyltryptamine (DMT) is produced in the human body.
2. When active in substantial doses, DMT can cause visions that closely mirror entity encounters.
3. Individuals under the influence of DMT have accepted food from non-human intelligences.
4. DMT is the active ingredient in the drink *ayahuasca*, a drink that is at once plant, god, and liquid.
5. "Eating the god" is an archetypal concept wherein the power of a deity is bestowed upon those who consume it.

My research has led me to propose the following hypothesis:

Extraterrestrial, spiritual, or interdimensional intelligences which exist in other realms can interact with human beings by altering chemical compounds (e.g. DMT) in the brain, leading to altered states of consciousness. In order to facilitate these changes in neural chemistry, these entities often draw upon the human race's rich symbolism of food and drink, offering "food mirages" which elicit a change in consciousness

in the observer. These simulacra are directly projected into the mind, an extension of the entity itself ("eating the god"), and are used to initiate, strengthen, sustain, or—most commonly—end an encounter.

Much of this hypothesis owes a debt to the efforts of researchers like Hancock and Hanks, whose work has suggested that DMT and similar psychoactive compounds may facilitate interactions with paranormal intelligences, acting as a sort of medium through which these beings can communicate. The theory is not without its strengths: it handily answers why concrete proof of mysterious beings has eluded investigators for centuries while simultaneously explaining why so many encounters feature a deeply personal psychological component. What you see in these experiences is what you bring to the table.

In my hypothesis these beings—as well as any craft they are piloting, clothes they are wearing, or food they are offering—are made manifest via DMT. Following this logic, these food mirages are in a sense composed of the same "material" as the entities themselves, and when they are symbolically consumed by witnesses they are in essence "eating the god." Rather than entities giving us a literal piece of themselves, they are instead using symbolism to administer a dose of the same medium that allows them to appear to us in the first place. Using these food mirages, nonhuman intelligences can exert control of the mind through allegory, a mechanism to regulate the experience of the observer.

How could non-physical food regulate the flow of DMT in the human mind? Suggestion is a powerful thing, and any entity wishing to initiate some type of change in a person would be well served to couch cues and triggers in the form of food. After all, we expect anything consumed to have some sort of affect upon us: coffee gives us energy; wine relaxes us; chocolate bars make us happy. How strong would that cause-effect relationship be if implanted directly into the mind?

Setting aside the possibility that these entities can directly interface human brain chemistry, the importance of pure symbolism to human consumption is still strong. Consider recent findings in the field of placebo research, where sugar pills have occasionally exhibited an efficacy rivaling prescription drugs. Any individual who is told by an authority figure that a substance will have a particular effect on them is more likely to report said effect, regardless of whether the substance is active or not—such is the power of the human brain. Harish Johari's words have never been truer: "As you eat, so is your mind; As is the food, so is your mind."

In addition to inducing altered states via a *physical* reaction like brain chemistry, it is reasonable to assume that the experience of food mirages could produce a *psychological* change to prolong or end an encounter. After all, substances like DMT are not a requisite for entering altered states of consciousness; meditation is a common method by which people slip in and out of trances every day without the help of any substances at all. A food mirage, wielding the full semiotic weight of its real-world counterpart, could function akin to a posthypnotic suggestion, wherein a seemingly unrelated idea triggers an abrupt, involuntary change in consciousness. Instead of conjuring long-forgotten places, people, and emotions like Proust's madeleine, the sensory input of these food mirages could instead shift the human mind into (or out of) an altered state. This was certainly the case in Andrew Paquette's experience, as well as that of the DMT user whose faerie pill significantly extended his DMT trip.

Given the tendency of entity food to appear at the end of most encounters, what if the act of eating—simple, mundane, earthly—acts as a trigger to move the human brain back towards its simple, mundane, earthly mindset? A post-ordinary suggestion, if you will.

An entity might also present a food mirage to help their message truly resonate, selecting a substance with symbolic meaning to the witness. If I ever met one of these intelligences and they wished to truly underscore a warning about the impending apocalypse, perhaps they would offer me some peanut butter pie to drive their point home. There are plenty of folks whose values are so entrenched that their subconscious would turn down LSD in a dream, but would eagerly throw back a pint of bitter. The flexibility of entity food to appear as any sort of mirage would allow for each experience to be tailored to the individual.

Purely symbolic consumables—especially liquids—have been utilized in a variety of metaphysical disciplines throughout the ages to elicit a change in the experiencer. In Taoist alchemy, adepts are instructed to visualize and create an internal "elixir" within the body, one which will bring the alchemist back to "the original state of Being and represents its attainment or recovery... the return to 'emptiness' (*xu*), the state in which no boundaries or distinctions occur between the absolute and the relative."[415]

Author and self-proclaimed out-of-body practitioner Anita Gamba claimed to have created a similar symbolic potion that she visualized in her ongoing efforts to combat Multiple Sclerosis.

> Many times, after I had detached from my body, but before I took off, I was present enough to pause and take some of my tonic. I got this idea from ancient texts which write about a drink called an elixir. This elixir, when taken, is a substance that is purported to cure all disease, open the brain to sacred knowledge and prolong life indefinitely.
>
> I decided to create my own elixir and use it when out of body on the off chance that it would do me some good. But, instead of an elixir, I called it a tonic. I visualized that this tonic would strengthen my DNA and eliminate any disease or abnormality that had occurred in my body.[416]

Though it is debatable whether or not the tonic had any objective effect on her body, Gamba's nonphysical tonic nonetheless proved useful in helping her craft her own reality in this out-of-body state.

But why would the entities under discussion use symbolism at all? Why not foist these changes upon us directly? Certainly a being capable of communicating telepathically, subverting inhibitions, and alleviating fear would have the ability to control our minds directly.

Perhaps the theater of entity food is an effort to ease the shock of encountering the unknown. The act of consumption is familiar to us, a universal act enjoyed by every man, woman, and child on planet Earth. This familiarity could be an effort to inject some normalcy into a strange situation, preventing us from panicking— not unlike the measures we take to make animals at home in a zoo.

Sure, we could place a tiger in a cement room behind bars, but it's not considered good practice in modern zoos. Among other things, animals under stress are dangerous, more likely to attack. They are unpredictable and uncooperative. By contrast, tigers in most of today's zoos enjoy a spacious recreation of their natural environment, complete with native flora and observation decks obscured from view. A simulation of the jungle is not only humane, but the familiarity keeps the tigers calm.

For all of its parsimony and strengths, there are flaws in my hypothesis as well. If entity food is so useful in ushering witness in and out of altered states of consciousness, then why is the literature replete with encounters that do not feature entity food at all? Perhaps these food mirages are more effective for controlling some witnesses than others, or maybe they are only required in longer encounters. In spite of these possibilities, I would be remiss if I did not transparently address such contradictions.

Another problem is that, even with the similarities mentioned in this book between faeries, aliens, and Sasquatch, hairy hominids seem to have a more physical component to them than UFOs or the Good Folk, a conclusion supported by how little their actions conform to the entity food model. Their offerings are infrequent and, on the rare occasion food is offered, Sasquatch tend to offer food that does not fit the overall trend, such as meat. One could argue that the brevity of the typical Sasquatch encounter precludes the offer of food, but the data does seem to suggest something a bit more tangible. An interdimensional or supernatural Sasquatch is still possible—a concept I am still very much open to—but my findings in this study seem to favor the flesh-and-blood hypothesis.

There is a physical component to alien and faerie phenomena that my hypothesis does not address either. The model I have proposed is predicated upon the idea that entity food is a "mirage," but the fact remains that many of these cases *do* possess a physical component—it is a glaring contradiction when I propose that entity food is nonexistent, yet Joe Simonton was able to produce his famous pancakes. Perhaps physical food such as the pancakes are the framework, the detritus, to which the food mirage is applied?

Proposed theories on the unexplained always run abreast of such problematic exceptions. "The problem with the UFO phenomenon is often that the best ideas always have holes in them," said Seriah Azkath, paranormal radio host. "Like you think, 'Oh, this fits perfectly!... except for that piece.' And no matter which way you look at it, there's always a piece that doesn't fit."[417]

The frustration this leads to cannot be denied, but such outliers are a blessing and a curse in this field. After all, if all the data ever collected was in complete agreement, we would have solved the unexplained long ago, and this book would never have been written. The fact that physical evidence such as Simonton's pancakes exist also serves as a reassuring pat-on-the-back—we are *not* wasting our time with a purely psychological phenomenon.

Where does all of this informed speculation leave us? I don't know. It's a statement I am comfortable making without reservations. I have none of the answers, only a rough, imperfect outline of a model that may give us greater insight in the future. What I do feel comfortable saying is that the vast majority of these phenomena contain a metaphysical element, a gut feeling that I can only avoid by cherry-picking the data. Whether this element is the result of advanced technology, brain chemistry, or spiritual communion is up for grabs, but the connection exists.

You don't have to run into an alien, a faerie, or a Sasquatch to be offered entity food. These beings are constantly pushing their meals on us each and every day—in the media. Sasquatch sell us beef jerky and barley wine. UFOs and aliens hawk hefeweizen, tequila, and an entire chain of restaurants. Faeries push everything from cereal (Rice Krispies and Lucky Charms) to cookies (Keebler), coffee (the Starbucks mermaid), tuna (Chicken of the Sea), vegetables (Jolly Green Giant), and margarine.

As initially noted, this book is merely a preliminary foray into the subject of entity food. The subject branches into potentially endless variations to study, countless other avenues of inquiry to follow, ideas that have only been lightly touched upon in these chapters. What about food from ghosts? Food from heavenly apparitions? Is there any validity to the claim that humans are being eaten by these entities?

Better minds than mine may be able to shed additional light not only on the entity food phenomena but on other niche areas as well. Looking at the big picture has perhaps not been in the best interest of the paranormal community—we may be, to flip a phrase on its head, not seeing the trees for the forest. Generations have grown up, had their imaginations kindled by our strange planet, and died without getting any closer to the answers; perhaps a shift in what demands our attention is in order. It is time we began examining the minutiae of the unexplained, for therein may lie the kernel of truth so many have long sought—not only is the devil in the details, but the truth may be as well.

Just be sure to take it all with a grain of salt.

Acknowledgments

So many individuals have assisted in the creation of this book that there will inevitably be an oversight or two. In that case, please take any omissions to be the result of a cluttered mind rather than malice.

First and foremost, thanks to Micah Hanks, for his guiding wisdom and unwavering kindness as I take my first step into the world of the unexplained. Without his encouragement, this book would simply be a series of random observations in my mind, and nothing more. An equal thanks to Red Pill Junkie, a Fortean force of nature whose generous donation of time and suggestions provided an invaluable polish for this project.

Special thanks to Albert Rosales, whose tireless work on cataloguing centuries of humanoid reports is one of the great unsung resources in this field.

Thanks to Anders Liljegren of the Archives for the Unexplained, for helping a wet-behind-the-ears researcher place some of his more obscure resources.

Thanks to Ben and Aaron of Mysterious Universe, for their enthusiasm when the project was still in its early stages. You two are the best—never stop bringing Fortean news to the masses.

Thanks to those with whom I had personal correspondence, pointing me toward leads and validating some of my ideas: Mikhail Gershtein, Denys Breysse, and Scott Corrales. Thanks also to the many listeners of The Gralien Report and Mysterious Universe who provided their insightful input.

Thanks also to Patrick Huyghe and Anomalist Books for the opportunity to share my work with the world.

Lastly, but certainly not least, thanks to my loved ones for supporting me and reassuring me that I haven't gone insane: Sarah, Mom, Dad, Jennifer, Jim, and—though they may not agree with that assessment when they grow up—Josh and Robey.

REFERENCES

INTRODUCTION

1   No author. En norsk Jente Indtagelse i Bjerg 1720. (1858, October 3). *Illustreret Nyhedsblad*, pp. 4-6. Retrieved from http://nb.no. Translated account by Old Jonny Brænne, retrieved from Magonia Exchange list (groups.yahoo.com/group/magonia_exchange), courtesy of Albert Rosales.

2   Olsdatter's original account was recorded August 6 and 7, 1720, in "Nordrehoughs [modern Norderhov] rectory at Ringeriget [modern Ringerike]."

3   Lady Wilde "Speranza" (1888). *Ancient Legends, Mystic Charms, and Superstitions of Ireland* (p. 31). Boston, MA: Ticknor and Company.

4   Fried, J., & Leach, M. (1949). Food tabu in the land of the dead. In *Funk & Wagnalls standard dictionary of folklore, mythology and legend*. (Vol. 1, pp. 409-410) New York, NY: Funk & Wagnalls Co.

5   Garry, J., & El-Shamy, H. (Eds.). (2005). *Archetypes and Motifs in Folklore and Literature*. Armonk, NY: M.E. Sharpe.

6   Garry & El-Shamy 2005.

7   Fried & Leach 1949.

8   Fried & Leach 1949.

9   Alley, J. R. (2007). *Raincoast Sasquatch: The Bigfoot/Sasquatch records of southeast Alaska, coastal British Columbia, & Northwest Washington from Puget Sound to Yakutat*. Blaine, WA: Hancock House. (Original work published 2003)

10   *Milwaukee Public Museum: Kwakiutl cosmology & ceremonial life*. (2014). Retrieved from http://www.mpm.edu/research-collections/artifacts/kwakiutl/cosmology-ceremonial-life

11   Garry & El-Shamy 2005.

12   Notwithstanding, of course, the possibility of an ancient global civilization, which has a good deal of merit in its own right.

13   Garry & El-Shamy 2005.

14   Purkiss, D. (2000). *Troublesome Things: A History of Fairies and Fairy Stories*. Westminster, UK: Penguin Books.

15   Latham, James E. (1987). Food. In *The Encyclopedia of Religion* (p. 387-393). M. Eliade (Ed.). New York, NY: Macmillan.

16   Gorbonyeva, A. (1991, August 31). *Komsomolets Kubani*.

17   A term used to describe the unexplained, named after the late writer and researcher of anomalous phenomena Charles Fort.

CHAPTER 1 – Lore: Faeries

18   Bord, J. (2014). *Fairies: Real Encounters with Little People* [Kindle edition]. London, UK: Michael O'Mara Books. (Original work published 1998)

19   The terms fairy/fae and fairies/fae folk will be used interchangeably.

20   Even though the term "gnome" originated with Paracelsus in the 16th century, the entity itself closely matches those of longstanding folk descriptions.

21   Herskovitz, M.J. (1990). *The Myth of the Negro Past*. Boston, MA: Beacon Press. (Original work published 1941)

22   Witthoft, J. & Hadlock, W.S. (1946). Cherokee-Iroquois Little People. *Journal of American Folklore, 59*, 413-422.

23   Bane, T. (2013). *Encyclopedia of fairies in world folklore and mythology*. Jefferson, NC: McFarland & Company, Inc.

24   Briggs, K. (1976). *An Encyclopedia of Fairies: Hobgoblins, Brownies, Bogies, and Other Supernatural Creatures* (p. 41). New York, NY: Pantheon Books.

25   Ashliman, D.L. (2005). *Fairy Lore: A Handbook*. Westport, CN: Greenwood.

26   Ashliman 2005.

27   MacGregor, A.A. (1937). *The Peat-Fire Flame: Folk-tales and Traditions of the Highlands and Islands*. Edinburgh: The Moray Press.

28   Bord 2014.

29   Smith, C. (2005, September). The Land of the Hidden People. *Fortean Times, 201*, 42-27.

30   Skoöanakönnun DV um álfatrú: Meirihluti þjóðarinnar trúir á álfa og huldufólk. (1998, July 22). *Dagblaðið Vísir - DV* (in Icelandic), p. 2. Retrieved August 11, 2014 from timarit.is.

31   Clark, J. (2010). *Hidden Realms, Lost Civilizations, and Beings from Other Worlds.* Canton, MI: Visible Ink Press.

32   Kennedy, P. (Ed.). (1866). *Legendary Fictions of the Irish Celts.* London, UK: Macmillan and Co.

33   Arrowsmith, N. & Moorse, G. (1977). *A Field Guide to the Little People.* New York, NY: Farrar Straus & Giroux.

34   Evans-Wentz, W.Y. (1966). *The Fairy-Faith in Celtic Countries.* New Hyde Park, NY: University Books.

35   Fried, J., & Leach, M. 1949.

36   Bane 2013.

37   Keightley, T. (1892). *The Fairy Mythology, Illustrative of the Romance and Superstition of Various Countries.* Retrieved from gutenberg.org.

38   Tongue, R. *County Folklore,* Vol. VIII (pp. 116-117). Cited in Briggs 1976.

39   Bane 2014, p. 139

40   MacGregor 1937.

41   Briggs 1976.

42   Briggs 1976.

43   MacGregor 1937.

44   Hartland, E.S. (1891). *The Science of Fairy Tales: An Inquiry into Fairy Mythology* (p. 45). London, UK: Walter Scott.

45   Bord 2014.

46   Rimmer, J. (1988, January). Transvection and UFOlogy. *Magonia.* Retrieved August 11, 2014 from http://magonia.haaan.com/2009/transvection

47　Rimmer, J. (1984). *The Evidence for Alien Abductions.* Wellingborough, UK: Aquarian Press. Citing S. Anglo's *The Damned Art*, RKP 1977.

48　Bane 2013.

49　Briggs 1976.

50　Briggs 1976.

51　Guiley, R.E. (2009). *The Encyclopedia of Demons and Demonology.* New York, NY: Checkmark Books.

52　Evans-Wentz 1966.

53　Evans-Wentz 1966.

54　Sanchez-Ocejo, V., & Ferrer, J. (2001, October 14). Chupacabras Said to Have Been in Chile Since 1970's. (M. Andrade, Trans.). Retrieved August 11, 2014 from http://www.rense.com/general15/chp.htm.

55　Evans-Wentz 1966.

CHAPTER 2 – Lore: ET & Bigfoot

56　Pope, N. (2004, March 2). Subject: Re: UFOs & Fairies? *UFO UpDates: A mailing list for the study of UFO-related phenomena.* Message posted to http://ufoupdateslist.com/2004/mar/m03-009.shtml.

57　Luis, G. (n.d.). UFO Files: Geraldo Bichara Case. Retrieved August 11, 2014 from http://www.ufociencia.com/2014/05/arquivo-ovni-caso-geraldo-bichara.html

58　Miller, J. G. (1994). Medical Procedural Differences: Alien Versus Human. In Pritchard, A., Pritchard, D.E., Mack, J. E., Kasey, P., & Yapp, C. (Eds.), *Alien Discussions: Proceedings of the Abduction Study Conference* (pp. 59-64). Cambridge, UK: North Cambridge Press.

59　BFRO Geographical Database of Bigfoot/Sasquatch Sightings & Reports. (2014). Retrieved May 8, 2014, from http://www.bfro.net/gdb/

60　Bane 2013.

61　Shearar, C. (2000). *Understanding Northwest Coast Art: A Guide to Crests, Beings and Symbols*. Seattle, WA: University of Washington Press.

62   Bane 2013.

63   Shearar 2000.

64   Alley 2007.

65   Taylor, S. (2011). BFRO Report #29355: Possible evidence collected after a woman is hit in the hand by a rock near Napavine. *BFRO*. Retrieved May 8, 2014 from http://www.bfro.net/gdb/show_report.asp?id=29355

66   Andersen, S. (2013, October 21). Comment 4. Message posted to http://bf-field-journal.blogspot.com/p/bigfoot-gifts.html

67   Corrales, S. (1992, August). UFOs in the Caribbean. *Fate 45*(8), pp. 62-72.

68   Vallée, J. & Aubeck, C. (2010). *Wonders in the Sky: Unexplained Aerial Objects from Antiquity to Modern Times*. Los Angeles, CA: Tarcher. Citing *Malleus Maleficarum*, H. Kramer & J. Sprenger (1486).

69   Bane 2013.

70   "Flap" is a Fortean term used to describe a highly concentrated period of paranormal activity. The 1973-1974 UFO/Bigfoot flap is covered extensively in Stan Gordon's *Silent Invasion*.

71   A Fortean term used to distinguish more complex and bizarre cases, attributed to Dr. J. Allen Hynek's United Nations address on UFOs (November 27, 1978).

CHAPTER 3 - Trends

72   Vallée, J. (1993). *Passport to Magonia*. Chicago, IL: Contemporary Books.

73   Pope 2004.

CHAPTER 4 – Food: Liquids

74   Pratt, B. (1991). Disturbing Encounters in NE Brazil. In T.

Good (Ed.), *UFO Report 1991* (pp. 102-124). London: Sidgwich & Jackson Ltd.

75   Rimmer 1984.

76   Machlin, M. & Beckley, T.G. (1981). *UFO* (p. 77). Cape Town, South Africa: Quick Fox.

77   Pogonov, V. I. & Regional Moscow Club for the Research of Anomalous Phenomenon (n.d.). Case 12. In A. Rosales (Ed.), *1990 Humanoid Sighting Reports*. Retrieved February 5, 2014 from http://www.ufoinfo.com/humanoid/humanoid-1990.pdf

78   Reid, K. (n.d.). Visitor Submitted Abduction Experiences – Alien abduction as a child. *Aliens the Truth*. Retrieved May 19, 2014 from http://www.aliensthetruth.com/Aliens_abductions.php?view=1&ID=23#.U3oFYS9_qLI

79   Anfalov, A. & Yaroslavl UFO Group (n.d.). Case 69. In A. Rosales (Ed.), *1953 Humanoid Sighting Reports*. Retrieved February 5, 2014 from http://www.ufoinfo.com/humanoid/humanoid-1953.pdf

80   Aleixo, H.B. (1973, November). Abduction at Bebdouro. *Flying Saucer Review (16)*6, 6-14.

81   Olaer, M. (2004). Alien Abduction. *Iwasabducted.com*. Retrieved on May 19, 2014 from http://www.iwasabducted.com/abduction-board/reports/638.htm

82   Martín, J. (1997, Autumn). Healed by "E.T.s" in Puerto Rico (G. Creighton, Trans.). *Flying Saucer Review* 42(3), 18-23.

83   Fenwick, L.J., Tokarz, H., and Muskat, J. (1984). Canadian Rock-Band Abducted? *Flying Saucer Review*, 29(3), pp. 2-9.

84   Johnson, F. (1980). *The Janos People* (p. 31). Suffolk, UK: Neville Spearman Limited.

85   Steiger, B. (1988). *The UFO Abductors*. New York City, NY: Berkley.

86   Turner, K. (1994). *Taken: Inside the Alien-Human Abduction Agenda*. Tallahassee, FL: Rose Printing Company, Inc.

87   Jasek, M. (2004). Abduction of the North Canol Road. *UFO BC*. Retrieved May 15, 2014 from www.ufobc.ca/yukon/n-canol-abd/

88   Evans-Wentz 1966.

89   Bane 2013.

90   No author En norsk Jente Indtagelse i Bjerg 1720, 1858.

91   Strieber, W. (1997). *Transformation*. New York, NY: Avon Books.

92   Bord 2014.

93   Arrowsmith, N. & Moorse, G. 1977.

94   Bane 2013.

95   Lopez, R.A.P. & Bound, R. F. (1974, November). Chaneques: Mexican Gnomes or Interplanetary Visitors? *Fate, 27,* pp. 51-57.

96   Shearar 2000.

97   Coleman, L. & Knatterud, E. (2006). Abductions by Modern Neandertals? *Cryptomundo*. Retrieved May 15, 2014 from http://cryptomundo.com/cryptozoo-news/abductions-neandertals/

98   Sidnacius. (2008, May 6). "In search of an illusive creature." *Merinews*. Retrieved June 16, 2014 from http://www.merinews.com/article/in-search-of-an-illusive-creature/133591.shtml

99   Semenduev, S. (1991). On the tracks of UFOs in Dagestan. *Iks: Newsletter of the Dagestan Center of the Study of UFOs and Anomalous Phenomena* 5, 2.

100   NUFORC report, 7/10/1975. (2007). *National UFO Reporting Center*. Retrieved May 20, 2014 from http://www.nuforc.org/webreports/060/S60035.html

101   Margaret. (n.d.). Case 33. In A. Rosales (Ed.), *1993 Humanoid Sighting Reports*. Retrieved February 5, 2014 from http://www.ufoinfo.com/humanoid/humanoid-1993.pdf

102   Clark, J. (2000). *Extraordinary Encounters: An Encyclopedia of Extraterrestrials and Otherworldly Beings*. Santa Barbara, CA: ABC-CLIO.

103   Strieber, W. (2011). *The Key*. New York, NY: Jeremy P. Tarcher. (Original work published 2001)

104   Wilson, C. (1998). *Alien Dawn: An Investigation into the Contact Experience*. New York, NY: Fromm International Publishing Corporation.

105 Valenze, D. (2011). *Milk: A Local and Global History*. Ann Arbor, MI: Sheridan Books.

106 Valenze 2011.

107 Many Abductees claim to be given false, more mundane memories of their experiences called *screen memories*.

108 Strieber 1997, *Transformation*.

109 Andrews, T. (2000). *Nectar and Ambrosia: An Encyclopedia of Food in World Mythology*. Santa Barbara, CA: ABC-CLIO.

110 Corrales, S. personal communication, June 9, 2014.

111 Webb, D.F. & Bloecher, T. *HUMCAT: Catalogue of Humanoid Reports 1956*. USA: CUFOs.

112 Kaminchuk, A. & Romanchenko, V. (2004, September 19). UFO Over Kiev. *Inoplanetyanin 12*.

113 Baschet, M., Bompoint, M., Dumas-Zajdela, F. (Producers), & Roux, J.M. (Director). (2002*). Enquête sur le monde invisible* [Motion picture]. France: Bac Films.

114 Jonsson, A. (n.d.). Visit to extraterrestrial civilizations. Retrieved May 14, 2014 from http://gratisenergi.se/anteeng.htm

115 Øverby, R. (2001). Intervju med ufokontaktpersonen Arve Jacobsen. Retrieved May 17, 2014 from http://galactic-server.com/rune/arve.html

116 Stranges, F. E. (1967). *Stranger at the Pentagon*. New Brunswick, NJ: Inner Light Publications.

117 No author. Contact with Aliens. (2009). Anomalous Phenomena. Retrieved May 17, 2014 from http://ufo-online.ru/file_3986.html

118 Alcock, J. P. (2006). *Food in the Ancient World*. Westport, CT: Greenwood Press.

119 Bullard, T. (1987). *UFO Abductions: The Measure of a Mystery* (Vol. 2). Bloomington, IN: The Fund for UFO Research.

120 Strieber 1997, *Transformation*.

121 NUFORC report, 7/23/1985. (2005). *National UFO Reporting Center*. Retrieved from http://www.nuforc.org/webreports/045/

S45661.html

122 Arrowsmith & Moorse 1977.

123 Briggs 1976.

124 Ashliman 2005.

125 Williamson, G.H. (1953) *Other Tongues—Other Flesh*. Amherst, WI: Amherst Press.

126 Bowen, C. (1968, March) The UFO's Caused by Drink. *Flying Saucer Review 14*(2), 30.

127 No author. Close Encounters: Everything you need to know about UFOs. (2014, June 28). *The Economist*. Retrived July 7, 2014 from http://www.economist.com/news/united-states/21605918-everything-you-need-know-about-ufos-0

128 Picasso, F. (n.d.). Case 19. In A. Rosales (Ed.), *1965 Humanoid Sighting Reports*. Retrieved February 5, 2014 from http://www.ufoinfo.com/humanoid/humanoid-1965.pdf

129 Wysmierski, M. (2000). Plínio Bragatto's Unexpected Trip. *Close Encounters of the Brazilian Kind, 1*, 24-29.

130 Angelucci, O. (1955). *The Secret of the* Saucers. Amherst, MA: Amherst Press.

131 Angelucci, O. (1959). *Son of the Sun*. Los Angeles, CA: DeVorss & Co.

132 Bishop, G. (2014, March 6). *Radio Misterioso: Nick Redfern: For Nobody's Eyes Only* [Audio podcast]. Retrieved from http://radiomisterioso.com/audio/Nick_Redfern_2_9_14.mp3

CHAPTER 5 – Food: Fruits

133 Granchi, I. (1990, December). A pleasant encounter in Brazil with "human-looking" little people. *Flying Saucer Review 35* (4), 20-21.

134 Bottrell, W. (1873). *Traditions and Hearthside Stories of West Cornwall*. Penzance, UK: Beare and Son.

135 Brewster, D. (1970, August). Our Last Monster. *Seattle Magazine*, 29-33.

136   Coleman & Knatterud 2006.

137   No author. UFO Sighting: andhrapradesh, India. (2005, October 27). *UFO Evidence: Scientific Study of the UFO Phenomenon
and the Search for Extraterrestrial Life*. Retrieved May 19, 2014 from
http://www.ufoevidence.org/sightings/report.asp?ID=7004

138   Strieber, W. & Strieber, A. (1997). *The Communion Letters*. New
York, NY: Harper Prism.

139   Hudson, B. (1993). Inside the ship. *Unsolved UFO Sightings*,
1(1), 4-5.

140   Lamarche, S. R. (1979). *Manifiesto OVNI de Puerto Rico, Santo
Domingo y Cuba*. San Juan, P.R.: Editorial Punto y Coma.

141   Sanchez-Ocejo, V. & Miami UFO Center (n.d.). Case 99. In A.
Rosales (Ed.), *1980 Humanoid Sighting Reports*. Retrieved February
5, 2014 from http://www.ufoinfo.com/humanoid/humanoid-1980.
pdf

142   Narcissov, V. (2000). Gelida. *Fourth Dimension and UFOs 3*, 4.

143   Klarer, E. (2009). *Beyond the Light Barrier: The Autobiography
of Elizabeth Klarer*. Flagstaff, AZ: Light Technology Publishing.
(Original work published 1980)

144   Strieber, W. (1987). *Communion*. New York, NY: Avon Books.

145   Jackson, E. (1996). *Food and Transformation: Imagery and Symbolism of Eating*. Toronto, Canada: Inner City Books.

146   Fieldhouse, P. (2002). Zoroastrianism. In *Encyclopedia of Food
and Culture (Scribner Library of Daily Life)*. (Vol. III, pp. 567-569)
New York, NY: Charles Scribner's & Sons.

147   Jackson 1996.

CHAPTER 6 – Food: Bread

148   Priyma, A. (2000). *XX Century: Chronicles of the Unexplained*
[online copy]. Retrieved from http://royallib.ru/book/priyma_alek-
sey/XX_vek_hronika_neobyasnimogo_fenomen_za_fenomenom.
html

149   Coleman & Knatterud 2006.

150 Keightley 1892.

151 Briggs 1976.

152 Anfalov n.d., *1953 Humanoid Sighting Reports*.

153 Azhazha, V. (1998). *Other Life* [online version]. Retrieved from http://royallib.ru/read/agaga_vladimir/inaya_gizn.html#0

154 Vallée 1993.

155 Keel, J. (1970). *UFOs: Operation Trojan Horse*. New York, NY: G.P. Putnam's Sons.

156 Bane 2013.

157 Blacker, C. (1967). Supernatural Abductions in Japanese Folklore. *Asian Folklore Studies, 26*(2), 111-147.

158 Feindt, C. (n.d.) *LL-??-1972*. Retrieved May 29, 2014 from http://www.waterufo.net/item.php?id=967

159 Andrews 2000.

160 Fried, J., & Leach, M. (1949). Bread. In *Funk & Wagnalls standard dictionary of folklore, mythology and legend*. (Vol. 1, pp. 162-163) New York, NY: Funk & Wagnalls Co.

161 Andrews 2000.

162 Gilman, P. (1967, September). Do the Cherubim Come from Mars? *Flying Saucer Review 13*(5), 19-21, 30.

163 Louise, R. (2013). The Miracle of Wheat: Evolution or Agriculture of the Gods? Retrieved May 30, 2014 from http://mysteriousuniverse.org/2013/10/the-miracle-of-wheat-evolution-or-agriculture-of-the-gods/

164 Andrews 2000.

CHAPTER 7 – Food: Pills

165 Budden, A. (1999). *The UFO Files: Psychic Close Encounters*. London, UK: Cassell & Co.

166 Bühler, W.K., Pereira, G., & Pires, N.M. (1985). *UFO Abduction at Mirassol: A Biogenetic Experiment* (W.C. Stevens, Trans.). Tucson, AZ: UFO Photo Archives.

167   Bullard, T. (1987). *UFO Abductions: The Measure of A Mystery* (Vol. 1). Mount Rainier, MD: Fund for UFO Research.

168   Guma, J. (1997, Winter). Another Astonishing South American Report (G. Creighton, Trans.). *Flying Saucer Review 42*(4), 6-10.

169   Hall, R. (1988) *Uninvited Guests: A Documented History of UFO Sighting, Alien Encounters & Coverups.* Santa Fe, NM: Aurora Press.

170   Bullard 1987, Vol. 2.

171   Sprinkle, L. (1975, November). A Preliminary Report on the Investigation of an Alleged UFO Occupant Encounter. *Flying Saucer Review 21*(3), 3-5.

172   Steiger 1988.

173   Endre, K. & RYUFOR Foundation Hungary (n.d.). Case 130. In A. Rosales (Ed.), *1980 Humanoid Sighting Reports.* Retrieved February 5, 2014 from http://www.ufoinfo.com/humanoid/humanoid-1980.pdf

CHAPTER 8 – Food: Miscellaneous

174   Angelucci 1959.

175   Øverby, R. (n.d.). Physical ufo-contact in former east-Germany in -57: The contacts of Martin Wiesengrün. Retrieved June 4, 2014 from http://galactic-server.com/rune/ariancont.html

176   Villarrubia Mauso, P. & Rangel, M. (n.d.) Case 52. In A. Rosales (Ed.), *1978 Humanoid Sighting Reports.* Retrieved February 5, 2014 from http://www.ufoinfo.com/humanoid/humanoid-1978.pdf

177   No author. Woman tells her story of being married to Bigfoot. (2004). *Pravda.* Retrieved June 4, 2014 from http://english.pravda.ru/news/society/sex/13-10-2004/59752-0/#.U490Ui9_qLI

178   Burns, J.W. (1954, December). "My Search for B.C.'s Giant Indians." *Liberty Magazine*, 38-39.

179   Reece, G. L. (2008) *Weird Science and Bizarre Beliefs: Mysterious Creatures, Lost Worlds and Amazing Adventures* (pp. 19-20). London, UK: I.B.Tauris.

180   Childress, D. H. (2010). *Yetis, Sasquatch, & Hairy Giants.* Gar-

dena, CA: SCB Distributors.

181   McClean, S. (2005). *Big News Prints*. Publisher: Author.

182   Fernández, P. M. & Mendoza, S. (2005, August). Supuesta abducción extraterrestre en Mérida. *Nacional* (Suppl.*Enigmas Express* [Vallejo ed.]) pp. 12-13.

183   Priyma, A. (2000). *From Mystery to Mystery* [online copy]. Retrieved June 5, 2014 from http://www.rulit.net/books/ot-tajny-k-tajne-read-20094-32.html

184   Bane 2013.

185   Pennant, T. (1796). *The History of the Parishes of Whiteford and Holywell (*pp. 131-132). London, UK: B. and J. White.

186   Collins, A. (1978, June). The Avely Abduction. *Flying Saucer Review 24*(1), 5-15.

187   Strieber, A. (ed.) (2004). Insight: Behind the News - Messages from Gray Monkeys. Retrieved June 9, 2014 from http://www.unknowncountry.com/insight/messages-gray-monkeys

188   Ivanov, I. (1990, December 4). Toropovo Anomalies. *Lenin's Path 144*, 4.

189   Keel, J. (1975). *Our Haunted Planet*. London, UK: Futura Publications. (Original work published 1971)

190   D. Breysse, personal communication, June 9, 2014.

191   Bigorne, J.M. (1976, April). "Forced Feeding" by UFO Entities. *Flying Saucer Review 21*(6), 20-23.

192   Vallée, J. (2008). *Messengers of Deception*. Brisbane, AU: Daily Grail Publishing. (Original work published 1979)

193   Ashliman 2005.

194   Briggs 1976.

195   Vallée & Aubeck 2010.

196   Baller, A.H. (1968, May). The mysterious defender. *Fate*, 123-126.

197   Cassano, A. (n.d.). 1970-79. *Avvistamenti UFO in Puglia*.Retrieved June 9, 2014 from http://www.cisupuglia.it/bari/bair1970.

htm

198   Gross, P. (2007). End May or beg, June, 1978, Pyrogovskaya Lake, Russia, Anatoly. Retrieved June 9, 2014 from http://ufologie. patrickgross.org/ce3/1978-05-russia-pyrogovskayalake.htm

199   Lamarche 1979.

200   Martin, J. (2001). *Vieques: Caribbean UFO Cover-Up of the Third Kind*. San Juan, PR: Cedicop, Inc.

201   de Athyayde, R. (1995, Winter). As Over 5000 Await The Virgin Mary UFO's "Put On A Show" In Brazil (A.J. Gevaerd, Trans.). *Flying Saucer Review 40*(4), 6-8.

202   Suenaga, C.T. (2011). Aliens who wanted to warn humanity. Retrieved July 24, 2014 from https://www.ufo.com.br/artigos/ extraterrestres-que-queriam-alertar-a-humanidade

203   Tsushbaya, G. (1994). *This Mysterious World*. Odessa, Ukraine: Odekov.

204   Randle, K. D. (1989). *The October Scenario*. New York City, NY: Berkley Books.

205   Bullard 1987, Vol. 2.

CHAPTER 9 – Relationships: Giving & Taking

206   Nunnelly, B.M. (2011). *The Inhumanoids: Real Encounters with Beings That Can't Exist*. Woolsery, UK: CFZ Press.

207   Clark 2000.

208   Picknett, L. (2012). *The Mammoth Book of UFOs*. London, UK: Constable & Robinson.

209   Vallée, J. (1990). *Confrontations: A Scientist's Search for Alien Contact*. New York, NY: Ballantine Books.

210   Lysaght, P. (2002). Wake and Funeral Hospitality in Ireland in the Nineteenth and Twentieth Centuries: Continuity and Change. In *Food and Celebration: From Fasting to Feasting*. Ljubljana, Slovenia: Zaloz'ba, ZRC.

211   Kvideland, K. (1993). Boundaries and the Sin-Eater. In *Boundaries and Thresholds: Papers from a Colloquium of the Katherine Briggs*

Club. H.E. Davidson (Ed.). Woodchester, U.K.: Thimble Press.

212 Danforth, L.M. (1982). *The Death Rituals of Rural Greece*. Princeton, NJ: Princeton University Press.

213 Jackson 1996.

214 Evans-Wentz 1966.

215 Purkiss 2000.

216 Arrowsmith & Moorse 1977.

217 Coxhead, J.R.W. (1959). *Devon Traditions and Fairy-tales*. Exmouth, UK: Raleigh Press.

218 Arrowsmith & Moorse 1977.

219 Evans-Wentz 1966.

220 Noël, C. (2014). *Our Life with Bigfoot: Knowing Our Next of Kin at Habituation Sites* [Kindle edition] (locations 964-968). US: CreateSpace Independent Publishing Platform

221 Jevning, W. (2014, February 23). *Bigfoot Hotspot Radio: EP 18 – Sasquatch Stories with Jim Grant AKA Bear* [Audio podcast]. Retrieved from https://www.youtube.com/watch?v=tOWFcRqdY_I

222 Shiel, L.A. (2006). *Backyard Bigfoot: The True Story of Stick Signs, UFOs, and the Sasquatch*. Lake Linden, MI: Jacobsville Books.

223 Keightley 1892.

224 Evans-Wentz 1966.

225 Wilson 1998.

226 Kelleher, C.A. & Knapp, G. (2005). *Hunt for the Skinwalker: Science Confronts the Unexplained at a Remote Ranch*. New York, NY: Pocket Books.

227 No author. (1965, March). World Round-Up of News and Comment About Recent Sightings. *Flying Saucer Review 11*(2), 24-30.

228 Rimes, N. (1969, January). Another Hospital Visited. *Flying Saucer Review 15*(1), 4-6.

229 Morris, E. (1979, November). The Winged Beings of Bluestone Walk. *Flying Saucer Review 25*(6), 24-27.

230   Licauco, J.T. (2005). *Dwarves and Other Nature Spirits: Their Importance to Man*. Philippines: Rex Book Store, Inc.

231   Kukushkin, V. (1997). *Chimeras of the X Location* [online copy]. Retrieved from http://royallib.ru/book/kukushkin_valeriy/himeri_ urochishcha_iks.html

232   No author. The Story of Emm. (1993, March/April). *Minnesota MUFON Newsletter, 40*, 3-4.

233   No author. (2001, December 11). Aliens Steal Grain in Saratov. *Megapolis-Express* (45).

234   Rife, P.L. (2001). *It Didn't Start with Roswell: 50 Years of Amazing UFO Crashes, Close Encounters and Coverups*. Bloomington, IN: iUniverse.

235   Keel 1970.

236   Lady Gregory. (1920). *Visions and Beliefs in the West of Ireland Collected and Arranged by Lady Gregory: with Two Essays and Notes by W.B. Yeats*. London, UK: The Knickerbocker Press. Retrieved from http://www.gutenberg.org/files/43973/43973-h/43973-h.htm

237   Kirk, R. (2012). *The Secret Commonwealth of Elves, Fauns, and Fairies* (pp. 49-50). Mineola, NY: Courier Dover Publications. (Original work published 1815)

238   Ashlima 2005.

239   Rogerson, P. (1977). Fairies and Fireballs. *Magonia*. Retrieved from http://magonia.haaan.com/2009/fireballs/

240   Kukushkin 1997.

241   Sanderson, I. T. (1974). *Uninvited Visitors: A Biologist Looks at UFO's*. London, UK: Universal-Tandem Publishing Company Ltd.

242   Vallée 1993.

243   Alley 2007.

244   Varner, G.R. (2006). *The Mythic Forest, the Green Man and the Spirit of Nature: The Re-emergence of the Spirit of Nature from Ancient Times Into Modern Society*. New York, NY: Algora Publishing.

245   Forth, G. (2008). *Images of the Wildman in Southeast Asia: An Anthropological Perspective* (p. 163). London, UK: Routledge.

246 Painthorse. (2012, June 12). Bf entering houses... [Online forum comment]. Retrieved June 16, 2014 from http://bigfootforums.com/index.php/topic/31643-bf-entering-houses/

247 Arrowsmith & Moorse 1977.

248 Bane 2013.

249 Evans-Wentz 1966.

250 Purkiss 2000.

251 Kirk 2012.

252 Bane 2013.

253 Wilson 1998.

254 Schwarz, B.E. (1971, March). Possible UFO-Induced Temporary Paralysis. *Flying Saucer Review 17*(2), 4-9.

255 Van Eyck, Z. (1997, July 6). "Close Encounters in Utah." Deseret News. Retrieved June 17, 2014 from http://www.deseretnews.com/article/570388/Close-encounters-in-Utah.html?pg=all

256 Gibbons, B. & Randles, J. (1982, January). Close Encounters with Animal Effects. *Flying Saucer Review 27*(4), 28.

257 Denikin. (2005, January). UFO in Belarus: 'Flying saucer' watches scientists "Shield of the Fatherland – 2004." *Secret Research 90*(1), 6.

258 Villarubia Mauso, P. (n.d.). Case 16. In A. Rosales (Ed.), *1990 Humanoid Sighting Reports*. Retrieved February 5, 2014 from http://www.ufoinfo.com/humanoid/humanoid-1990.pdf

CHAPTER 10 – Connections: *Sattvic* Diet

259 Keel, J. (2002). *The Complete Guide to Mysterious Beings*. New York, NY: Tom Doherty Associates, LLC. (Original work published 1970 as *Strange Creatures from Time and Space*)

260 Spencer, C. (1993). *The Heretic's Feast: A History of Vegetarianism* (pp.69-84). London: Fourth Estate.

261 Bernard, T. (1999). *Hindu Philosophy*. Delhi, India: Motilal Banarsidass Publishing.

262	Agte, V.V., & Chiplonkar, S.A. (2007, April). Linkage of concepts of good nutrition in yoga and modern science. *Current Science* 92(7), 956-961.

263	Johari, H. (2000). *Ayurvedic Healing Cuisine: 200 Vegetarian Recipes for health, Balance, and Longevity.* Rochester, VT: Healing Arts Press. (Original work published in 1994)

264	Guha, D. S. (1985, June). Food in the Vedic Tradition. *India International Centre Quarterly, 12*(2), 141-152.

265	Johari 2000.

266	Johari 2000.

267	Schwarz, B.E. (1977, October). Talks with Betty Hill: 2 – The things that happen around her. *Flying Saucer Review 23*(3), 11-14.

268	Tsakiris, A. (2014, January 15). *Skeptiko Episode 198: Mike Clelland struggles to understand contact with alien consciousness* [Audio podcast]. Retrieved from http://www.skeptiko.com/mike-clelland-contact-with-alien-consciousness/

269	Bullard 1987, Vol. 1.

270	Collins 1978.

271	Turner, K. (1992). *Into the Fringe.* New York, NY: Berkley Books.

272	Briggs 1976.

273	Klarer 2009.

274	Gross, P. (2008). 1965 - Mexico, San Angel. Retrieved August 11, 2014 from http://ufologie.patrickgross.org/ce3/1965-mexico-sanangel.htm

275	Strieber 1997. *Transformation.*

CHAPTER 11 – Connections: Sleep Paralysis

276	Adler, S. R. (2010). *Sleep Paralysis: Night-mares, Nocebos, and the Mind-Body Connection.* Piscataway Township, NJ: Rutgers University Press.

277	Burton, R. (1927). *The Anatomy of Melancholy.* F. Dell & P.

Jordan-Smith (Eds.). New York, NY: Farrar & Rinehart (Original work published 1620)

278   Adler 2010.

279   Terrillon, J.C., & Marques-Bonham, S. M. (2001). Does Recurring Sleep Paralysis Involve More Than Cognitive Neurosciences? *Journal of Scientific Exploration 15*(1), 97-123.

280   Sinistrari. (1700) *De delictis et poenis.* Venice, Italy: Albriccium.

281   Aina, O.F., & Famuyiwa, O.O. (2007, March). *Ogun Oru:* A Traditional Explanation for Nocturnal Neuropsychiatric Disturbances among the Yoruba of Southwest Nigeria. *Transcultural Psychiatry 44*(1), 44-54.

282   Hanks, M. (2010). *Magic, Mysticism, & the Molecule: The Search for Sentient Intelligence from Other Worlds.* US: CreateSpace Independent Publishing Platform.

283   Paquette, A. (2010). *Dreamer: 20 Years of Psychic Dreams and How They Changed My Life.* Hampshire, UK: John Hunt Publishing Ltd.

CHAPTER 12 – Connections: Sexuality

284   Fried & Leach 1949.

285   Bane, 169.

286   Coulter, C.R., & Turner, P. (Eds.). (2012). Agdistis. In *Encyclopedia of Ancient Deities* (Vol. 1, p. 24). Jefferson, NC: McFarland & Company, Inc. (Original work published 2000).

287   Dalton, J.P. (2011). *The Taming of the Demons: Violence and Liberation in Tibetan Buddhism.* New Haven, CT: Yale University Press.

288   Arrowsmith & Moorse 1977.

289   Bane 2013.

290   Purkiss 2000.

291   Arrowsmith & Moorse 1977.

292   Steiger 1988.

293   Little, G.L. (1994). *Grand Illusions: The Spectral Reality Underly-*

ing Sexual UFO Abductions, Crashed Saucers, Afterlife Experiences, Sacred Ancient Sites, and Other Enigmas. Vancouver, BC: White Buffalo Books.

294   Turner 1992.

295   Turner, K. (1994). *Masquerade of Angels* (pp. 229-238). Roland, AR: Kelt Works.

296   Mack, J. (1999). *Passport to the Cosmos* (p. 124). New York, NY: Three Rivers Press.

297   Newman, L.S., & Baumeister, R.F. (1996). Toward and Explanation of the UFO Abduction Phenomenon: Hypnotic Elaboration, Extraterrestrial Sadomasochism, and Spurious Memories. *Psychological Inquiry 7*(2), 99-126.

CHAPTER 13 – Connections: Absorption, Ointment, & the Entity Diet

298   Meldrum, J. (2006). *Sasquatch: Legend Meets Science* (p. 188). New York, NY: Forge Books.

299   Clark 2000.

300   Rife 2001.

301   Barakitis, J. (2006). CONTACT with Hollow Earth Beings. Retrieved June 19, 2014 from http://ufoexperiences.blogspot.com/search?q=cartago

302   Mack, J. (1995). *Abduction: Human Encounters with Aliens* (p. 179). New York, NY: Ballantine Books.

303   Valerian, V. (1988). *The Matrix: Understanding Aspects of Covert Interaction with Alien Culture, Technology and Planetary Power Structures* (p. 61) Scotia, NY: Arcturus Book Service.

304   Kottmeyer, M.S. (2005, November 10). Editorial: A mystery until now? Dunking Dr. Jacobs in the food vat. In *Magonia (59)*. Retrieved June 19, 2014 from http://www.users.waitrose.com/~magonia/ms59.htm

305   Jacobs, D. (1998). *The Threat.* New York, NY: Simon & Schuster.

306   No author. (n.d.). MUFON Case 10767: Shiny brightly slowly

hovering disc on cloudless night. Retrieved June 19, 2014 from http://mufoncms.com/cgi-bin/report_handler.pl?req=view_long_desc&id=10767

307 Mack 1995.

308 Steiger 1988.

309 Lear, J. (1987). LEAR.TXT. Retrieved from http://www.text-files.com/ufo/alear1.txt

310 Corso, P.J. & Birnes, W.J. (1997). *The Day After Roswell*. New York, NY: Pocket Books.

311 Jones, S. (2007, July 1). Abducted by aliens – and a scar to prove it. *Southern Daily Echo*. Retrieved June 21, 2014 from http://www.dailyecho.co.uk/news/1509904.abducted_by_aliens_and_a_scar_to_prove_it/

312 Stringfield, L. (1979, November). Retrievals of the Third Kind – Part 3. *Flying Saucer Review 25*(6), 8-14.

313 Jackson 1996.

314 Kirk 2012.

315 Rogers, C. (1869). *Scotland Social and Domestic: Memorials of Life and Manners in North Britain*. London: Charles Griffin and Co. Citing Robert Kirk.

316 Briggs 1976.

317 Arrowsmith & Moorse 1977.

318 Bane 2013.

319 Homer. (1876). *Iliad*. W.L. Collins (Ed.). Philadelphia, PA: J.B. Lippincott and Co.

320 Hartland 1891.

321 Heiden, R.W. (1982, March) A 1949 Brazilian Contactee – Part 1. *Flying Saucer Review, 27*(5), 28-29.

322 Thomas, J. (1979, September). Humanoid and Abduction Reports Widespread. *The MUFON UFO Journal 130*, 15-16.

323 Creighton, G. (1976, November) Soaking Wet "Space Flight." *Flying Saucer Review 22*(4), 23.

324   Bullard 1987, Vol. 2.

325   Purkiss 2000.

326   Briggs 1976.

327   Hartland 1891.

328   Bane 2013.

329   Brewster 1970.

330   Creighton, G. (1965, January). The Most Amazing Case of All: Part I – A Brazilian Farmer's Story. *Flying Saucer Review 11*(1), 13-17.

331   Creighton, G. (1966, September). Even More Amazing: The A.V.B. Case Continued. *Flying Saucer Review 12*(5), 22-25.

332   Creighton, G. (1966, November). Even More Amazing… Part III. *Flying Saucer Review 12*(6), 14-16.

333   Bullard 1987, Vol. 2.

334   Bühler, Pereira, & Pires 1985.

335   Granchi, I. (1984, October). Abduction at Botucatu. *Flying Saucer Review 30*(1), 22-25.

336   Bullard 1987 Vol. 2.

337   Bennet, C., McQueen, N., & Cowan, R. (2001). *Sex, Drugs, Violence and the Bible*. Gibsons, B.C., Canada: Forbidden Fruit Publishing. Books.

338   Uagga, A. Q. (n.d.). *James Bong's Ultimate SpyGuide to Marijuana* [Google eBook]. Retrieved from books.google.com

339   Moreno, M. (1992). "Pancāmirtam: God's Washing as Food." In R.S. Khare (Ed.), *The Eternal Food: Gastronomic Ideas and Experiences of Hindus and Buddhists* (147-178). Albany: State University of New York Press.

340   Feinberg, G., & Shapiro, R. (1980). *Life Beyond Earth: The Intelligent Earthling's Guide to Life in the Universe*. New York, NY: William Morrow.

CHAPTER 14 – Connections: Entheogens

341   James, W. (2008). *Varieties of Religious Experience: A Study in Human Nature.* Rockville, MD: Arc Manor (Original work published 1902)

342   Bäckman, L., & Hultkrantz, Å. (1977). *Studies in Lapp Shamanism.* Stockholm, Sweden: Almqvist & Wiksell International.

343   Dubois, T. (2009) *An Introduction to Shamanism.* Cambridge, UK: Cambridge University Press.

344   Bullard, T. E. (1989, April). UFO Abduction Reports: The Supernatural Kidnap Narrative Returns in Technological Guise. *The Journal of American Folklore 102*(404), 147-170.

345   Dubois 2009.

346   Wasson, R.G. (1972). *Soma: Divine Mushroom of Immortality.* New York: Harvest Books.

347   Wasson 1972.

348   Andrews 2000.

349   Metzner, R. (Ed.). (1999). *Ayahuasca: Hallucinogens, Consciousness, and the Spirit of Nature.* New York, NY: Thunder's Mouth Press.

350   Dubois 2009.

351   Hancock, G. (2013, January). Giving up the Green Bitch: Reflections on Cannabis, Ayahuasca and the mystery of plant teachers [Web log post]. Retrieved from http://www.grahamhancock.com/forum/HancockG3.php

352   Hancock, 2013.

353   Stafford, P. (1993). Psychedelics Encyclopedia (3rd ed). Berkeley, CA: Ronin Publishing.

354   A.T. Weil, personal communication, May 1, 1972.

355   Harner, M. (2000). Discovering the Way. In L. E. Luna & S. F. White (Eds.), *Ayahuasca Reader: Encounters with the Amazon's Sacred Vine* (pp. 98-101). Santa Fe, NM: Synergetic Press.

356   Payaguaje, F. (2000). At the End You See God (excerpt from *The Yajé Drinker*). In L. E. Luna & S. F. White (Eds.), *Ayahuasca Reader: Encounters with the Amazon's Sacred Vine* (pp. 67-80). Santa

Fe, NM: Synergetic Press.

357   Hancock, 2013.

358   Payaguaje 2000.

359   Perriam, D. Personal communication, January 19, 2015.

360   Stafford 1993.

361   Langon, E. J. M. (2000). A Visit to the Second Heaven: A Siona Narrative of the Yagé Experience. In L. E. Luna & S. F. White (Eds.), *Ayahuasca Reader: Encounters with the Amazon's Sacred Vine* (pp. 21-30). Santa Fe, NM: Synergetic Press.

362   Stafford 1993.

363   Hausinger, A.V. (2005, October 7). Visitors – Oct 1, 2005. Retrieved from http://www.iwasabducted.com/abductionboard/reports/670.htm

364   Smith, Y.R. (2014). *Coronado: The President, The Secret Service, and Alien Abductions* [Kindle edition].

365   Turner 1994, *Masquerade of Angels.*

366   McKenna, D. J., Towers, G.H.N., & Abbott, F. (1984, April). Monoamine oxidase inhibitors in South American hallucinogenic plants: tryptamine and ⊠-carboline constituents of *ayahuasca. Journal of Ethnopharmacology 10*(2), 195-223.

367   McKenna, D. J. (1999). Ayahuasca: An Ethnopharmacologic History. In R. Metzner (Ed.), *Ayahuasca: Hallucinogens, Consciousness, and the Spirit of Nature* (pp. 40-62). New York, NY: Thunder's Mouth Press.

368   Strassman, R. (2000). *DMT: The Spirit Molecule.* Rochester, VT: Park Street Press.

369   Hanks 2010.

370   Holden, J. (n.d.). *USDA National Nutrient Database for Standard Reference, Release 22.* Retrieved July 15, 2014 from http://www.ars.usda.gov/main/site_main.htm?modecode=12-35-45-00

371   Knowles, J. (2014). Altered States of the Fourth Kind. In J. Knight (Ed.), *Contact: Them or Us* (pp. 138-167). US: CreateSpace Independent Publishing Platform.

372 Pup [Screen name] (2006, February 10). DMT trip accounts. Message posted to http://dmt.tribe.net/thread/9e832018-5fbc-4ff6-b4e5-e314184f687c

373 Grimes, D. & Dunlop, G. (2014, December 20). *Grimerica talks lucid dreaming with Robert Waggoner* [Podcast]. Retrieved from http://www.grimerica.ca/waggoner/

374 Rogan, J. (2013, May 23). *Joe Rogan Experience #360* [Video podcast]. Retrieved from https://www.youtube.com/watch?v=tsu2-I2q6dg

375 disinformation [Screen name] (2010, October 26). *Graham Hancock: Elves, Aliens, Angels and Ayahuasca* [Video file]. Retrieved from https://www.youtube.com/watch?v=0qgMFO0KU-I

376 Lagrou, E. M. (2000). Two Ayahuasca Myths from the Cashinahua of Northwestern Brazil. In L. E. Luna & S. F. White (Eds.), *Ayahuasca Reader: Encounters with the Amazon's Sacred Vine* (pp. 31-35). Santa Fe, NM: Synergetic Press.

377 Adamson, R. (1999). The Experience of Ayahuasca: Teaching of the Amazonian Plant Spirits. In R. Metzner (Ed.), *Ayahuasca: Hallucinogens, Consciousness, and the Spirit of Nature* (pp. 118-128). New York, NY: Thunder's Mouth Press.

378 Ravenswood, S. (1999). Ethereal Serpents Held Me in Thrall. In R. Metzner (Ed.), *Ayahuasca: Hallucinogens, Consciousness, and the Spirit of Nature* (pp. 118-128). New York, NY: Thunder's Mouth Press.

379 White, D. (2013, January 7). I was taken in Merseyside. PLEAS HELP. Message posted to http://bufog.freeforums.org/i-was-taken-in-merseyside-pleas-help-t570.html

380 Wasson 1972.

381 Wasson 1972.

382 Jones, C. (2007). *Encyclopedia of Hinduism*. New York, NY: Infobase Publishing.

383 White, D.G. (1996) *The Alchemical Body: Siddha Traditions in Medieval India*. Chicago, IL: The University of Chicago Press.

384 Dubois 2009.

385   Jung, C.G. (1978) *Flying Saucers: A Modern Myth of Things Seen in the Skies* (pp. 24-26). Princeton, NJ: Princeton University Press.

386   Mishlove, J. (Host), & Bloch, A. (Director). (YEAR). *#S425: Aliens and Archetypes* [Television series episode]. In A. Bloch (Producer), *Thinking Allowed*. San Mateo, CA: Pacific Mountain Network.

387   Bullard 1987, Vol. 2.

388   Basterfield, K. (2002). Waking Paralysed: Abduction or Sleep Paralysis? *Australasian UFOlogist Magazine* 6(1), 12-20.

389   Halliday, R. (2010). *Edinburgh After Dark: Vampires, Ghosts and Witches of the Old Town*. Edinburgh, UK: Black & White Publishing.

390   Granchi, I. (1977, October). Brazilian CE4 Case. *APRO Bulletin* 26(4), 1-4.

391   Alley 2007.

392   Ralph of Coggeshall. (n.d.). *Radulhpi de Coggeshall Chronicon Anglicanum*. Retrieved December 11, 2014 from http://gallica.bnf.fr/ark:/12148/bpt6k50317j/f6.image.r=raoul%20de%20coggeshall.langFR

393   Terence McKenna Archive [Screen name] (2011, July 11). *The Definitive UFO Tape (Terence McKenna) [FULL]* [Video file]. Retrieved from https://www.youtube.com/watch?v=LrgveoEVuq4

CHAPTER 15 – Connections: Eating the God & Rebirth

394   Lagrou 2000

395   Fox, R. (n.d.). Food and Eating: An Anthropological Perspective. Retrieved July 22, 2014 from http://www.sirc.org/publik/food_and_eating_11.html

396   Machen, J.G. (1921). *The Origin of Paul's Religion*. New York, NY: The Macmillan Company.

397   Fried & Leach 1949.

398   Jackson 1996.

399   Lagrou 2000.

400   Mack 1999.

401   Martin, R. (1999, October 5). Great Zulu Shaman And Elder Credo Mutwa: A Rare, Astonishing Conversation. *The Spectrum, 1*(5), 1, 17-32.

402   Mack 1999.

403   Creighton, G. (2001, Spring). The Khoury Case (Australia). *Flying Saucer Review 46*(1), 14-15.

404   Chalker, B. (2005). *Hair of the Alien: DNA and Other Forensic Evidence of Alien Abduction.* New York, NY: Simon & Schuster.

405   Adamson 1999.

406   Jackson 1996.

407   Martín, J. (1997, Autumn). Healed by "E.T.s" in Puerto Rico (G. Creighton, Trans.). *Flying Saucer Review 42*(3), 18-23.

408   Mack 1999.

409   Freke, T., & Gandy, P. (2001). *The Jesus Mysteries: Was the "Original Jesus" a Pagan God?* New York, NY: Harmony Books.

CHAPTER 16 – Entity Food: A Working Model of Meaning & Thought

410   Short, B. (2012, May). Additive, Responsive Shape [Web log post]. Retrieved from http://numinousintrusions.blogspot.com/2012/05/additive-responsive-shape.html

411   No author. (1971, July). World round-up. *Flying Saucers Review 17*(4), 31-33.

412   Young, J.Z. (1968). Influence of the mouth on the evolution of the brain. In P. Person (Ed.) *Biology of the mouth.* Washington, DC: American Association for the Advancement of Science.

413   Lyman, B. (1989). *A Psychology of Food: More Than a Matter of Taste.* New York, NY: Van Nostrand Reinhold Co.

414   Jung 1978.

415   Pregadio, F. (2012). *The Way of the Golden Elixir: A Historical Overview of Taoist Alchemy.* Mountain View, CA: Golden Elixir

Press.

416   Gamba, A. (2014). *Boundless: One Woman's Journal of Her Out-of-Body Experiences* [Kindle edition].

417   Azkath, S. (2014, July 26). *Where Did the Road Go?: Micah Hanks on the UFO Phenomenon* [Audio podcast]. Retrieved from http://wheredidtheroadgo.com/2014/07-26-14MicahHanks.mp3

BIBLIOGRAPHY

Adamson, R. (1999). The Experience of Ayahuasca: Teaching of the Amazonian Plant Spirits. In R. Metzner (Ed.), *Ayahuasca: Hallucinogens, Consciousness, and the Spirit of Nature* (pp. 118-128). New York, NY: Thunder's Mouth Press.

Adler, S. R. (2010). *Sleep Paralysis: Night-mares, Nocebos, and the Mind-Body Connection.* Piscataway Township, NJ: Rutgers University Press.

Agte, V.V., & Chiplonkar, S.A. (2007, April). Linkage of concepts of good nutrition in yoga and modern science. *Current Science 92*(7), 956-961.

Aina, O.F., & Famuyiwa, O.O. (2007, March). *Ogun Oru:* A Traditional Explanation for Nocturnal Neuropsychiatric Disturbances among the Yoruba of Southwest Nigeria. *Transcultural Psychiatry 44*(1), 44-54.

Alcock, J. P. (2006). *Food in the Ancient World.*Westport, CT: Greenwood Press.

Aleixo, H.B. (1973, November). Abduction at Bebdouro. *Flying Saucer Review (16)*6, 6-14.

Alley, J. R. (2007). *Raincoast Sasquatch: The Bigfoot/Sasquatch records of southeast Alaska, coastal British Columbia, & Northwest Washington from Puget Sound to Yakutat.* Blaine, WA: Hancock House. (Original work published 2003)

Andersen, S. (2013, October 21). Comment 4. Message posted to http://bf-field-journal.blogspot.com/p/bigfoot-gifts.html

Andrews, T. (2000). *Nectar and Ambrosia: An Encyclopedia of Food in World Mythology.* Santa Barbara, CA: ABC-CLIO.

Anfalov, A. & Yaroslavl UFO Group (n.d.). Case 69. In A. Rosales

(Ed.), *1953 Humanoid Sighting Reports*. Retrieved February 5, 2014 from http://www.ufoinfo.com/humanoid/humanoid-1953.pdf

Angelucci, O. (1955). *The Secret of the* Saucers. Amherst, MA: Amherst Press.

Angelucci, O. (1959). *Son of the Sun*. Los Angeles, CA: DeVorss & Co.

Arrowsmith, N. & Moorse, G. (1977). *A Field Guide to the Little People*. New York, NY: Farrar Straus & Giroux.

Ashliman, D.L. (2005). *Fairy Lore: A Handbook*. Westport, CN: Greenwood.

Azhazha, V. (1998). *Other Life* [online version]. Retrieved from http://royallib.ru/read/agaga_vladimir/inaya_gizn.html#0

Azkath, S. (2014, July 26). *Where Did the Road Go?: Micah Hanks on the UFO Phenomenon* [Audio podcast]. Retrieved from http://wheredidtheroadgo.com/2014/07-26-14MicahHanks.mp3

Bäckman, L., & Hultkrantz, Å. (1977). *Studies in Lapp Shamanism*. Stockholm, Sweden: Almqvist & Wiksell International.

Baller, A.H. (1968, May). The mysterious defender. *Fate*, 123-126.

Bane, T. (2013). *Encyclopedia of fairies in world folklore and mythology*. Jefferson, NC: McFarland & Company, Inc.

Barakitis, J. (2006). CONTACT with Hollow Earth Beings. Retrieved June 19, 2014 from http://ufoexperiences.blogspot.com/search?q=cartago

Baschet, M., Bompoint, M., Dumas-Zajdela, F. (Producers), & Roux, J.M. (Director). (2002). *Enquête sur le monde invisible* [Motion picture]. France: Bac Films.

Basterfield, K. (2002). Waking Paralysed: Abduction or Sleep Paralysis?

Australasian UFOlogist Magazine 6(1), 12-20.

Bennet, C., McQueen, N., & Cowan, R. (2001). *Sex, Drugs, Violence and the Bible*. Gibsons, B.C., Canada: Forbidden Fruit Publishing. Books.

Bernard, T. (1999). *Hindu Philosophy*. Delhi, India: Motilal Banarsidass Publishing.

BFRO Geographical Database of Bigfoot/Sasquatch Sightings & Reports. (2014). Retrieved May 8, 2014, from http://www.bfro.net/gdb/

Bigorne, J.M. (1976, April). "Forced Feeding" by UFO Entities. *Flying Saucer Review 21*(6), 20-23.

Bishop, G. (2014, March 6). *Radio Misterioso: Nick Redfern: For Nobody's Eyes Only* [Audio podcast]. Retrieved from http://radiomisterioso.com/audio/Nick_Redfern_2_9_14.mp3

Blacker, C. (1967). Supernatural Abductions in Japanese Folklore. *Asian Folklore Studies, 26*(2), 111-147.

Bord, J. (2014). *Fairies: Real Encounters with Little People* [Kindle edition]. London, UK: Michael O'Mara Books. (Original work published 1998)

Bottrell, W. (1873). *Traditions and Hearthside Stories of West Cornwall*. Penzance, UK: Beare and Son.

Bowen, C. (1968, March) The UFO's Caused by Drink. *Flying Saucer Review 14*(2), 30.

Brewster, D. (1970, August). Our Last Monster. *Seattle Magazine*, 29-33.

D. Breysse, personal communication, June 9, 2014.

Briggs, K. (1976). *An Encyclopedia of Fairies: Hobgoblins, Brownies, Bogies, and Other Supernatural Creatures.* New York, NY: Pantheon Books.

Budden, A. (1999). *The UFO Files: Psychic Close Encounters.* London, UK: Cassell & Co.

Bühler, W.K., Pereira, G., & Pires, N.M. (1985). *UFO Abduction at Mirassol: A Biogenetic Experiment* (W.C. Stevens, Trans.). Tucson, AZ: UFO Photo Archives.

Bullard, T. (1987). *UFO Abductions: The Measure of A Mystery* (Vol. 1). Mount Rainier, MD: Fund for UFO Research.

Bullard, T. E. (1989, April). UFO Abduction Reports: The Supernatural Kidnap Narrative Returns in Technological Guise. *The Journal of American Folklore 102*(404), 147-170.

Bullard, T. (1987). *UFO Abductions: The Measure of a Mystery* (Vol. 2). Bloomington, IN: The Fund for UFO Research.

Burns, J.W. (1954, December). "My Search for B.C.'s Giant Indians." *Liberty Magazine*, 38-39.

Burton, R. (1927). *The Anatomy of Melancholy.* F. Dell & P. Jordan-Smith (Eds.). New York, NY: Farrar & Rinehart (Original work published 1620)

Cassano, A. (n.d.). 1970-79. *Avvistamenti UFO in Puglia.* Retrieved June 9, 2014 from http://www.cisupuglia.it/bari/bair1970.htm

Chalker, B. (2005). *Hair of the Alien: DNA and Other Forensic Evidence of Alien Abduction.* New York, NY: Simon & Schuster.

Childress, D. H. (2010). *Yetis, Sasquatch, & Hairy Giants.* Gardena, CA: SCB Distributors.

Clark, J. (2000). *Extraordinary Encounters: An Encyclopedia of*

Extraterrestrials and Otherworldly Beings. Santa Barbara, CA: ABC-CLIO.

Clark, J. (2010). *Hidden Realms, Lost Civilizations, and Beings from Other Worlds.* Canton, MI: Visible Ink Press.

Coleman, L. & Knatterud, E. (2006). Abductions by Modern Neandertals? *Cryptomundo.* Retrieved May 15, 2014 from http://cryptomundo.com/cryptozoo-news/abductions-neandertals/

Collins, A. (1978, June). The Avely Abduction. *Flying Saucer Review 24*(1), 5-15.

Corrales, S. (1992, August). UFOs in the Caribbean. *Fate 45*(8), pp. 62-72.

S. Corrales, personal communication, June 9, 2014.

Corso, P.J. & Birnes, W. J. (1997). *The Day After Roswell.* New York, NY: Pocket Books.

Coulter, C.R., & Turner, P. (Eds.). (2012). Agdistis. In *Encyclopedia of Ancient Deities* (Vol. 1, p. 24). Jefferson, NC: McFarland & Company, Inc. (Original work published 2000).

Coxhead, J.R.W. (1959). *Devon Traditions and Fairy-tales.* Exmouth, UK: Raleigh Press.

Creighton, G. (1965, January). The Most Amazing Case of All: Part I – A Brazilian Farmer's Story. *Flying Saucer Review 11*(1), 13-17.

Creighton, G. (1966, September). Even More Amazing: The A.V.B. Case Continued. *Flying Saucer Review 12*(5), 22-25.

Creighton, G. (1966, November). Even More Amazing... Part III. *Flying Saucer Review 12*(6), 14-16.

Creighton, G. (1976, November) Soaking Wet "Space Flight." *Flying*

Saucer Review 22(4), 23.

Creighton, G. (2001, Spring). The Khoury Case (Australia). *Flying Saucer Review 46*(1), 14-15.

Dalton, J.P. (2011). *The Taming of the Demons: Violence and Liberation in Tibetan Buddhism.* New Haven, CT: Yale University Press.

Danforth, L.M. (1982). *The Death Rituals of Rural Greece.* Princeton, NJ: Princeton University Press.

de Athyayde, R. (1995, Winter). As Over 5000 Await The Virgin Mary UFO's "Put On A Show" In Brazil (A.J. Gevaerd, Trans.). *Flying Saucer Review 40*(4), 6-8.

Denikin. (2005, January). UFO in Belarus: 'Flying saucer' watches scientists "Shield of the Fatherland – 2004." *Secret Research 90*(1), 6.

disinformation [Screen name] (2010, October 26). *Graham Hancock: Elves, Aliens, Angels and Ayahuasca* [Video file]. Retrieved from https://www.youtube.com/watch?v=0qgMFO0KU-I

Dubois, T. (2009) *An Introduction to Shamanism.* Cambridge, UK: Cambridge University Press.

Endre, K. & RYUFOR Foundation Hungary (n.d.). Case 130. In A. Rosales (Ed.), *1980 Humanoid Sighting Reports.* Retrieved February 5, 2014 from http://www.ufoinfo.com/humanoid/humanoid-1980.pdf

Evans-Wentz, W.Y. (1966). *The Fairy-Faith in Celtic Countries.* New Hyde Park, NY: University Books.

Feinberg, G., & Shapiro, R. (1980). *Life Beyond Earth: The Intelligent Earthling's Guide to Life in the Universe.* New York, NY: William Morrow.

Feindt, C. (n.d.) *LL-??-1972.* Retrieved May 29, 2014 from http://www.waterufo.net/item.php?id=967

Fenwick, L.J., Tokarz, H., and Muskat, J. (1984). Canadian Rock-Band Abducted? *Flying Saucer Review, 29*(3), pp. 2-9.

Fernández, P. M. & Mendoza, S. (2005, August). Supuesta abducción extraterrestre en Mérida. *Nacional* (Suppl. *Enigmas Express* [Vallejo ed.]) pp. 12-13.

Fieldhouse, P. (2002). Zoroastrianism. In *Encyclopedia of Food and Culture (Scribner Library of Daily Life).* (Vol. III, pp. 567-569) New York, NY: Charles Scribner's & Sons.

Forth, G. (2008). *Images of the Wildman in Southeast Asia⊠: An Anthropological Perspective.* London, UK: Routledge.

Fox, R. (n.d.). Food and Eating: An Anthropological Perspective. Retrieved July 22, 2014 from http://www.sirc.org/publik/food_and_eating_11.html

Freke, T., & Gandy, P. (2001). *The Jesus Mysteries: Was the "Original Jesus" a Pagan God?* New York, NY: Harmony Books.

Fried, J., & Leach, M. (1949). Bread. In *Funk & Wagnalls standard dictionary of folklore, mythology and legend.* (Vol. 1, pp. 162-163) New York, NY: Funk & Wagnalls Co.

Fried, J., & Leach, M. (1949). Food tabu in the land of the dead. In *Funk & Wagnalls standard dictionary of folklore, mythology and legend.* (Vol. 1, pp. 409-410) New York, NY: Funk & Wagnalls Co.

Gamba, A. (2014). *Boundless: One Woman's Journal of Her Out-of-Body Experiences* [Kindle edition]. US: CreateSpace Independent Publishing Platform.

Garry, J., & El-Shamy, H. (Eds.). (2005). *Archetypes and Motifs in Folklore and Literature.* Armonk, NY: M.E. Sharpe.

Gibbons, B. & Randles, J. (1982, January). Close Encounters with Animal Effects. *Flying Saucer Review 27*(4) , 28.

Gilman, P. (1967, September). Do the Cherubim Come from Mars? *Flying Saucer Review 13*(5), 19-21, 30.

Gorbonyeva, A. (1991, August 31). *Komsomolets Kubani.*

Granchi, I. (1977, October). Brazilian CE4 Case. *APRO Bulletin 26*(4), 1-4.

Granchi, I. (1984, October). Abduction at Botucatu. *Flying Saucer Review 30*(1), 22-25.

Granchi, I. (1990, December). A pleasant encounter in Brazil with "human-looking" little people. *Flying Saucer Review 35* (4), 20-21.

Gross, P. (2007). End May or beginning of June 1978, Pyrogovskaya Lake, Russia, Anatoly. Retrieved June 9, 2014 from http://ufologie. patrickgross.org/ce3/1978-05-russia-pyrogovskayalake.htm

Gross, P. (2008). 1965 - Mexico, San Angel. Retrieved August 11, 2014 from http://ufologie.patrickgross.org/ce3/1965-mexico-sanangel.htm

Guha, D. S. (1985, June). Food in the Vedic Tradition. *India International Centre Quarterly*, *12*(2), 141-152.

Guiley, R.E. (2009). *The Encyclopedia of Demons and Demonology*, p. 68. New York, NY: Checkmark Books.

Guma, J. (1997, Winter). Another Astonishing South American Report (G. Creighton, Trans.). *Flying Saucer Review 42*(4), 6-10.

Hall, R. (1988) *Uninvited Guests: A Documented History of UFO Sighting, Alien Encounters & Coverups.* Santa Fe, NM: Aurora Press.

Halliday, R. (2010). *Edinburgh After Dark: Vampires, Ghosts and Witches of the Old Town.* Edinburgh, UK: Black & White Publishing.

Hancock, G. (2013, January). Giving up the Green Bitch: Reflections on Cannabis, Ayahuasca and the mystery of plant teachers [Web

log post]. Retrieved from http://www.grahamhancock.com/forum/
HancockG3.php

Hanks, M. (2010). *Magic, Mysticism, & the Molecule: The Search for Sentient Intelligence from Other Worlds*. US: CreateSpace Independent Publishing Platform.

Harner, M. (2000). Discovering the Way. In L. E. Luna & S. F. White (Eds.), *Ayahuasca Reader: Encounters with the Amazon's Sacred Vine* (pp. 98-101). Santa Fe, NM: Synergetic Press.

Hartland, E.S. (1891). *The Science of Fairy Tales: An Inquiry into Fairy Mythology*. London, UK: Walter Scott.

Hausinger, A.V. (2005, October 7). Visitors – Oct 1, 2005. Retrieved from http://www.iwasabducted.com/abductionboard/reports/670.htm

Heiden, R.W. (1982, March) A 1949 Brazilian Contactee – Part 1. *Flying Saucer Review, 27*(5), 28-29.

Herskovitz, M.J. (1990). *The Myth of the Negro Past*. Boston, MA: Beacon Press. (Original work published 1941)

Holden, J. (n.d.). *USDA National Nutrient Database for Standard Reference, Release 22*. Retrieved July 15, 2014 from http://tinyurl.com/dr9zo

Homer. (1876). *Iliad*. W.L. Collins (Ed.). Philadelphia, PA: J.B. Lippincott and Co.

Hudson, B. (1993). Inside the ship. *Unsolved UFO Sightings, 1*(1), 4-5.

Ivanov, I. (1990, December 4). Toropovo Anomalies. *Lenin's Path 144*, 4.

Jackson, E. (1996). *Food and Transformation: Imagery and Symbolism of Eating*. Toronto, Canada: Inner City Books.

Jacobs, D. (1998). *The Threat*. New York, NY: Simon & Schuster.

James, W. (2008). *Varieties of Religious Experience: A Study in Human Nature*. Rockville, MD: Arc Manor (Original work published 1902)

Jasek, M. (2004). Abduction of the North Canol Road. *UFO BC*. Retrieved May 15, 2014 from www.ufobc.ca/yukon/n-canol-abd/

Jevning, W. (2014, February 23). *Bigfoot Hotspot Radio: EP 18 – Sasquatch Stories with Jim Grant AKA Bear* [Audio podcast]. Retrieved from https://www.youtube.com/watch?v=tOWFcRqdY_I

Johari, H. (2000). *Ayurvedic Healing Cuisine: 200 Vegetarian Recipes for health, Balance, and Longevity*. Rochester, VT: Healing Arts Press. (Original work published in 1994)

Johnson, F. (1980). *The Janos People*. Suffolk, UK: Neville Spearman Limited.

Jones, C. (2007). *Encyclopedia of Hinduism*. New York, NY: Infobase Publishing.

Jones, S. (2007, July 1). Abducted by aliens – and a scar to prove it. *Southern Daily Echo*. Retrieved June 21, 2014 from http://www.dailyecho.co.uk/news/1509904.abducted_by_aliens_and_a_scar_to_prove_it/

Jonsson, A. (n.d.). Visit to extraterrestrial civilizations. Retrieved May 14, 2014 from http://gratisenergi.se/anteeng.htm

Jung, C.G. (1978) *Flying Saucers: A Modern Myth of Things Seen in the Skies*. Princeton, NJ: Princeton University Press.

Kaminchuk, A. & Romanchenko, V. (2004, September 19). UFO Over Kiev. *Inoplanetyanin*.

Keel, J. (1970). *UFOs: Operation Trojan Horse*. New York, NY: G.P. Putnam's Sons.

Keel, J. (1975). *Our Haunted Planet*. London, UK: Futura Publications. (Original work published 1971)

Keel, J. (2002). *The Complete Guide to Mysterious Beings*. New York, NY: Tom Doherty Associates, LLC. (Original work published 1970 as *Strange Creatures from Time and Space*)

Keightley, T. (1892). *The Fairy Mythology, Illustrative of the Romance and Superstition of Various Countries*. Retrieved from gutenberg.org.

Kelleher, C.A. & Knapp, G. (2005). *Hunt for the Skinwalker: Science Confronts the Unexplained at a Remote Ranch*. New York, NY: Paraview Pocket Books.

Kennedy, P. (Ed.). (1866). *Legendary Fictions of the Irish Celts*. London, UK: Macmillan and Co.

Kirk, R. (2012). *The Secret Commonwealth of Elves, Fauns, and Fairies*. Mineola, NY: Courier Dover Publications. (Original work published 1815)

Klarer, E. (2009). *Beyond the Light Barrier: The Autobiography of Elizabeth Klarer*. Flagstaff, AZ: Light Technology Publishing. (Original work published 1980)

Knowles, J. (2014). Altered States of the Fourth Kind. In J. Knight (Ed.), *Contact: Them or Us* (pp. 138-167). US: CreateSpace Independent Publishing Platform.

Kottmeyer, M.S. (2005, November 10). Editorial: A mystery until now? Dunking Dr. Jacobs in the food vat. In *Magonia (59)*. Retrieved June 19, 2014 from http://www.users.waitrose.com/~magonia/ms59.htm

Kukushkin, V. (1997). *Chimeras of the X Location* [online copy]. Retrieved from http://tinyurl.com/nzgvxwu

Kvideland, K. (1993). Boundaries and the Sin-Eater. In *Boundaries and Thresholds: Papers from a Colloquium of the Katherine Briggs Club*. H.E.

Davidson (Ed.). Woodchester, U.K.: Thimble Press.

Lady Gregory. (1920). *Visions and Beliefs in the West of Ireland Collected and Arranged by Lady Gregory: with Two Essays and Notes by W.B. Yeats.* London, UK: The Knickerbocker Press. Retrieved from http://www. gutenberg.org/files/43973/43973-h/43973-h.htm

Lady Wilde "Speranza" (1888). *Ancient Legends, Mystic Charms, and Superstitions of Ireland.* Boston, MA: Ticknor and Company.

Lagrou, E. M. (2000). Two Ayahuasca Myths from the Cashinahua of Northwestern Brazil. In L. E. Luna & S. F. White (Eds.), *Ayahuasca Reader: Encounters with the Amazon's Sacred Vine* (pp. 31-35). Santa Fe, NM: Synergetic Press.

Lamarche, S. R. (1979). *Manifiesto OVNI de Puerto Rico, Santo Domingo y Cuba.* San Juan, P.R.: Editorial Punto y Coma.

Langon, E. J. M. (2000). A Visit to the Second Heaven: A Siona Narrative of the Yagé Experience. In L. E. Luna & S. F. White (Eds.), *Ayahuasca Reader: Encounters with the Amazon's Sacred Vine* (pp. 21-30). Santa Fe, NM: Synergetic Press.

Latham, James E. (1987). Food. In *The Encyclopedia of Religion* (p. 387-393). M. Eliade (Ed.). New York, NY: Macmillan.

Lear, J. (1987). LEAR.TXT. Retrieved from http://www.textfiles.com/ ufo/alear1.txt

Licauco, J.T. (2005). *Dwarves and Other Nature Spirits: Their Importance to Man.* Philippines: Rex Book Store, Inc.

Little, G.L. (1994). *Grand Illusions: The Spectral Reality Underlying Sexual UFO Abductions, Crashed Saucers, Afterlife Experiences, Sacred Ancient Sites, and Other Enigmas.* Vancouver, BC: White Buffalo Books.

Lopez, R.A.P. & Bound, R. F. (1974, November). Chaneques: Mexican Gnomes or Interplanetary Visitors? *Fate, 27,* 51-57.

Louise, R. (2013). The Miracle of Wheat: Evolution or Agriculture of the Gods? Retrieved May 30, 2014 from http://mysteriousuniverse. org/2013/10/the-miracle-of-wheat-evolution-or-agriculture-of-the-gods/

Luis, G. (n.d.). UFO Files: Geraldo Bichara Case. Retrieved August 11, 2014 from http://www.ufociencia.com/2014/05/arquivo-ovni-caso-geraldo-bichara.html

Lyman, B. (1989). *A Psychology of Food: More Than a Matter of Taste.* New York, NY: Van Nostrand Reinhold Co.

Lysaght, P. (2002). Wake and Funeral Hospitality in Ireland in the Nineteenth and Twentieth Centuries: Continuity and Change. In *Food and Celebration: From Fasting to Feasting*. Ljubljana, Slovenia: Zaloz̆ba, ZRC.

MacGregor, A.A. (1937). *The Peat-Fire Flame: Folk-tales and Traditions of the Highlands and Islands*. Edinburgh: The Moray Press.

Machen, J.G. (1921). *The Origin of Paul's Religion*. New York, NY: The Macmillan Company.

Machlin, M. & Beckley, T.G. (1981). *UFO*. Cape Town, South Africa: Quick Fox.

Mack, J. (1995). *Abduction: Human Encounters with Aliens*. New York, NY: Ballantine Books.

Mack, J. (1999). *Passport to the Cosmos*. New York, NY: Three Rivers Press.

Margaret. (n.d.). Case 33. In A. Rosales (Ed.), *1993 Humanoid Sighting Reports*. Retrieved February 5, 2014 from http://www.ufoinfo.com/humanoid/humanoid-1993.pdf

Martín, J. (1997, Autumn). Healed by "E.T.s" in Puerto Rico (G. Creighton, Trans.). *Flying Saucer Review 42*(3), 18-23.

Martin, R. (1999, October 5). Great Zulu Shaman And Elder Credo Mutwa: A Rare, Astonishing Conversation. *The Spectrum, 1*(5), 1, 17-32.

Martín, J. (1997, Autumn). Healed by "E.T.s" in Puerto Rico (G. Creighton, Trans.). *Flying Saucer Review 42*(3), 18-23.

Martin, J. (2001). *Vieques: Caribbean UFO Cover-Up of the Third Kind.* San Juan, PR: Cedicop, Inc.

McClean, S. (2005). *Big News Prints.* Publisher: Author.

McKenna, D. J., Towers, G.H.N., & Abbott, F. (1984, April). Monoamine oxidase inhibitors in South American hallucinogenic plants: tryptamine and ⊠-carboline constituents of *ayahuasca. Journal of Ethnopharmacology 10*(2), 195-223.'

McKenna, D. J. (1999). Ayahuasca: An Ethnopharmacologic History. In R. Metzner (Ed.), *Ayahuasca: Hallucinogens, Consciousness, and the Spirit of Nature* (pp. 40-62). New York, NY: Thunder's Mouth Press.

Meldrum, J. (2006). *Sasquatch: Legend Meets Science.* New York, NY: Forge Books.

Metzner, R. (Ed.). (1999). *Ayahuasca: Hallucinogens, Consciousness, and the Spirit of Nature.* New York, NY: Thunder's Mouth Press.

Miller, J. G. (1994). Medical Procedural Differences: Alien Versus Human. In Pritchard, A., Pritchard, D.E., Mack, J. E., Kasey, P., & Yapp, C. (Eds.), *Alien Discussions: Proceedings of the Abduction Study Conference* (pp. 59-64). Cambridge, UK: North Cambridge Press.

Milwaukee Public Museum: Kwakiutl cosmology & ceremonial life. (2014). Retrieved August 11, 2014 from http://www.mpm.edu/research-collections/artifacts/kwakiutl/cosmology-ceremonial-life

Mishlove, J. (Host), & Bloch, A. (Director). (YEAR). *#S425: Aliens and Archetypes* [Television series episode]. In A. Bloch (Producer), *Thinking*

Allowed. San Mateo, CA: Pacific Mountain Network.

Moreno, M. (1992). "Pan⊠cāmirtam: God's Washing as Food." In R.S. Khare (Ed.), *The Eternal Food: Gastronomic Ideas and Experiences of Hindus and Buddhists* (147-178). Albany: State University of New York Press.

Morris, E. (1979, November). The Winged Beings of Bluestone Walk. *Flying Saucer Review 25*(6), 24-27.

Narcissov, V. (2000). Gelida. *Fourth Dimension and UFOs 3*, 4.

Newman, L.S., & Baumeister, R.F. (1996). Toward and Explanation of the UFO Abduction Phenomenon: Hypnotic Elaboration, Extraterrestrial Sadomasochism, and Spurious Memories. *Psychological Inquiry 7*(2), 99-126.

No author. En norsk Jente Indtagelse i Bjerg 1720. (1858, October 3). *Illustreret Nyhedsblad*, pp. 4-6. Retrieved from http://nb.no. Translated account by Old Jonny Brænne, retrieved from Magonia Exchange list (groups.yahoo.com/group/magonia_exchange), courtesy of Albert Rosales.

No author. (1965, March). World Round-Up of News and Comment About Recent Sightings. *Flying Saucer Review 11*(2), 24-30.

No author. (1971, July). World round-up. *Flying Saucers Review 17*(4), 31-33.

No author. The Story of Emm. (1993, March/April). *Minnesota MUFON Newsletter, 40*, 3-4.

No author. (2001, December 11). Aliens Steal Grain in Saratov. *Megapolis-Express* (45).

No author. Woman tells her story of being married to Bigfoot. (2004). *Pravda*. Retrieved June 4, 2014 from http://tinyurl.com/ne8bn43

No author. UFO Sighting: andhrapradesh, India. (2005, October 27). *UFO Evidence: Scientific Study of the UFO Phenomenon and the Search for Extraterrestrial Life.* Retrieved May 19, 2014 from http://www. ufoevidence.org/sightings/report.asp?ID=7004

No author. Contact with Aliens. (2009). Anomalous Phenomena. Retrieved May 17, 2014 from http://ufo-online.ru/file_3986.html

No author. Close Encounters: Everything you need to know about UFOs. (2014, June 28). *The Economist.* Retrived July 7, 2014 from http://www.economist.com/news/united-states/21605918-everything-you-need-know-about-ufos-0

No author. (n.d.). MUFON Case 10767: Shiny brightly slowly hovering disc on cloudless night. Retrieved June 19, 2014 from http://tinyurl.com/mf3a78l

Noël, C. (2014). *Our Life with Bigfoot: Knowing Our Next of Kin at Habituation Sites* [Kindle edition] (locations 964-968). US: CreateSpace Independent Publishing Platform

NUFORC report, 7/23/1985. (2005). *National UFO Reporting Center.* Retrieved from http://www.nuforc.org/webreports/045/S45661.html

NUFORC report, 7/10/1975. (2007). *National UFO Reporting Center.* Retrieved May 20, 2014 from http://www.nuforc.org/webreports/060/S60035.html

Nunnelly, B.M. (2011). *The Inhumanoids: Real Encounters with Beings That Can't Exist.* Woolsery, UK: CFZ Press.

Olaer, M. (2004). Alien Abduction. *Iwasabducted.com.* Retrieved on May 19, 2014 from http://www.iwasabducted.com/abductionboard/reports/638.htm

Øverby, R. (n.d.). Physical ufo-contact in former east-Germany in -57: The contacts of Martin Wiesengrün. Retrieved June 4, 2014 from http://galactic-server.com/rune/ariancont.html

Øverby, R. (2001). Intervju med ufokontaktpersonen Arve Jacobsen. Retrieved May 17, 2014 from http://galactic-server.com/rune/arve. html

Painthorse. (2012, June 12). Bf entering houses... [Online forum comment]. Retrieved June 16, 2014 from http://bigfootforums.com/ index.php/topic/31643-bf-entering-houses/

Paquette, A. (2010). *Dreamer: 20 Years of Psychic Dreams and How They Changed My Life*. Hampshire, UK: John Hunt Publishing Ltd.

Payaguaje, F. (2000). At the End You See God (excerpt from *The Yajé Drinker*). In L. E. Luna & S. F. White (Eds.), *Ayahuasca Reader: Encounters with the Amazon's Sacred Vine* (pp. 67-80). Santa Fe, NM: Synergetic Press.

Pennant, T. (1796). *The History of the Parishes of Whiteford and Holywell*. London, UK: B. and J. White.

D. Perriam, personal communication, January 19, 2015.

Picasso, F. (n.d.). Case 19. In A. Rosales (Ed.), *1965 Humanoid Sighting Reports*. Retrieved February 5, 2014 from http://www.ufoinfo.com/ humanoid/humanoid-1965.pdf

Picknett, L. (2012). *The Mammoth Book of UFOs*. London, UK: Constable & Robinson.

Pogonov, V. I. & Regional Moscow Club for the Research of Anomalous Phenomenon (n.d.). Case 12. In A. Rosales (Ed.), *1990 Humanoid Sighting Reports*. Retrieved February 5, 2014 from http:// www.ufoinfo.com/humanoid/humanoid-1990.pdf

Pope, N. (2004, March 2). Subject: Re: UFOs & Fairies? *UFO UpDates: A mailing list for the study of UFO-related phenomena*. Message posted to http://ufoupdateslist.com/2004/mar/m03-009.shtml
Pratt, B. (1991). Disturbing Encounters in NE Brazil. In T. Good (Ed.), *UFO Report 1991* (pp. 102-124). London: Sidgwich & Jackson

Ltd.

Pregadio, F. (2012). *The Way of the Golden Elixir: A Historical Overview of Taoist Alchemy*. Mountain View, CA: Golden Elixir Press.

Priyma, A. (2000). *XX Century: Chronicles of the Unexplained* [online copy]. Retrieved from http://tinyurl.com/ogjcdoa

Priyma, A. (2000). *From Mystery to Mystery* [online copy]. Retrieved June 5, 2014 from http://www.rulit.net/books/ot-tajny-k-tajne-read-20094-32.html

Pup [Screen name] (2006, February 10). DMT trip accounts. Message posted to http://dmt.tribe.net/thread/9e832018-5fbc-4ff6-b4e5-e314184f687c

Purkiss, D. (2000). *Troublesome Things: A History of Fairies and Fairy Stories*. Westminster, UK: Penguin Books.

Ralph of Coggeshall. (n.d.). *Radulhpi de Coggeshall Chronicon Anglicanum*. Retrieved December 11, 2014 from http://tinyurl.com/qy2633d

Randle, K. D. (1989). *The October Scenario*. New York City, NY: Berkley Books.

Ravenswood, S. (1999). Ethereal Serpents Held Me in Thrall. In R. Metzner (Ed.), *Ayahuasca: Hallucinogens, Consciousness, and the Spirit of Nature* (pp. 118-128). New York, NY: Thunder's Mouth Press.

Reece, G. L. (2008) *Weird Science and Bizarre Beliefs: Mysterious Creatures, Lost Worlds and Amazing Adventures*. London, UK: I.B.Tauris.

Reid, K. (n.d.). Visitor Submitted Abduction Experiences – Alien abduction as a child. *Aliens the Truth*. Retrieved May 19, 2014 from http://tinyurl.com/q8aqcgk
Rife, P.L. (2001). *It Didn't Start with Roswell: 50 Years of Amazing UFO*

Crashes, Close Encounters and Coverups. Bloomington, IN: iUniverse.

Rimes, N. (1969, January). Another Hospital Visited. *Flying Saucer Review 15*(1), 4-6.

Rimmer, J. (1984). *The Evidence for Alien Abductions.* Wellingborough, UK: Aquarian Press. Citing S. Anglo's *The Damned Art*, RKP 1977.

Rimmer, J. (1988, January). Transvection and UFOlogy. *Magonia.* Retrieved August 11, 2014 from http://magonia.haaan.com/2009/transvection

Rogan, J. (2013, May 23). *Joe Rogan Experience #360* [Video podcast]. Retrieved from https://www.youtube.com/watch?v=tsu2-I2q6dg

Rogers, C. (1869). *Scotland Social and Domestic: Memorials of Life and Manners in North Britain.* London: Charles Griffin and Co. Citing Robert Kirk.

Rogerson, P. (1977). Fairies and Fireballs. *Magonia.* Retrieved from http://magonia.haaan.com/2009/fireballs/

Sanchez-Ocejo, V. & Miami UFO Center (n.d.). Case 99. In A. Rosales (Ed.), *1980 Humanoid Sighting Reports.* Retrieved February 5, 2014 from http://www.ufoinfo.com/humanoid/humanoid-1980.pdf

Sanderson, I. T. (1974). *Uninvited Visitors: A Biologist Looks at UFO's.* London, UK: Universal-Tandem Publishing Company Ltd.

Schwarz, B.E. (1971, March). Possible UFO-Induced Temporary Paralysis. *Flying Saucer Review 17*(2), 4-9.

Schwarz, B.E. (1977, October). Talks with Betty Hill: 2 – The things that happen around her. *Flying Saucer Review 23*(3), 11-14.

Semenduev, S. (1991). On the tracks of UFOs in Dagestan. *Iks: Newsletter of the Dagestan Center of the Study of UFOs and Anomalous Phenomena 5,* 2

Shearar, C. (2000). *Understanding Northwest Coast Art: A Guide to Crests, Beings and Symbols*. Seattle, WA: University of Washington Press.

Shiel, L.A. (2006). *Backyard Bigfoot: The True Story of Stick Signs, UFOs, and the Sasquatch*. Lake Linden, MI: Jacobsville Books.

Short, B. (2012, May). Additive, Responsive Shape [Web log post]. Retrieved from http://numinousintrusions.blogspot.com/2012/05/additive-responsive-shape.html

Sidnacius. (2008, May 6). "In search of an illusive creature." *Merinews*. Retrieved June 16, 2014 from http://www.merinews.com/article/in-search-of-an-illusive-creature/133591.shtml

Sinistrari. (1700) *De delictis et poenis*. Venice, Italy: Albriccium.

Skoöanakönnun DV um álfatrú: Meirihluti þjóðarinnar trúir á álfa og huldufólk. (1998, July 22). *Dagblaðið Vísir - DV* (in Icelandic), p. 2. Retrieved August 11, 2014 from timarit.is.

Smith, C. (2005, September). The Land of the Hidden People. *Fortean Times, 201*, 42-27.

Smith, Y.R. (2014). *Coronado: The President, The Secret Service, and Alien Abductions* [Kindle edition].

Spencer, C. (1993). *The Heretic's Feast: A History of Vegetarianism*. London: Fourth Estate.

Sprinkle, L. (1975, November). A Preliminary Report on the Investigation of an Alleged UFO Occupant Encounter. *Flying Saucer Review 21*(3), 3-5.

Stafford, P. (1993). Psychedelics Encyclopedia (3rd ed). Berkeley, CA: Ronin Publishing.

Steiger, B. (1988). *The UFO Abductors*. New York City, NY: Berkley.

Stranges, F. E. (1967). *Stranger at the Pentagon*. New Brunswick, NJ: Inner Light Publications.

Strassman, R. (2000). *DMT: The Spirit Molecule*. Rochester, VT: Park Street Press.

Strieber, A. (ed.) (2004). Insight: Behind the News - Messages from Gray Monkeys. Retrieved June 9, 2014 from http://www.unknowncountry.com/insight/messages-gray-monkeys

Strieber, W. (1987). *Communion*. New York, NY: Avon Books.

Strieber, W. & Strieber, A. (1997). *The Communion Letters*. New York, NY: Harper Prism.

Strieber, W. (1997). *Transformation*. New York, NY: Avon Books.

Strieber, W. (2011). *The Key*. New York, NY: Jeremy P. Tarcher. (Original work published 2001)

Stringfield, L. (1979, November). Retrievals of the Third Kind – Part 3. *Flying Saucer Review 25*(6), 8-14.

Suenaga, C.T. (2011). Aliens who wanted to warn humanity. Retrieved July 24, 2014 from https://www.ufo.com.br/artigos/extraterrestres-que-queriam-alertar-a-humanidade

Taylor, S. (2011). BFRO Report #29355: Possible evidence collected after a woman is hit in the hand by a rock near Napavine. *BFRO*. Retrieved May 8, 2014 from http://www.bfro.net/gdb/show_report.asp?id=29355

Terence McKenna Archive [Screen name] (2011, July 11). *The Definitive UFO Tape (Terence McKenna) [FULL]* [Video file]. Retrieved from https://www.youtube.com/watch?v=LrgveoEVuq4

Terrillon, J.C., & Marques-Bonham, S. M. (2001). Does Recurring Sleep Paralysis Involve More Than Cognitive Neurosciences? *Journal of*

Scientific Exploration 15(1), 97-123.

Thomas, J. (1979, September). Humanoid and Abduction Reports Widespread. *The MUFON UFO Journal 130*, 15-16.

Tongue, R. *County Folklore*, Vol. VIII (pp. 116-117). Cited in Briggs 1976.

Tsakiris, A. (2014, January 15). *Skeptiko Episode 198: Mike Clelland struggles to understand contact with alien consciousness* [Audio podcast]. Retrived from http://www.skeptiko.com/mike-clelland-contact-with-alien-consciousness/

Tsushbaya, G. (1994). *This Mysterious World*. Odessa, Ukraine: Odekov.

Turner, K. (1992). *Into the Fringe*. New York, NY: Berkley Books.

Turner, K. (1994). *Taken: Inside the Alien-Human Abduction Agenda*. Tallahassee, FL: Rose Printing Company, Inc.

Turner, K. (1994). *Masquerade of Angels*. Roland, AR: Kelt Works.

Uagga, A. Q. (n.d.). *James Bong's Ultimate Spy Guide to Marijuana* [Google eBook]. Retrieved from books.google.com

Valenze, D. (2011). *Milk: A Local and Global History*. Ann Arbor, MI: Sheridan Books.

Valerian, V. (1988). *The Matrix: Understanding Aspects of Covert Interaction with Alien Culture, Technology and Planetary Power Structures*. Scotia, NY: Arcturus Book Service.

Vallée, J. (1990). *Confrontations: A Scientist's Search for Alien Contact*. New York, NY: Ballantine Books.

Vallée, J. (1993). *Passport to Magonia*. Chicago, IL: Contemporary Books.

Vallée, J. (2008). *Messengers of Deception*. Brisbane, AU: Daily Grail Publishing. (Original work published 1979)

Vallée, J. & Aubeck, C. (2010). *Wonders in the Sky: Unexplained Aerial Objects from Antiquity to Modern Times*. Los Angeles, CA: Tarcher. Citing *Malleus Maleficarum*, H. Kramer & J. Sprenger (1486).

Van Eyck, Z. (1997, July 6). "Close Encounters in Utah." Deseret News. Retrieved June 17, 2014 from http://www.deseretnews.com/article/570388/Close-encounters-in-Utah.html?pg=all

Varner, G.R. (2006). *The Mythic Forest, the Green Man and the Spirit of Nature: The Re-emergence of the Spirit of Nature from Ancient Times Into Modern Society*. New York, NY: Algora Publishing

Villarubia Mauso, P. (n.d.). Case 16. In A. Rosales (Ed.), *1990 Humanoid Sighting Reports*. Retrieved February 5, 2014 from http://www.ufoinfo.com/humanoid/humanoid-1990.pdf

Villarrubia Mauso, P. & Rangel, M. (n.d.) Case 52. In A. Rosales (Ed.), *1978 Humanoid Sighting Reports*. Retrieved February 5, 2014 from http://www.ufoinfo.com/humanoid/humanoid-1978.pdf

Wasson, R.G. (1972). *Soma: Divine Mushroom of Immortality*. New York: Harvest Books.

Webb, D.F. & Bloecher, T. *HUMCAT: Catalogue of Humanoid Reports 1956*. USA: CUFOs.

A.T. Weil, personal communication, May 1, 1972.

White, D. (2013, January 7). I was taken in Merseyside. PLEAS HELP. Message posted to http://bufog.freeforums.org/i-was-taken-in-merseyside-pleas-help-t570.html

White, D.G. (1996) *The Alchemical Body: Siddha Traditions in Medieval India*. Chicago, IL: The University of Chicago Press.

244 A Trojan Feast

Williamson, G.H. (1953) *Other Tongues—Other Flesh*. Amherst, WI: Amherst Press.

Wilson, C. (1998). *Alien Dawn: An Investigation into the Contact Experience*. New York, NY: Fromm International Publishing Corporation.

Witthoft, J. & Hadlock, W.S. (1946). Cherokee-Iroquois Little People. *Journal of American Folklore, 59*, 413-422.

Wysmierski, M. (2000). Plínio Bragatto 's Unexpected Trip. *Close Encounters of the Brazilian Kind, 1*, 24-29.

Young, J.Z. (1968). Influence of the mouth on the evolution of the brain. In P. Person (Ed.) *Biology of the mouth*. Washington, DC: American Association for the Advancement of Science.

245

INDEX

Printed in May 2024
by Rotomail Italia S.p.A., Vignate (MI) - Italy